PRESENTED TO:

_____

FROM:

_____

LIVING WATERS!

DAILY DEVOTIONAL STUDIES from
JOHN FOR EVERYDAY LIFE

DARYL KRAFT

GRACE *upon* GRACE
FOUNDATION

COEUR D'ALENE, IDAHO

Living Waters!
Daily Devotional Studies from the Gospel of John for Everyday Life

Copyright 2023 by Daryl Kraft
Published by Grace Upon Grace Foundation
Coeur d'Alene, Idaho 83815
www.gugf.org

Cover and interior design by Gearbox, StudioGearbox.com

ISBN: 978-1-7923-7260-5 (Living Waters Devotional, Volume One)
ISBN: 978-1-7923-7260-5 (Living Waters Devotional, Volume Two)
ISBN: 978-1-7923-7260-5 (Living Waters Devotional, Two Volume Set)

Printed in China 12 11 10 9 8 7 6 5 4 3 2

Unless otherwise indicated, all Scripture quotations cited in this book are taken from *The New American Standard Bible®* ("NASB™"). Copyright 1960, 1962, 1963, 1968, 1971, 1972, 1975, 1977, 1995 by The Lockman Foundation, a Corporation Not for Profit, La Habra, California. Used by permission. All rights reserved. (www.Lockman.org).

Verses marked NIV are taken from *The New International Version®* Study Bible, 10th Anniversary Edition, Copyright 1995 by the Zondervan Corporation. Used by permission. All rights reserved.

Verses marked NKJV are taken from the *New King James Version*. Copyright 1982 by Thomas Nelson, Inc. Used by permission. All rights reserved.

Verses marked KJV are taken from the King James Version.

Verses marked TLB are taken from *The Living Bible*. Copyright 1971 by Tyndale House Publishers, Inc., Wheaton, IL. Used by permission. All rights reserved.

Verses marked AMP are taken from *The Amplified Bible*. Copyright 1954, 1958, 1962, 1964, 1965, 1987 by the Lockman Foundation. Used by permission. All rights reserved. (www.Lockman.org).

Verses marked NLT are taken from the Holy Bible, New Living Translation. Copyright 1996, 2004 by Tyndale House Publishers, Inc. Wheaton, IL. Used by permission. All rights reserved.

Verses marked EDB are taken from the Everyday Bible. Copyright 1996, 2004 by Tyndale House Publishers, Inc. Wheaton, IL. Used by permission. All rights reserved.

Verses marked MES are taken from THE MESSAGE. Copyright 2003 by Eugene H. Peterson. Used by permission of NavPress Publishing Group.

Verses marked IG-ENT are taken from *The Interlinear Greek-English New Testament* 2nd Edition. Copyright 1958, 1959 by Editorial Interlineation Samuel Bagster and Sons Ltd.

Emphasis of certain words or phrases within Bible quotations have been added by the author for emphasis unless otherwise indicated. Bracketed words within a Bible quotation have been added by the author for clarification unless otherwise indicated.

To *Every* Christian who believes

that the Christian Life is something

they must do (and not do).

FOREWORD

*... these have been written so that **you may believe** that Jesus is the Christ, the Son of God; and that **believing** you may have life in His name.*

JOHN 20:31

Why did God lead John to write his gospel? He gives us the answer in the verse above. It is a remarkably simple message, yet one with profound life-changing impact.

He wanted us TO BELIEVE, and through that belief, TO LIVE.

For John, it is belief in Jesus that eternally saves us; and that same belief which guides us every day of our life in Christ. The life of a believer, as described by John, is not complicated. It is freedom-giving, easy, and joyous! It is not a list of dos and don'ts for us to follow or scripture verses we try hard to apply to our lives. Rather, it is a living person—who is our *total* and *complete* Savior, actively working His will in our lives each day. The life of a Christian is not something divided into complex doctrinal subcomponents, but is a seamless whole—initiated, guided, nurtured, and perfected by God—from our first breath as a born-again believer until our entrance into glory. It is a belief that manifests as fullness of unspeakable peace and overflowing *Living Waters* of joy in our daily living.

For many, the Christian life is still a profound mystery—what it is, and how it is lived. Considering the book of John each day in this devotional will clarify answers to both questions. Some understand their life in terms of "doing" (or "not doing") certain things: like reading the Bible daily, praying regularly, loving others unconditionally, witnessing relentlessly, tithing faithfully; *not* cheating on their spouse, *not* lying, *not* having angry or lustful thoughts, *not* taking God's name in vain, and *not* breaking any of the other Ten Commandments. For the Apostle John, however, the life every Christian is blessed by God to live is vastly more miraculous and transcendent than all these human notions. It is a life no more complicated than *God manifesting Himself* IN His family of believers—from cradle to glory—*without any of their earthly plans or human help!*

I pray that God will open the book of John to you as you read it throughout the year. If you feel *any* stress, guilt, sense of failure, *any* inadequacies before God, *any* fear that you are not living up to what God is expecting of you—this book is for you! *Enjoy the journey into **Christ your Savior** and experience His Living Water bubbling up **within you!***

THE
WORD IS
A LIVING
PERSON!

———

JOHN 1:1-5

JANUARY 1

In the beginning ... God.

—JOHN 1:1

January 1 each year is a "beginning" of sorts, within the limited context of time itself. It is not, however, what the Apostle John is referring to in this verse. John's "beginning" is not an invention of man's calendar. It is a point of reference for our faith. It cuts through all of man's philosophy, education, and scientific speculations concerning the universe including how it came into being. John simply says that before any and all of it—there was God. Nothing is before God. Nothing created God. Nothing is bigger than God.

John was writing his gospel (which means "God's *Good News*") to believers living in the first century, many of whom were suffering under great persecution. John begins his good-news message by addressing a fundamental concern that everyone was facing: Do you think the troubles that afflict and threaten to overwhelm you are insurmountable? He then answers his own question by telling us that God existed *before* our troubles and is bigger than our troubles. So He can comfort us in and direct us through each of them. He also tells us God will accomplish good in our life through each of our difficulties and all will soon pass.

"*In the beginning ... God*"—also forces us to recognize that we have no ability or capacity to understand this truth within the scope of our limited human intellect. To the extent that we can accept this understanding at all is proof positive that the "*In the beginning*" God has placed *His* own faith *in us* to believe and understand. This is the first step along a wonderful journey into knowing God as the One who has done it all for us ... and the One who is all we need.

LIVING WATER FOR TODAY:

Where were you when I laid the foundation of the earth? *Tell Me, if you have understanding.* —JOB 38:4

For today, take comfort in the fact that God was ***in the beginning*** and is bigger than your every problem. Begin your new year knowing that *your* God will faithfully guide your path and refresh you with His Life (as *living water*) each and every day—in every circumstance of your life. *Praise the Lord!*

JANUARY 2

*In the beginning was the Word, and the **Word was with God**, and the **Word was God**. He was in the beginning with God.*

—John 1:1-2

John uses the Greek word *Logos* (meaning "spoken word with creative power") in these verses with a specific purpose in mind. *Logos* is not like any other noun. It translates into English as the proper name: "Word." John is introducing Jesus to his reader; and he begins with four categorical phrases— *"In the beginning was the **Word**,"* *"the **Word** was with God," "the **Word** was God,"* ... and *"**He** was in the beginning with God."* In the last phrase John uses the pronoun *"He,"* referring to the *Word*, to make clear that he is not speaking about a philosophical concept, but a real person. He is referring to none other than Jesus, God Himself, and uses *Logos* as a proper name to emphasize a life-changing truth that directly relates to us: *Jesus is God's spoken word with creative power.*

Now, if we didn't study any further, how revolutionary is this truth? Jesus is God IN US speaking with creative power! Or—all of scripture is Jesus—the spoken word of God speaking to you and me with creative power! Or—our Bible is not merely a set of dos and don'ts for us to try to apply and live up to in our human effort. The Bible is Jesus speaking creative words of power *INTO US* to transform us into a new creation. This is the purpose of *all* scripture: to mold us more into Christ's likeness as the Potter molds the clay.

LIVING WATER FOR TODAY:

*For the **word of God is living and active** and sharper than any two-edged sword, and piercing as far as the division of soul and spirit, of both joints and marrow, and able to judge the thoughts and intentions of the heart.*

—Hebrews 4:12

For today, consider the truth that Jesus is God's spoken word with creative power which makes the Bible *living, active, and life-changing* TO YOU. Pray earnestly that God will reveal this miraculous truth to you—that it is not *YOU* trying to apply scripture to your life; but rather, the creative power of God through scripture actively transforming your life as you just read it or hear it! *Praise the Lord!*

JANUARY 3

All things came into being through Him, and apart from Him nothing came into being that has come into being.

—JOHN 1:3

The world is a cesspool of irrational beliefs and "pseudo-science" that pose as rational thought. There are people who believe (earnestly) in just about every conceivable thing imaginable: UFOs and ancient intelligent aliens, vampires, werewolves, and zombies, even a flat earth (yes, believe it or not, some *still* do). The pandemic problem in this world is *not* a matter of *lack of faith* (not believing in something), but rather in humanity's unthinking willingness to *rush to believe* and accept *anything* as long as it is *not* a belief in God. We are only three verses into John's good news and he presents us with just such a major challenge to our faith: what will you believe about how things came into being? This choice is as relevant today as it was in John's day—a choice between two fundamental worldviews.

The labels for these worldviews are *Naturalism* and *Theism*. *Naturalism*, the source of most of our science and scientific theory, teaches what is often referred to as the "Big Bang" theory, a notion that all matter was originally compressed into a tiny point of nothingness, perhaps within a black hole (don't ask where the black hole came from), and finally exploded into the billions of galaxies we see today. *Theism*, by contrast, simply believes that God is the source of all created things. Compare these two beliefs and then ask yourself which one takes more faith to believe? John is showing us how dark a system can be without God. While mocking and laughing at those who believe God created all things, Naturalists believe that a tiny pinpoint of "nothing" exploded into a whole bunch of "something." One day, our scientists may discover that what they call the "Big Bang" was actually the moment God spoke: *"Let there be light."*

LIVING WATER FOR TODAY:

For from Him and through Him and to Him are all things. To Him be the glory forever. Amen.—ROMANS 11:36

For today, consider the truth that all things are from God. There is nothing that has come into being apart from Him, *including* every aspect of spiritual growth that you may have previously believed you must discipline yourself to achieve. *It's all from God!*

JANUARY 4

*Then God said, "**Let there be light**"; and there was light.*
—GENESIS 1:3

When John refers to the creation of all things by God in *John 1:3*, he is referring back to *Genesis 1:3* when God said: *"Let there be Light."* Many Christians make the common mistake of taking this verse from *Genesis* for granted without a moment of thought about the implications and consequences it continues to have for *their* daily living. Since we cannot fully understand this truth, it is easier to relegate it to some back recess of our mind, which is then ultimately forgotten in the immediacy of our daily challenges. We can then read scores of verses like *Philippians 1:6* (below) and fail to connect the dots that the Christian life is entirely a matter of this same Creator God's immense creative power at work *in us*. Once God blesses us with this understanding, it revolutionizes our thinking about every aspect of our living as Christians.

The truth about God's enormous creative power is foundational to connecting the dots to what Christianity really is. God's creative power is not some esoteric factoid from history past. It is a vitally relevant description of our How-Great-Thou-Art Almighty God—*TODAY!* It is this God who tells us that HE is the **Potter** molding our clay *(Romans 9:21)*; the **Vine** flowing sustenance to our branches *(John 15:5)*; the **Living Water** springing up into eternal life in us *(John 4:14)*; and the **Good Shepherd** guiding and protecting us His sheep *(John 10:11)*. The picture is clear: We are the clay, the branches, the vessel being filled with His Living Water, and the sheep *(all of which can do nothing for themselves)*.

LIVING WATER FOR TODAY:

For I am confident of this very thing, that
He who began a good work in you will perfect it
until the day of Christ Jesus.—PHILIPPIANS 1:6

For today, rejoice in the fact that the Creator of all the universe and life itself *lives in you!* Be comforted in knowing that He promises to continue His good work in your life until it is perfected according to His purpose. You are freed to simply rest in His creative power *in you. Praise Him—and rest!*

LET THERE BE LIGHT

In Genesis 1:3 God spoke four words *"Let there be light"* and He no sooner said the words then the sun appeared. No waving of hands or dancing for Him—He just spoke four words. Do you know how big the sun is? It is large enough to swallow one million, four hundred thousand (1,400,000) earths without so much as a burp! And how big is the earth?

I don't know how many readers will have flown around the world. I have done it several times when visiting an orphanage we were helping to support in India. I remember that trip was exceedingly tiring. You sit in a jumbo jet and fly at 600 miles per hour for 13 hours straight to Hong Kong. You land and have a layover; then fly another 6 hours, another layover, and then yet another 6 hours to finally reach India. The whole trip is about 25 hours of flying. After all of this exhaustive flying you are only *half* way around the planet earth! Think of that!

God didn't just make the sun and one planet. When He spoke *"Let there be light"* He created billions of galaxies that contain billions upon billions of stars like our sun, and countless moons and planets as well. He did all of that by speaking just four words. So, is that God powerful and capable enough to do what He promised He would do for you and in you (to transform you from glory to glory into His image, *2 Corinthians 3:18)*? Or is your God so tuckered out from His creation work that He now no longer can do what He promised without your help?

This should lead you to the question: **What does "being a Christian" really mean?**

[Hint: See page 20]

January 5

In Him was life, and the life was the Light of men.

—John 1:4

John has already told us that Jesus is GOD and Jesus is the WORD. Now he tells us that Jesus is LIFE! The phrase *"in Him was life"* refers to the *eternal* kind of life that Christ *IS*. His life is not the *created* kind of life that we have, but the uncreated and eternal life unique to God Himself. Take care not to trivialize this term by thinking of it only as a metonym, or that it refers merely to a future event or heavenly place reserved for Christians when they die (like a "ticket" that is useful only upon entering the turnstiles at heaven's gate). The *eternal* life John is referring to doesn't start in the future but is unveiled *and lived* in the NOW. It isn't about a Christian persevering until they get to heaven, but a taste of "heaven" progressively experienced in the present. This *eternal* life is presently ours to fully enjoy the moment God reveals His Son Jesus in us (just like He did to Paul in *Galatians 1:15-16*). After all, the phrase refers specifically to Christ's *quality of life* in every aspect of our lives; He is the living God/Word/Life dwelling in us which has real and profound benefits.

In Christ, we have God's quality of *love*; we have *His joy, peace, patience, kindness, goodness,* and *faithfulness*—in real time, in the midst of real circumstances—for every aspect of our daily living *(Galatians 5:22-23)*. Can you think of a circumstance that Jesus, *the Creator God*, could not handle? This only scratches the surface of what His *eternal* life means *to* us, *in* us, and *for* us. We have God's quality of *wisdom, righteousness, sanctification,* and *redemption (1 Corinthians 1:30)*—which are all gifts given to us from our Father, all packaged in the person of Christ.

Living Water for Today:

*Every good thing given and **every perfect gift is from above,** coming down from the Father of lights, with whom there is no variation or shifting shadow.*—James 1:17

For today, embrace the liberating reality that all truly good peace, all true joy (not just momentary, earthly fun), and all true unconditional love you hold for others have all been instilled in you as a gift from your *"Father of lights."* He NEVER varies. For example, He is not mad at you one minute and happy the next. He is *ALWAYS* gifting you daily with His quality of life—as *living water* springing up in you to eternal life.

JANUARY 6

*In Him was life, **and the life was the Light of men.***

—JOHN 1:4

The term *"Light"* in scripture is commonly used by the biblical writers to signify God's quality of life, which is *true* love, peace, joy, contentment, and freedom from condemnation and death; while darkness signifies sin's quality of life: misery, guilt, condemnation, and death. All of God's life comes down *from* God *in* Christ *to* us and enlightens us. It also stands in stark contrast to a dark world.

This does not mean that we become smarter than those who do not believe. It means that we are spiritually enlightened (by God) in ways that the nonbeliever is not. *First Corinthians 1:18* tells us, *"For the word of the cross* [or our salvation] *is foolishness to those who are perishing, but to us who are being saved it is the power of God."* The nonbeliever may be the nicest and most intelligent person you know, yet everything that scripture says about Christ bearing our sins on the cross to become our forgiveness and eternal life is ridiculous to them. *This is because they do not have the Spirit of God enlightening them.*

That living light not only gives enlightenment regarding our salvation, but also wisdom concerning our daily living, families, businesses, and everything that leads to *true* happiness, joy, hope, and freedom. This allows all believers to live in contrast to the world's guilt, hopelessness, pain, and fake happiness. In *John 8:12 (TLB)* the phrase, *"living light will flood your path"* means that we are empowered by the Creator God to live this way. He etches His truth into our lives as we walk and live daily in His Light.

LIVING WATER FOR TODAY:

*On the other hand, I am writing a new commandment to you, which is **true in Him and in you**, because the darkness is passing away and **the true Light is already shining.*** —1 JOHN 2:8

For today, notice this verse does not say "true TO you" but rather "true ... IN you." Recognize that the nexus of this verse is operating inside of you. The darkness is (progressively) passing away and *"the true Light is already shining"*—meaning the Light of Christ, God's spoken word with creative power, is already in you—enlightening you. *Praise God!*

CONNECTING THE THEOLOGICAL DOTS

I will never forget an ER doctor friend saying to me several years ago, "Daryl, I see every day the profound darkness that God has saved us from." He was referring to all of the drug and alcohol abuse, all the anger, all the depression, all the attempted and successful suicides, all of the self-inflicted disease so prevalent in the world.

These are the things that God is in the process of saving us from every day. Does this mean that if you are a Christian (and have the Light) you will be perfect? Far from it! We all battle with our flesh daily. Does this mean that if you are a Christian and still have a drug or alcohol problem, or facing loneliness, or depression, or some other debilitating disease that you are not a good enough Christian for God? Or that God has rejected you in some fashion and taken away the Light? Or that you probably didn't have the Light in you in the first place (so you are not really a Christian)? Or that you need to try harder to "follow" God more earnestly? No, no, no, and again, no.

God has placed each of His children (young and old, immature to mature in spiritual understanding, drug addicts, alcoholics, and those afflicted with every form of disease) on His ever-brightening path of the righteous *(Proverbs 4:18)*. This is the *path* we all travel on, not a *destination* where we have already arrived. None of us will be fully transformed until the Lord returns for His children. For now, we all still struggle with our flesh, just as the Apostle Paul did *(Romans 7:14-25)*. Take hope from this word from John: *"Beloved, now we are children of God, and it has not appeared as yet what we will be. We know that when He appears, **we will be like Him**, because we will see Him just as He is" (1 John 3:2).*

Today, God ministers to all His children, regardless of differences, through His spoken word with creative power. This reflects how truly unique the word of God is because it guides, protects, and nourishes both the youngest and oldest Christian, those afflicted with loneliness, depression, addiction, and self-inflicted diseases, precisely in their present circumstances. You can be confident in God's wisdom and timing in faithfully shepherding *you* along His path of the righteous *(John 14:26; Philippians 1:6, 2:13).*

January 7

*Then Jesus again spoke to them, saying, "**I am the Light of the world; he who follows Me will not walk in darkness,** but will have the Light of life."*

—John 8:12

Today we jump to *John 8:12* to continue this theme of Christ as living light in us. The phrase *"he who follows Me"* refers to *ALL* believers in Christ. Jesus is not discussing how God grades, sorts, or classifies Christians depending on whether they are sufficiently "following" Him (or *not following* Him at any given moment) based on some performance criteria. Look at the context of this verse and it will become clear. Jesus is talking to a general gathering of people and refers to all those who just *believe* in Him as His followers. To be a follower of Jesus is not burdensome *(Matthew 11:30)*. It is not something we "perform" or try to do. It is His faith in us to believe—which faith is itself a gift from God *(Ephesians 2:8)*—that makes us followers of Christ. A follower of Christ is simply one who is being led (as all believers are) by the Spirit of God *(Romans 8:4)*.

John 8:12 in *The Living Bible* makes this even clearer. It reads, *"Later, in one of his talks, Jesus said to the people, 'I am the Light of the world. So if you follow me, you won't be stumbling through the darkness, for living light will flood your path.'"* You won't be going through this life making one bad choice after another, continually messing up your life, living in constant pain, regret, misery, and guilt. The phrase *"living light will flood your path"* is referring to Christ's life progressively becoming our life; or through Christ indwelling us we are enlightened to see and believe what an unbeliever does not see and believe. We desire what the unbeliever does not desire. Again, this does not come from us. *It is Christ's life within us enlightening our path.* Whether we are aware of it or not—*Christ is working in us!*

Living Water for Today:

"To him the doorkeeper opens, and the sheep hear his voice, and **he calls his own sheep by name and leads them out.** *⁴When he puts forth all his own, he goes ahead of them, and the sheep follow him because they know his voice."* —John 10:3-4

For today, enjoy the freedom of knowing that while you may feel like nothing more than a dumb sheep, you are HIS dumb sheep and HE has caused you to know His voice. *He is calling you by name and guiding you along His path of light.*

January 8

*The Light shines in the darkness, and **the darkness did not comprehend it**.*

—John 1:5

"The darkness did not comprehend it" is better understood as the darkness did not *overcome* it. This is something to really praise God for. Let's take a closer look. God's Light in our life is greater than any of Satan's oppositions to it. Praise God! This also means that all the propensities of our flesh cannot overcome God's life in us. Again, I say: Praise God!

For today, pray to comprehend this thought: Light Always Dispels Darkness. It is the light that tells me what is dark. When the warring in my flesh seems completely out of control, I have something greater in me—the Light. You can bring any amount of darkness to the light and the light will *ALWAYS* prevail. The same is true of God's Light in us. Yes, we often struggle with our flesh *(Galatians 5:17)*, but our flesh will *NEVER* defeat the Light. What tremendous hope this gives us!

And here is maybe the best part. This verse: *"The Light shines in the darkness, and the darkness did not comprehend it"* means that every time we remember a verse or read God's word—*every time*—it brings light. It brings the living, spoken word with creative power, which will always prevail over our fleshly feelings. We may not see or feel it instantly but it *is* working. We have all experienced worrying about something and feeling the weight of it, then God causes a verse like *Psalm 46:10 (NIV)* to come to mind (or we read it), *"Be still and know that I am God"* *(the NASB translates it as "Cease striving and know that I am God")*; and we realize those words aren't just black ink on white paper—but are living words by God with creative power. We know this because we feel our shoulders begin to relax as we say: *I praise You God for reminding me of this right now.*

Living Water for Today:

*You are from God, little children, and have overcome them; because **greater is He who is in you than he who is in the world**.* —1 John 4:4

***For today**, regardless of your circumstances, be confident in this: Light Always Dispels Darkness. Christ in you is greater than anything Satan can toss your way. Read God's word and trust its living and operative power working in you, to bring about the very thing that it (God's word) is speaking to you about. *Praise the Lord!*

WHAT DOES "BEING A CHRISTIAN" REALLY MEAN?

For many, if not most Christians, the answer to this profoundly simple question proves to be painfully obscure—filled with nuances of worry, doubt, fear, and frustration. Some see this doctrinally as Christ dying on the cross as a propitiation for our sins—which is certainly true—but that does not answer the question. Others see it in terms of how well they *perform* as disciples of Christ.

In truth, these responses miss the question's core meaning. Here is the question again: ***What does BEING a Christian really mean?*** Is it "what you are" or "what you do"? If action is involved, whose action is it—*your* action or *God's*? Most Christians believe that "being a Christian" is a combination of God's effort and their own—but is it really? Let's work through this step by step.

To BE a Christian simply means that God has chosen you to BE in His family. You didn't earn it, deserve it, or even make the choice *(John 15:16)*—He did—and He did so before the foundation of the world *(Ephesians 1:3-4)*. Then, during your life, God made you aware of His choice by revealing Christ in you—just like He did to the Apostle Paul *(Galatians 1:15-16)*. He facilitated this revelation by giving you the faith to believe in Him *(Ephesians 2:8)*; and by believing, you were given God's life—Eternal life *(John 3:16)*. At this point, you ARE a Christian—not based on anything you *do* but what you *are*—GOD'S CHOSEN VESSEL (albeit made of clay) CONTAINING CHRIST. That is everything you need to know about BEING a Christian. It has nothing to do with your performance and everything to do with His mercy. You BEING a Christian is entirely a matter of grace—an act of unmerited favor bestowed on you by God. Most Christians can accept this as true. But how does BEING a Christian affect your daily living? This is where many get confused between *BELIEF in Christ* and *TRUSTING Him*. To explore this difference, see "Connecting the Theological Dots" on page 32.

LIVING WATER FROM JOHN 1:1-5

January 1	In the beginning, as a point of reference for our faith, there was the Word, and there was God, and they were One.
January 2	Jesus is God's spoken word with creative power.
January 3	God is the source of all created things.
January 4	The power of God that spoke light throughout the universe is daily working His creative power in our lives.
January 5	Christ, our eternal Light and Life, lives in us, and never wavers or varies.
January 6	The light of Christ enlightens us to the truth of God's word.
January 7	The Spirit of God—Living Light—guides and directs our path.
January 8	God's shining Light in us will always prevail over Satan and our flesh.

PRAYER

Father, I pray that You would enlighten me to what it truly means to have Your spoken word with creative power living within me. In four simple words You spoke "Let there be Light" and billions upon billions of galaxies full of stars, planets, moons, asteroids, comets, and nebulae came into being—so many that our scientists to this very day are still trying to count them all. Your word with creative power did it all. You neither requested nor required the universe to cooperate. All of creation has no choice but to instantly respond to Your command. Grant me the faith to believe that this same word (my Bible) with creative power will complete Your work in me as You have promised: to guide, direct, sanctify, transform, nourish, and protect me each and every day. And just like the galaxies are filled with Your majestic wonders, as Your creation, there is nothing more for me to do. I believe Your word is powerful enough to complete all that it has been sent forth to accomplish in my life. Dear Lord—I believe—help my unbelief at times when I'm tempted to believe I need to help You help me.
Amen.

CHRIST IS GRACE!

JOHN 1:6-14

A SPECIAL WORD TO THE READER...

The next series of devotionals relating to *John 1:6-14 (January 9-16)* touch upon John's initial efforts to reveal a liberating truth that will (as God prepares your heart to understand it) *completely revolutionize* your understanding of the central role that believing and trusting God plays in the Christian's life. These verses are, in fact, the first indicators of a vital truth that John returns to scores of times throughout his gospel. Should we assume that John was so lacking in good writing skills that this repetition is nothing more than mediocre redundancy? Or should we prayerfully recognize that under the inspiration of the Holy Spirit, John is not being redundant at all, but in truth, expressing *THE* most vital truth in all of scripture for every Christian to understand.

Assuming John's words are sourced from divine *inspiration* rather than *mediocrity* is only part of the challenge. There is yet another subtle trap that may catch us unawares. These verses in John contain "familiar" words that most Christians will likely *assume* that they already understand their meaning. For the next several days you will read the word "believe" and wonder why I am going over the same thing again and again. If you have this thought, then you have fallen into the trap. I encourage you to slow down your reading and pray for the Lord to deepen your understanding. Each day emphasizes something more wonderful than the day before. I have defined words and subdivided verses into their component phrases in order to carefully discuss how each word and phrase relate to other words and phrases in context. This is to help and encourage you. Regardless of what I do, however, it is only the work of the Holy Spirit in your heart that can (and will) enlighten you concerning the liberating truth contained in these verses—a truth that, once understood, will confirm (without doubt) that scripture is, indeed, the greatest love letter you have ever read; full of grace and truth beyond what you have ever experienced.

JANUARY 9

*There came a man sent from God, whose name was John. ⁷He came as a **witness**, to testify about the Light, **so that all might believe through him**.*
—JOHN 1:6-7

God inspired the Apostle John, the human author of the Gospel of John, to begin his book by introducing us to a different John. We know (from *Matthew 3:1*) that this is John the Baptist, whom God called the forerunner of Jesus (the Messiah) as prophesied in the Old Testament (or as John 1:7 describes him: a *witness* to Jesus).

What was John called by God to be a witness of? *To declare that Jesus is the Light which enlightens every person.* And to what end? *That all might believe in Him.* This is the first of scores of references in John to the fact that *belief alone in Jesus saves*. This same theme is echoed throughout scripture! **BELIEF ALONE, WITHOUT WORKS, SAVES!**

Scripture also tells us the liberating good news that God is the *source* of the belief we have in Jesus. Yes, you read right. The belief every Christian has in Jesus is NOT something originating from us (and is not the result of any work we do *for* God). It is *entirely* a free gift *from* God *(Ephesians 2:8-9)*. God initiated our salvation by first gifting to us the very "belief" in Jesus that He then uses to: (i) rescue us from darkness and (ii) transfer us into the kingdom of His beloved Son *(Colossians 1:13-14)*.

You might ask: If God does it all, then why is John called to be a witness? And by extension: Why should we witness to others? In truth, God has always chosen to reveal Himself through the agency of men and women. The difference is we don't witness to please God, or to gain salvation from Him through our effort. We simply live our lives rejoicing in God's love and grace for us. The "witness" flows effortlessly from within us as *living waters* of salvation to others. To *witness* is not what we DO but who we ARE!

LIVING WATER FOR TODAY:

*For God so loved the world, that He gave His only begotten Son, that **whoever believes in Him** shall not perish, but have eternal life.*—JOHN 3:16

For today, consider again this famous verse, which declares that just *believing in Jesus saves you*. Pray for God to enlighten you to this truth and to remove any need you may feel to try to please Him by "adding" any of your own efforts to the belief He gave you.

January 10

*He came as a witness, to testify about the Light, so that **all might believe** through Him.*
⁸He was not the Light, but he came to testify about the Light.

—John 1:7-8

The Apostle John makes clear from the very outset of his gospel that John the Baptist was NOT the Light. He was only a witness to the Light. In a few more verses we will learn that John's witness was to declare that Jesus is God, every bit God, and God's gift of eternal life to us. We will explore this more beginning on *January 11*.

For today, we must not move too quickly beyond this life-changing word: BE-LIEVE. Many of us have been taught that we need to do something *more* than just believe in Christ Jesus to be saved. Some are told that they need to pray a certain prayer of salvation. Others are taught that they need to make a public statement about accepting Christ to a large group of people in order to be saved. Still others have been instructed that they must invite Christ into their lives and be baptized to be saved. TO BE CLEAR, there is nothing wrong if you have done (or hold as true) any of these things. I am only pointing out that scripture simplifies it to ONE word: Believe. Praise God for this! Some are taught that they are not saved until they commit their lives entirely to the Lord. I personally heard this explanation for years. But scripture says: Believe.

If you are skeptical of this, no worries; just make a mental note and keep reading. By the time we finish the book of John, we will see scores of verses that say the same thing: just believing (or faith in) Christ saves us. Isn't that wonderful?

LIVING WATER FOR TODAY:

*"Sirs, what must I do to be saved?" ³¹They said, "**Believe in the Lord Jesus, and you will be saved.**"*—Acts 16:30b-31a

For today, set aside all of the complicated and qualifying things you "think" you know about your salvation; and begin afresh with the simplicity that is repeated again and again in scripture. A worthless, undeserving life is consumed by God's love and eternal life—and filled to overflowing with His joy and peace—all because of this simple truth. *Believing in Christ Jesus* saves you irrevocably for all time, and forever. *Praise the Lord!*

A PERSONAL TESTIMONY:

BELIEVE IN JESUS AND BE SAVED

The power contained within this simple section of scripture came home to me a couple years ago. One of my sons and I were hunting with a guide in Idaho. We had heard by reputation that this man was a Christian and we looked forward to getting to know him on the trip.

At the end of a long day, we typically end up in camp comprised of a simple tent occupied by everyone in the group; hunters and guides. There is really nothing else to do but have the evening meal, then climb into our sleeping bags and talk about the day or whatever else comes up. As God often orchestrates things, on one of these nights, after a couple of hours of general chatting, our guide suddenly broke down in tears. This big strong man began sharing how deeply troubled he had been about whether he was really saved—whether he was truly a Christian. He shared through his tearful anguish how another Christian friend told him he couldn't be saved if he continued to hunt animals. I can still see the tears flowing from his heart as he struggled under the harsh (and unscriptural) burden laid upon him by another (and I am sure, well-meaning) Christian.

We rejoiced with this guide as we returned to the simplicity of scripture. What power and freedom are in these words: *Believe in Jesus and be saved.*

No matter whether we hunt animals, or have been divorced five times, or had numerous affairs, or still struggle with a drinking, drug, or pornography addiction, or a smoking habit, or can enumerate any number of such personal failures, praise the Lord for this simple, yet absolute, truth: just believing that Jesus is our total forgiveness and eternal life—saves us. AND when we reach our last breath on earth, *Heaven is our home!* Praise God for this simple yet powerful truth!

JANUARY 11

*He came as a witness, to testify about the Light, so that all might believe **through** him.*
—JOHN 1:7

Let's take another day to drill yet deeper into this glorious truth about what actually saves us. As briefly mentioned on *January 9,* God's good news gets even better when we consider that John tells us that God *gives us* the belief (or the believing) in Christ that saves us. Look at the words carefully in *verse seven.* Does it say that all might believe IN Him? No—it says *all might believe THROUGH Him. This means* that even our faith in Christ comes *through* (or *from*) Christ.

We all have witnessed this often. Two people can hear the same good news gospel: that you can't save yourself and none of us—no matter how many good works we try to accumulate—can merit God's holiness and righteousness. God simply chose to rescue us from this certain death by sending His Son Jesus to substitute Himself for us, and through His death on the cross accomplished that rescue mission for all of us. Just believe and be saved to eternal life.

One person will believe this is true, while the other thinks it is foolishness. Is one smarter or more sophisticated than the other? Not at all. Is it a matter that one *believes* and the other doesn't? No, they both believe in what they believe. The difference is that *God has given* to one a life-saving belief. Apart from God's mercy, we would all believe that the gospel is foolishness *(1 Corinthians 1:18). We have nothing to boast of in ourselves.*

LIVING WATER FOR TODAY:

And on the basis of faith in His name, it is the name of Jesus
which has strengthened this man whom you see and know;
*and the faith **which comes through Him** has given him*
this perfect health in the presence of you all.—ACTS 3:16

For today, rejoice in the fact that God's eternal plan for you has been and continues to be carried out entirely by God. You believe in Jesus as your Savior because God gave you that faith to believe—it is not of yourself, it is the gift of God! *Praise the Lord!*

JANUARY 12

*There was the **true Light** which, coming into the world, **enlightens every man**.*
—JOHN 1:9

Here is a good example of how important it is to look to scripture to interpret scripture. It is clear that *verse nine* infers that no human is capable of self-enlightenment and can only be enlightened through the *true Light*. But superficially, we could interpret this one verse out of context to mean that *everyone* is saved by God because Jesus (the true Light) enlightens every man. We need the safeguard of other scriptural verses to give us an accurate understanding.

John 3:19-20 states: *"This is the judgment, that the Light has come into the world, and men loved the darkness rather than the Light, for their deeds were evil. ²⁰For everyone who does evil hates the Light, and does not come to the Light for fear that his deeds will be exposed."* The "Light" in these two verses is the same Light referred to in *John 1:9*. But even though the Light came, men still loved the darkness more "... *for their deeds were evil.*" They don't like to come to the Light because they fear that their evil deeds will be exposed. There is no automatic salvation for these folks. These verses make it clear that some fear the Light and hate it (by running from it)—while others love the Light and respond by embracing it as true.

So the phrase *"enlightens every man"* in *John 1:9* is not referring to Jesus bringing salvation to every person. But rather, that Christ Jesus brought light into the world—both to reveal God's judgment AND His forgiveness.

LIVING WATER FOR TODAY:

Light is sown like seed for the righteous *and gladness for the upright in heart. ¹²Be glad in the* LORD, *you righteous ones, and give thanks to His holy name.*—PSALM 97:11-12

For today, give thanks to the Lord that He has come into the world as Light. And He has sown His light *within you* like a seed, which not only reveals to you the pathway to salvation, but continues throughout your life to shine in the dark places of your heart as He transforms you from glory to glory into His image. *Thank You Lord Jesus!*

There is a brother who comes to the Bible study I teach. He has been coming for about ten years now. He is a highly educated man, recognized as one of the top nuclear physicists in the world. I've been to his house. His library of books must be at least a 20'x30' room with books from floor to ceiling. He told me once that he has read every book in that library seven or eight times. He is a VERY smart man.

One day, I asked him when he came to believe in Christ. His answer was very revealing. He said he grew up being taught, through various institutions and universities in America, that there was no God; but rather, everything that exists came from the "Big Bang" event millions upon millions of years ago—wherein a point of "mathematical nothingness" exploded into everything we see today. He said he grew up with this but it never set right with him.

Then at one point in his life, while he was still a widower, he met what would become his second wife. She was attending my Bible study and asked that he come along. It was the first time in his life that he heard about Jesus and that believing in Him brings salvation and eternal life. He just came, and sat, and listened. And what was the bottom line?

These are his words: "I knew what you were saying was the truth."

How powerful is that? In the face of his massive worldly knowledge, and the cacophony of worldly teachings he had been steeped in for his entire life, God pierced it all and enlightened him to understand the truth that set him free: that Christ Jesus came to save him—to bring salvation to mankind because man, in all his so-called wisdom, education, philosophy, and efforts, can't save himself.

JANUARY 13

He was in the world, and the world was made through Him, and the world did not know Him. ¹¹He came to His own, and those who were His own did not receive Him.
—JOHN 1:10-11

John is making it abundantly clear in these verses that the Light he is talking about is not something ethereal or intangible. This Light is Jesus and He is very tangible. He created the entire world, then entered it through the birth canal of a young woman and was born in Bethlehem of Judea. He grew up and walked about the very world that He had made. He came to His people—the Jewish people of Israel—but they would not receive Him. Think of that! Those same people were being gravely oppressed by the occupying forces of the Roman Empire and were eagerly yearning for their prophesied Messiah, yet they did not recognize Him when they came face to face with Him.

My wife and I have had the opportunity to travel to Israel several times. Each visit brings home afresh the words that John is communicating here. The Light is a real person. He created the world and lived His life in it. This is the Light that lives in every Christian. He understands what it means to live in this world. We have walked along the same hot and dusty paths Jesus walked and visited places (still existing) where He taught. We have entered the tomb that many believe is the very one Jesus was buried in (but could not hold Him). Walking those paths and visiting those places made His sojourn on earth so palpably tangible and real to us. John's use of the word "world" in *verse ten* is referring to this convergent environment of people, culture, and geography.

Just as the Creator God came and said *"Let there be light"* in *Genesis 1:3*, He also came as Light to shine in a darkened world, and to enlighten even our darkened hearts.

LIVING WATER FOR TODAY:

*The **LORD** is my light and my salvation; whom shall I fear? The **LORD** is the defense of my life; whom shall I dread?*—PSALM 27:1

For today, consider the fact that God's light is in your life. *Light is NEVER passive.* Light is not an inanimate object outside of you; but a person living within you— defending and bringing salvation (God's wisdom, comfort, direction, etc.) to you each day!

CONNECTING THE THEOLOGICAL DOTS

On page 20 we asked the question: *What does "being a Christian" really mean?* We suggested that the answer to this question provides insight into the difference between *believing* and *trusting*. *Being a Christian* boils down to God: (i) choosing us as vessels (albeit made of clay) to contain His Son, and (ii) giving us the life-saving faith to *believe*. Most Christians can acknowledge this truth with little difficulty. The confusion creeps in when we consider how BEING a Christian "should" affect our daily living (or when we see another "so-called" Christian acting in demonstrably "unchristian" ways). It was in the midst of just such confusion that Paul asked his famous question in *Galatians 3:1-3, "You foolish Galatians ... are you so foolish? Having begun by the Spirit, are you now being perfected by the flesh?"* Like the Galatians, we suffer this same confusion today.

Let's talk straight about this in practical terms. We become a Christian—then we hear that we *should* act a certain way, do specific things, and refrain from engaging in other things. These messages are delivered through conversations with other Christians, Christian literature, or often from the pulpit. This leads most Christians to infer what Paul wrote in *2 Corinthians 3:18: "But we all ... are being transformed into the same image* [as Christ] *from glory to glory, just as from the Lord, the Spirit"* as relating to an *EXTERNAL* (how we act) transformation.

Actually, Paul is referring to an *INTERNAL* work of God in our lives. What we do does not make the person—what God does makes the person. Some of us vessels are pretty banged up—nevertheless, we are still *vessels chosen by God*. Every Christian knows that they shouldn't get angry or have lustful thoughts. But does it work to determine each morning not to do these things? Take it from me—it doesn't. This is the flesh that we all struggle with our entire lives *(Galatians 5:17)*. It is hypocritical to deny this. Still God is working! What we can't change in a day, God genuinely transforms over time—sometimes over years or decades—in a way that we could never do for ourselves. Our *BELIEVING* in God for salvation becomes *TRUSTING* in Him for our transformation!

Let me give you an example. At my business, we have a lady who has worked in the company for many years. She recently discovered she has cancer. Throughout the diagnostic process, she used up all her medical sick leave and was facing the prospect of major surgery involving two to four weeks of recovery time with no income coming in. When I heard this, my heart instantly responded *we can't let this happen*. I immediately asked our Human Resource Manager to draft a new policy that under such circumstances the company would grant an additional two weeks paid time off, to be reviewed every two weeks thereafter to meet the human needs of the employee.

Now, here is the crucial part of this example: thirty years ago this thought would *never* have occurred to me. I would have said in my heart *too bad, she should have planned ahead and not used up all of her medical sick days*. I likely would have let her go because she could no longer do her job. Yes, I was THAT selfish! I was THAT cruel hearted! I was THAT depraved! Oh, you might assume that I wasn't a Christian then. No, I prayed all the prayers of salvation. I taught Sunday school, and attended services regularly. But I still had a dark, greedy, selfish, cruel heart when it came to running my business and making money. I assure you, I didn't just "decide" one day to change my heart. But over the course of 30 years, God changed my heart toward my co-workers. *I can take absolutely no credit for any of it!* Through it all, I was just a clay pot—a chosen vessel that had the Creator God living and working in me.

What is the lesson from all of this? With all of our fleshly shortcomings, thoughts, addictions, attitudes, and destructive behaviors, none of which we have the power to change in ourselves, we are still *His chosen vessels*. HE is the Potter—WE are the clay. Here is what matters: *Believing* in God saves us—*trusting* in God to transform us gives us peace! In this life we actually see little of His transforming work in us, as though we are looking into a mirror dimly *(1 Corinthians 13:12)*.

Over the course of our lives, our Creator God works our clay. He touches our heart and gently creates it anew. He performs His internal transforming work in us according to His purpose *and His timing*. We are but vessels containing and reflecting His glorious workmanship. Some will say, *"Well, my job is to speed this transformation work along by praying and reading my Bible."* I ask, *"Who has quickened you to pray? Who has placed the thought in your mind to read your Bible?"* In reality, without God's continual drawing us to Himself we would never even think of Him *(Romans 3:10-11)*. Any desire we have to know God all flows from His faithful working in us as He has promised *(Philippians 2:13, 1:6)*. Rest in Him ... and rejoice! This is the difference between *believing* and *trusting*.

January 14

*But **as many as received Him**, to them He gave the right to become children of God,*
even to those who believe in His name.

—John 1:12

Here is yet another verse that reiterates the essential truth that *belief alone saves* you. I must confess that I misunderstood this verse for many years. When John begins the verse with *"as many as received Him"* he is not referring to OUR HUMAN INITIATIVE of inviting Christ into our life, but rather GOD's INITIATIVE in putting Christ in us and making us *recipients* of Him. Now, you may ask, how do we know that this is the correct interpretation? Again, we look to scripture to interpret scripture.

In *Acts 10:47*, we read: *"Surely no one can refuse the water for these to be baptized who have **received** the Holy Spirit just as we did, can he?"* The word *"received"* in this verse is the same Greek word for *"received"* in *John 1:12*. *Acts 10:47* doesn't say that the Holy Spirit was poured out upon all those who were inviting God to come into their life. No, the context of the verse is unambiguous, those who "received" the Holy Spirit (that is, the ones that the *"gift of the Holy Spirit had been poured out on," Acts 10:45*) were simply listening to what Peter was saying. Peter wasn't done talking yet when the Holy Spirit acted. *John 1:12* could actually be paraphrased: *"But as many as are **recipients** of Him, to them He gave the right to become children of God, even to those who believe in His name."*

You and I, whether we realize it or not according to scripture, came to faith in Christ in the same way. At some point in our life, as we heard the gospel, the Holy Spirit enlightened us (remember *January 9*). He enlightened us to understand: (i) that we can't save ourselves and are lost apart from Christ, and (ii) that Jesus, through His death on the cross, is God's gift of eternal life to us. Praise Him!

Living Water for Today:

*But **when God**, who ... called me through His grace, **was***
pleased [16]to reveal His Son in me so that I might preach
Him among the Gentiles ....—Galatians 1:15-16

For today, give thanks to God for His grace *toward you*. Like Paul, God was *pleased* to reveal His Son *IN* you. Not TO you but IN you! It was God's choosing and doing alone. And it *pleased* Him to do it! How great is His love for you?

JANUARY 15

*Who were born, not of blood nor of the will of the flesh **nor of the will of man**, but of God.*
—JOHN 1:13

I spent most of my adult life believing that I had something to do with my salvation. It was up to me to choose to accept Jesus as my personal Savior (or not). If you are like me, *John 1:13* will take you some time to get used to. We received a hint of this truth yesterday *(January 14)* when we read Paul's personal testimony of his own salvation. According to Paul, God didn't present Christ to Paul so he could accept or reject Him. What actually happened was much more glorious. It reflects the greatest of all mercies and grace. God didn't just offer us salvation; HE FLAT OUT CHOSE TO SAVE US! I know ... I know; if you have always thought it was up to you to decide, this truth can be hard to take, but that doesn't make it any less true.

Today, John 1:13, delivers this same truth with blunt force. John gives us NO wiggle room to squirm away from this scriptural reality. *John 1:12-13* are really *one* sentence. *Verse 12* begins by telling us that those who receive the Lord, even those who believe on His name, are given the right to become children of God. *Verse 13* continues by telling us how this miraculous transfer occurs: *"Who were born (see* born again in *John 3:3), NOT of blood* (through family heritage), *NOR the will of the flesh* (by physical reproduction), *NOR the will of man* (by you deciding to accept or reject Jesus), *BUT of God."* That unequivocally declares the simple truth of it. True freedom in our Christian life flows as living waters from this wonderful truth! We are God's children because God (not us) chose to act on our behalf to save us from this dark world!

LIVING WATER FOR TODAY:

> *For He says to Moses, "***I WILL HAVE MERCY ON WHOM I HAVE MERCY, AND I WILL HAVE COMPASSION ON WHOM I HAVE COMPASSION.***" [16]So then it does not depend on the man who wills or the man who runs, **but on God who has mercy**.*—ROMANS 9:15-16

For today, consider how much you hear the abundance of chatter about man's free will. While every sentient human being has the capacity to make a variety of daily decisions, recognize and praise the Lord that He alone has chosen to give *you* a new birth and transfer *you* into His family. Praise God that your "free will" has nothing to do with it!

CONCERNING "FREE WILL"

Does God enlighten man to understand the truth? Jump in a time capsule with me and set the date for 1525 A.D., nearly five centuries ago. This will place us in a dynamic time in church history when the leaders of the Reformation were challenging the Catholic church to allow the Bible to be translated out of Latin into the common languages of the people so everyone could read God's word for themselves.

Martin Luther, one of the great leaders during this Reformation period translated the Bible into German and wrote many books concerning Christian doctrine and scripture. In the following quote, he is explaining why he would not want "free will" even if it was possible for him to have it.

When an associate of mine gave this quote to me, I had to reach for a Kleenex:

"I frankly confess that, for myself, even if it could be, I should not want "free-will" to be given me, nor anything to be left in my own hands to enable me to endeavor after salvation; not merely because in face of so many dangers, and adversities and assaults of devils, I could not stand my ground; but because even were there no dangers, I should still be forced to labour with no guarantee of success. But now that God has taken my salvation out of the control of my own will, and put it under the control of His, and promised to save me, not according to my working or running, but according to His own grace and mercy. I have the comfortable certainty that He is faithful and will not lie to me, and that He is also great and powerful, so that no devils or opposition can break Him or pluck me from Him. Furthermore, I have the comfortable certainty that I please God, not by reason of the merit of my works, but by reason of His merciful favour promised to me; so that, if I work too little, or badly, He does not impute it to me, but with fatherly compassion pardons me and makes me better. This is the glorying of all the saints in their God."

Martin Luther, *The Bondage of the Will* (Grand Rapids, Revell, 1957), 313-314.

JANUARY 16

*And the Word became flesh, and dwelt among us, and we saw His glory, glory as of the only begotten from the Father, **full of grace and truth**.*
—JOHN 1:14

We learned on *January 2* that John referred to Jesus by one of His proper names "Word." In a court of law John's eyewitness testimony would be admitted into evidence—that God manifested Himself in the flesh in the person of Jesus; and Jesus tangibly lived on earth dwelling in the community. John further observed that Jesus expressed a "glory" that only the Son of God could possess—full of grace and truth.

The phrase *"full of grace and truth"* means that Jesus was completely focused on the task of revealing God's grace and truth to humanity. Not about God's grace and "something else," or grace AND law, or grace AND what God expects from us in return. No, Christ was filled up and consumed with sharing God's grace toward us.

The word "grace" is used so frequently that it can lose the potency and power of its true meaning. Spiro Zodhiates, in his *Greek Word Dictionary*, gives this definition: *"A favor done by God without expectation of anything in return; the absolute free expression of the loving kindness of God to men. Finding its only motive in the bounty and the benevolence of the Giver; it is unearned and unmerited favor."* According to this definition, we can't save ourselves. No matter how well we act, how hard we work, how earnest our desire, how smart our minds, how compassionate our hearts—we can never merit God's righteousness. Only God's unmerited lovingkindness can save us from certain eternal death.

LIVING WATER FOR TODAY:

*But God, being rich in mercy, because of His great love with which He loved us, ⁵**even when we were dead in our transgressions**, made us alive together with Christ (by grace you have been saved).*—EPHESIANS 2:4-5

For today, to quicken this verse to you, ask yourself what a dead person can do to be more acceptable to God. Can they exercise their "free will" or work harder for Him? What a silly thought! Thank God on this day that when you were dead (and you had no understanding of your need for Christ), He was alive—rich in mercy and grace—to make you alive (spiritually) together with His Son. *PTL!*

...OR IT WOULDN'T BE GRACE!

Follow along with this summary:

- We can't be deserving of God's grace ... *Or it wouldn't be grace*;

- We can't earn it in any way ... *Or it wouldn't be grace*;

- We can't barter or negotiate for it ... *Or it wouldn't be grace*;

- We can't be obligated to do anything in return ... *Or it wouldn't be grace*;

- We can't add a helping hand to God's grace ... *Or it wouldn't be grace*;

- We can't have any responsibility to work hard and make ourselves a better Christian ... *Or it wouldn't be grace*;

- We can't suffer shame for our failures ... *Or it wouldn't be grace*;

- We can't be punished for our failures ... *Or it wouldn't be grace*.

Grace is *unmerited* favor and kindness from God; it is God accomplishing a salvation for us that we could never accomplish for ourselves. It is God sanctifying us over the course of our life by growing the qualities of His life in our life—at His pace—without any help from us. It is God treating us kindly day after day after day, even though we still continue to fail every day. It is God caring for us (and everything that concerns us) out of His immense kindness and love.

THAT IS GRACE!

LIVING WATER FROM JOHN 1:6-14

January 9	John the Baptist (sent from God) testified that Jesus is the Light, so that all might believe through him.
January 10	Believing in Christ Jesus saves us irrevocably for all time.
January 11	Our faith in Christ comes through (or from) Christ. God gives us the very belief in Christ that saves us.
January 12	Christ Jesus brought light into the world to reveal both God's judgment and His forgiveness.
January 13	Jesus lived in the world He created, and the world did not know (comprehend, perceive, or recognize) Him.
January 14	Enlightenment from the Holy Spirit has given us the right to become children of God.
January 15	This is the greatest of all mercies and grace! God alone chose to give us a new birth and transfer us into his family.
January 16	Through His life, Jesus revealed God's grace and truth to humanity.

PRAYER

Father, I pray that today and in the coming days You will open my eyes and enlighten my heart concerning my "role" in Your eternal plan, not only Your plan of salvation for me, but how You mold all of my life like the Potter does the clay. Make it increasingly real to me how the clay can do NOTHING, while the Potter does EVERYTHING! I grow weary of trying to add my own self-effort to "help" You, and I occasionally sense the freedom that exists by letting go of all my self-efforts; yet like Paul in Romans 7, my flesh relentlessly hungers for self-significance. I want to please You because I love You, yet I pray that you will make real in my heart that the only thing that pleases you is Christ and His transforming work in me. I have nothing to boast of in myself. I only desire to behold Your wondrous workmanship revealed in me. Grant me the patience to trust in your ways and timing. I give You all the honor and glory for what you are accomplishing in me. I desire only Your ways in my life, which I know are pleasant, peaceful, and marked by happiness.
Amen.

GOD ALWAYS TREATS US KINDLY

JOHN 1:15-34

January 17

*For of His fullness we have all received, and **grace upon grace**.*
—John 1:16

I will never forget some years ago a young husband came to me. His wife had serious back problems and he recognized that he was often impatient with her. He said, "Daryl, I'm afraid to even pray for more patience for fear that God will cause me to injure my back, so I'll have more patience with her." Boy, this memory is as vivid to me now (as I write this devotional day), as it was when he said it. It reflected a concept about God, as the hard taskmaster, that I held for the first 40 years of my Christian life. This concept, expressed by this young husband, may reflect *the biggest misunderstanding about God* held by all people, even among Christians! Let's look at this verse more closely.

Verse 16 tells us *"… of His fullness we have all received, and **grace upon grace**."* This means that God ALWAYS deals with us kindly, never harshly, never hurtfully; or to say it in a way that addresses that young husband's fear: He never hurts us so we will have more patience in a similar regard with someone else. *The Living Bible* reads, *"We have all benefited from the rich blessings He brought to us—blessing upon blessing heaped upon us!"* Notice John did not say *"**to be** heaped upon us"* as some sort of future event; but rather, he shared the revolutionary good news that this grace upon grace (or blessing upon blessing) has *already* been heaped upon us as a fact fully accomplished by God! It is not a grace (or a blessing) that is dependent in any way upon our performance.

John is telling us that we have all received (past tense) grace upon grace, or we all have received God's full blessing upon blessing heaped upon us *already*. How has this happened and what does it mean? Tomorrow, in *verse 17*, we learn the answers.

LIVING WATER FOR TODAY:

*But we proved to be **gentle** among you, as a **nursing mother tenderly cares for her own children**.*

—1 Thessalonians 2:7

For today, consider this wonderful word picture offered by Paul. It is an insightful example of how our heavenly Father always treats us. Paul was a man *"breathing threats and murder" (Acts 9:1)* before meeting the Lord on the road to Damascus. Now he is as gentle to others as the Lord was gentle to him—*and is always gentle to us!*

JANUARY 18

*For the Law was given through Moses; **grace and truth were realized through Jesus Christ.***
—JOHN 1:17

How did God make it possible to heap blessing upon blessing and grace upon grace on us? He sent His Son Jesus to fulfill the Law and usher into reality an entirely new basis for us to have a deeper relationship with Him. The Law was all about *our* performance: Do this and be blessed—Do that and be cursed. From humanity's sinful perspective the requirements of the Law looked simple; yet we relentlessly and consistently failed. Here is this legal mindset in action today: We get angry at the guy driving in front of us on the freeway, or the waiter at a restaurant, or our spouse. We see our sinful flesh manifest every day and wonder how many chances we will get before God punishes us? *That is a thought process still operating under the Law.* The Law was God's way of showing humanity that in our own efforts we can *never* achieve God's righteousness.

This stands in stark contrast to the grace and truth we realize today through Jesus Christ. It is no longer what *we* do to meet God's righteous standards; but what *Christ has done* on our behalf. God sent His Son to dwell among us and removed us from the equation. He replaced us with Jesus, who completely and perfectly fulfilled the Law. Grace and truth replaced requirements and penalty! This brings us to the very best of the good news: God now deals with every believer today solely out of His mercy and kindness (regardless of how we have acted in the past, or are acting currently, or will act in the future). This is His *"blessing upon blessing heaped upon us!"* Praise the Lord!

The liberating truth is in this *verse 17*: We are no longer under law but grace. *Every day* God heaps upon us grace upon grace and blessings upon blessings because Christ lives in us *as our righteous fulfillment of the Law!*

LIVING WATER FOR TODAY:

*For **Christ is the end of the law** for righteousness to everyone who believes.*—ROMANS 10:4

For today, recognize that Christ has fulfilled the Law—not only for our eternal salvation but also for our daily living. Even when our flesh is acting out at any given moment during the day God still treats us with mercy and kindness. *Praise the Lord!*

JANUARY 19

*No one has seen God at any time; the **only begotten God who is in the bosom of the Father**, He has explained Him.*

—JOHN 1:18

John has already identified Jesus as God *(see January 2)*. The phrase *"only begotten God"* is referring to the uniqueness of Christ; and, again, that He is God. John is saying that while no one has seen God the Father at any time, that does not mean He has left us without a means to observe and know Him. He does not want us ignorant of His heart's intent for us. He sent forth His Son who was *"in the bosom of the Father,"* meaning the heart's desire of both Jesus and the Father were the same—full of love, forgiveness, kindness, compassion, mercy, and grace. With that imprinted in His heart, Jesus came to dwell among us for the purpose of "explaining" or "revealing" His loving, forgiving, kind, compassionate, merciful, and gracious Father to us. Was God's desire for His children to exhaust themselves endlessly in a vain self-effort to fulfill the Law? No! You will not find that in the life of Jesus.

The Message translates this same verse: *"No one has ever seen God, not so much as a glimpse. This one-of-a-kind God-Expression, who exists at the very heart of the Father, has made him plain as day."* John is telling us that we can know the Father and understand His heart's intention as *"plain as day."* How? By observing the life of Jesus! The Father and the Son are not separate, but One. Look at Jesus' perfect and sinless life (that fulfilled all aspects of the Law's requirements on our behalf), His death on the cross (substituting Himself for us and wiping away our sins and failures), and His triumphant resurrection over death itself (providing us hope for our present and future life)—all of it reveals God's loving intention for us. The closer we look at Jesus, the more we see the Father's mercy and grace for us!

LIVING WATER FOR TODAY:

Fixing our eyes on Jesus, *the author and perfecter of faith.*—HEBREWS 12:2A

For today, consider Jesus' life on earth: He dwelt among sinners, comforted His followers with parables, healed the blind and crippled, forgave sin, raised the dead, fed the hungry, and offered His own life on the cross. This is the Jesus who lives *in us* to reveal and explain the Father's heart to us every day. *Praise Him!*

January 20

*I did not recognize Him, but He who sent me to baptize in water said to me, "He upon whom you see the Spirit descending and remaining upon Him, this is the **One who baptizes in the Holy Spirit.**" 34I myself have seen, and have testified that **this is the Son of God.***
—John 1:33-34

Having established that Jesus is God, the Apostle John then tells us about John the Baptist, a prophet sent by God to be a "voice crying in the wilderness" *(verse 23)* proclaiming the arrival of Jesus. While John the Baptist was baptizing people in Bethany beyond the Jordan *(verse 28)*, the religious leaders from Jerusalem sent messengers to ask questions of him. Why? Because their holy scriptures (the Old Testament) clearly spoke of a coming Messiah/Savior. They wanted to know if John the Baptist was that Messiah. He denied it and told them that while he was baptizing in water the Messiah (Jesus) was already among them and would baptize in the Holy Spirit *(verses 19-34)*.

In this context, water baptism was a symbol of spiritual cleansing. It didn't actually cleanse anybody. It was a physical parable of a spiritual reality. It indicated the repentant heart of the one being baptized. John the Baptist declared that Jesus was coming to baptize, not in water, but in the Holy Spirit. What is the significance of this?

For Christ Jesus to baptize in the Holy Spirit means that He immersed us in His Spirit including putting His Spirit *in* us. It was not a one-time event but continuous. This spiritual baptism accomplishes the *total cleansing* that water baptism signified. God's Spirit now surrounds us and is in us; fully accomplishing our cleansing—satisfying God *every* day, in *every* way. We are totally cleansed! We still have our flesh, of course, but we are perpetually clean, righteous, sanctified, and redeemed because God has baptized/immersed us in Christ and Christ's Spirit is in us.

Living Water for Today:

*But by His doing you are in **Christ Jesus,** who became to us wisdom from God, and **righteousness and sanctification, and redemption.**—*1 Corinthians 1:30

For today, rejoice that at this very moment, as you read this devotional, Christ is baptizing you with His Holy Spirit; God has immersed you *in Christ* who is your *total* righteousness, sanctification, and redemption. *Praise Him for His loving grace and mercy!*

Let's expand on the verse we ended yesterday's devotional with *(1 Corinthians 1:30)* since it reflects upon the same principle as Christ baptizing us in the Holy Spirit. I truly love this verse: *"But by His* [the Father's] *doing you are in Christ Jesus, who became to us **wisdom from God**, and **righteousness** and **sanctification**, and **redemption**."* This verse paints a wonderful picture of our relationship with Christ. God has taken all believers and placed them IN Christ. It doesn't say that we are walking "hand-in-hand" with Christ, or that we are "riding on His shoulders" but that we are totally enclosed in Christ. There is no portion or aspect of us hanging outside of Christ. He has completely encased us in Christ and Christ has become our total wisdom, righteousness, sanctification, and redemption before God.

The verse is also clear that all of this was accomplished entirely by God. We had nothing to do with it. None of it depends on us deserving it or acting in some way to earn it. None of it depends upon our understanding what we are reading in this verse (or this devotional) and then changing the way we act. All of it is grace upon grace—"undeserving-favor" heaped upon "undeserving-favor" from God. Can our minds fully comprehend this? I know I can't.

Take righteousness from this verse as an example: it means, *"right with God in every way."* You can fill in the blank here to personalize and appreciate the full meaning in this one word. Say, "Christ makes my '_____' right with God." Fill it in with anything you can think of, anything that you struggle with, anything that you are ashamed of. ***Christ has made it right with God!***

Do you worry about failing as a parent? Christ has made you a perfect parent before God. Do you regret certain poor decisions you have made in your life? Christ has wiped out all those decisions and made them right with God. So many examples could be written here. I encourage you to fill in the blank for yourself.

This verse draws me into praise and worship to Him. It brings me into a deeper understanding of the next verse, which is really the remaining portion of the sentence begun in verse 30: *"… so that, just as it is written, 'Let him who boasts, boast in the Lord.'"* We have nothing to boast of in ourselves. We can only boast in Him!

JANUARY 21

The next day he saw Jesus coming to him and said, **"Behold, the Lamb of God who takes away the sin of the world!"**

—JOHN 1:29

How does Christ make us right with God in every way? This is answered in today's verse. John the Baptist saw Jesus coming and proclaimed: *"Behold, the Lamb of God who takes away the sin* [the shortcomings, failures, mistakes, and wrong choices] *of the world!"*

Why is Christ being referred to in this verse as the *"Lamb of God?"* It is a direct reference to the Old Testament. When God gave the *Children of Israel* the Law (at their request) He knew they would fail. So, out of His love and mercy, He provided a way for them to "transfer" their sins and failures onto an innocent lamb without blemish to represent them, then sacrifice that lamb in a burnt offering to God. It was temporary, but gave the *Israelites* a means to remain in fellowship with their God. All of this, of course, pointed to Christ—God's eternal solution for dealing with the sins of the world.

John the Baptist referred to Jesus as the *"Lamb of God"* because His ultimate sacrifice on the cross would take away *all* our failures, *all* our impatience, *all* our wrong choices, *all* our immoral thoughts, *all* our addictions, *all* our wrong feelings, *everything* about us that falls short of the righteousness of God.

What can we conclude from this? As I personally contemplated this question, I realized that I have lived over 80 years now and can make this observation as a true statement: I have *never* felt kicked around by God. I have *never* felt anything other than God's gentleness in dealing with me. Of course, I can also add that I have *often* felt the consequences of sin radiating from my flesh—its unhappiness, stress, resentment, anger, selfishness, worry, etc.—which is *not* gentle. None of which comes from God.

LIVING WATER FOR TODAY:

Therefore if anyone is in Christ, he is a new creature; the old things passed away; behold, new things have come. **18Now all these things are from God, who reconciled us to Himself through Christ.**—2 CORINTHIANS 5:17-18A

For today, know that you have been placed by God into Christ, the Lamb of God, and have been made a new creation in Him. You are *fully* reconciled to God through Christ!

JANUARY 22

*As far as the **east is from the west**, so far has He removed our transgressions from us.*
—PSALM 103:12

Yesterday, we read how John the Baptist declared: *"Behold, the Lamb of God who takes away the sin of the world!"* Let's contemplate just how far away God has removed our transgressions from us. Today's verse explains it. King David, the author of *Psalm 103*, tells us that God has removed our transgressions *"as far as the east is from the west."* Isn't that an interesting way to describe it? You can travel around the world heading east and never travel west. This is not so if you begin your journey south. Eventually, you will be traveling north again. This is never the case when traveling east to west. This is a wonderful way for King David to say that our sin has been removed from us to a point of infinite distance. Nothing is farther apart than the east is from the west.

This may sound like a trivial turn of phrase, nothing more than eloquent literary poetry, but it is much more than that. It is telling us a compelling truth: that all our sins and transgressions committed throughout our entire lives have been completely removed from us. God has removed *all* our wrong choices, *all* our impatience, *all* our critical attitudes, *all* the millions and billions of times we did not fully trust Him. He has removed it *all* as far as the unmeasurable distance between east and west.

As wonderful as this truth is, it brings us to a much more liberating insight that God is drawing us to see. Many Christians live in fear, believing that Christ will reveal all their sins at His Judgment Seat, like on a 60-foot, big-screen television! How can this possibly be if He has already removed them to a place so far away that it is beyond our ability to fathom? Why do we still struggle with guilt, believing the lie that we are displeasing God, rather than praising Him in our hearts each day for His love and mercy for us?

LIVING WATER FOR TODAY:

*I, even I, am the one who **wipes out your transgressions** for My own sake, and **I will not remember your sins**.*—ISAIAH 43:25

For today, trust in the fact that God will *never* go back on His promise: *"I will not remember your sins."* This is total salvation (and grace heaped upon grace) for us!

January 23

*Among them we too all formerly lived in the **lusts of our flesh** ... and of the mind, and were by nature children of wrath, even as the rest.*

—Ephesians 2:3

Many dear Christians cannot accept the glorious freedom Christ has made possible through His death on the cross as the Lamb of God who takes away the sin of the world. They cannot believe that their sins are forgotten by God *(Isaiah 43:25)* and removed as far as the east is from the west *(Psalm 103:12)* when they see their sins played out in their lives every day. Those sins look more "real" than the scripture that tells them the opposite. But scripture doesn't say that the Christian will not sin. On the contrary, scripture says our sins (which we continue to commit) will be remembered no more and removed from us as far as the east is from the west. What is the basis for the distinction that scripture is making here? Today's verse explains it.

Prior to Christ revealing Himself *in* us, we *"were by nature children of wrath."* That means it was our nature to live 24/7 solely in the lust of our flesh (and mind) according to the evil and ungodly desires within us. We had no thought or attraction to God at all *(Romans 3:11)*. There was no Spirit of God within us, enlightening us, overcoming those desires, and giving us (for the first time) an attraction to God.

But God did not leave us in this pitiful condition. He reconciled us to Himself through Christ by placing us *in Christ* and crucifying us on the cross with Him *(Galatians 2:20)*, which killed our old nature and made us a new creation with a new nature in Christ! That is who we are before God today. Do we still suffer from sinful thoughts and actions that arise from our flesh? Yes, but that is not who we are. *"The old things passed away; behold, new things have come"* (2 Corinthians 5:17).

LIVING WATER FOR TODAY:

*I have been **crucified with Christ; and it is no longer I who live**, but Christ lives in me; and the **life which I now live in the flesh I live by faith in the Son of God**, who loved me and gave Himself up for me.*—Galatians 2:20

For today, acknowledge your faith in the Son of God, who loves you and gave Himself up for you! It is His nature that draws you to God and transforms you into His image.

A PERSONAL TESTIMONY

A VESSEL OF GOD'S MERCY

As I have grown to realize the extent of God's grace and mercy toward me, I can only describe it as a powerfully humbling experience. If you've ever attended my Bible studies or listened online, you may have heard me say that the only thing I want on my tombstone is the phrase: "A VESSEL OF GOD'S MERCY." This comes from *Romans 9:23-24*, which declares: *"And He did so to make known the riches of **His glory upon vessels of mercy**, which He prepared beforehand for glory, even us, whom He also called, not from among Jews only, but also from among Gentiles."* For those of you who are around to arrange my memorial service, you can place a photo of my face on the bulletin, and right on that photo print the words: "A VESSEL OF GOD'S MERCY."

The truth is, I haven't done anything! In fact, I'm rather like the poster boy for grace upon grace as a personal testimony. Forty years ago, the guy writing this devotional repeatedly thought to himself I DON'T WANT TOO MUCH GOD for fear He would take the fun out of my life. Now, I recognize that my life has been one constant stream of grace *upon* grace *upon* even more grace. I often argue with the Apostle Paul as to which one of us is the "chiefest of sinners." Yet God has *always* treated me with mercy and kindness.

Paul, in *Romans 7:25* and *8:1-2*, puts this last week of devotionals into a concise nugget. *Romans 7:25* reads, *"Thanks be to God through Jesus Christ our Lord! So then, on the one hand I myself with my mind am serving the law of God, but on the other, with my flesh the law of sin."* The next *verses (8:1-2)* is all you need to experience liberation as a Christian for the rest of your life: *"Therefore there is now no condemnation for those who are in Christ Jesus. ²For the law of the Spirit of life in Christ Jesus has set you free from the law of sin and of death."*

Thanks be to God that we have a new heart—a heart that has an attraction for God and through that attraction is serving the law of God. But Paul does not overlook, *"with my flesh the law of sin."* He is acknowledging that he personally still sins. And because He still sins, he unequivocally declares, once again, that there is *now* (since the "Spirit of life" has come) NO condemnation (meaning no wrong or pronouncement of guilt for anything, forever) for those who are IN CHRIST JESUS. *Praise God!*

LIVING WATER FROM JOHN 1:15-34

January 17	As believers, we have all received God's full blessing upon blessing heaped upon us—grace upon grace.
January 18	Grace and truth through Jesus perfectly fulfilled the Law; Christ lives in us as our complete righteousness.
January 19	Jesus' perfect and sinless life as the expression of God, reveals His loving intention for us.
January 20	Our spiritual baptism in the Holy Spirit fully accomplishes our cleansing—satisfying God every day, in every way.
January 21	Jesus, the Lamb of God, takes away all our sins— everything about us that falls short of the righteousness of God.
January 22	God has removed our sins as far as the immeasurable distance between east and west—and He will never think of them again!
January 23	God rescued us from the lusts of our flesh and mind and made us a new creation (with a new nature) in Christ.

PRAYER

Lord, there is not one thing about any of this that I deserve. I don't deserve to be among those You have chosen to be recipients of Your immense mercy and kindness. I certainly have not earned such loving grace through sinless and righteous living. From my perspective, I continue to sin every day; yet, as 1 Corinthians 1:30 promises, You have placed **me**—*IN CHRIST and made* **me** *righteous, sanctified, and redeemed in Him. You have promised that You will remember* **my** *sins no more and separate them from* **me** *as far as the east is from the west. You continue to draw* **me** *to Yourself. You quicken* **me** *to pray and gain nourishment from Your word. You guide* **me** *daily in the path that You have chosen for* **me**. *The only response I have is to give you all the praise and glory forever and forever.*
My boast is in You!
Amen.

JESUS
CHANGES LIVES

—

JOHN 1:35-51

January 24

Again the next day John was standing with two of his disciples, *³⁶and he looked at Jesus as He walked, and said, "Behold, the Lamb of God!"* *³⁷The two disciples heard him speak, and they followed Jesus.*

—John 1:35-37

In these verses we learn of a fascinating event that made me uncomfortable for years (I will tell you why in a moment). John the Baptist is standing with two of his "disciples" (meaning "followers"). Jesus walks into view. John sees him and declares, *"Behold, the Lamb of God."* It is unclear whether this was a broad proclamation or spoken specifically to these two followers. Regardless, the two did exactly what you would expect them to do—they left off following John and began following Jesus.

We get a deeper insight into John the Baptist's attitude by reading *John 3:28-30*, where he likens himself to a friend of the bridegroom, who *"rejoices greatly"* at the bridegroom's voice. It is in this context where we read the famous statement *"He must increase, but I must decrease."* This is not something that John the Baptist grudgingly conceded. On the contrary, *John 1:7 (January 9-10)* declared that his sole interest was for *all* people to hear the gospel about Christ *and believe.* He had no jealousy and no interest in maintaining or increasing his own ministry. He pointed them all to Jesus.

What a wonderful reality check for us today. For many years I was highly active in a missionary endeavor in India that ministered both eternal hope and the ability to become self-sustaining—food, clothing, shelter and training in essential trades. The project had many challenges but was generally quite successful. Over the years, I grew proud of this work to the point that I became secretly jealous of other ministries in the region. John's attitude always pricked my conscience in those days because it was so loving and gracious. Today, by God's mercy, He has brought me to rejoice in every ministry that points people to Christ. He has transferred me from *my works* to *His grace.*

Living Water for Today:

John [the Baptist] *answered and said, "A **man can receive nothing unless it has been given him from heaven."*** —John 3:27

For today, look at all the Christian ministries in your community (are you a Christian worker?); rejoice that God is providing so many witnesses pointing to His Son Jesus.

JANUARY 25

*One of the two who heard John speak and followed Him, was Andrew, Simon Peter's brother. ⁴¹He found first his own brother Simon and said to him, "We have found the Messiah" (which translated means Christ). ⁴²He brought him to Jesus. Jesus looked at him and said, **"You are Simon the son of John; you shall be called Cephas"** (which is translated Peter).*

—John 1:40-42

John began by telling us that ***Jesus is God*** *(January 2)*; that we are eternally saved simply through ***believing in Him***—not through the church we attend or any effort on our part *(January 9-11, 14)*; that what Christ accomplished on the cross for us is the sole basis for ***God dealing with us entirely out of His mercy and kindness***—never according to what we deserve *(January 17-18, 20)*; and now, John tells us the next amazing fact: ***Jesus changes people's lives!*** He doesn't just save us from hell to glory, He becomes an increasingly vital part of our lives throughout our remaining earthly life.

Andrew runs off to find his brother Simon and brings him to Jesus. The first thing Jesus does is change Simon's name to Cephas, which means Peter. What does that mean? Scripture often uses the meaning of names to teach us something. Simon (which is the same as Simeon in *Genesis 49:5-7*) was the brother of Levi and they were violent men, whose *"swords are implements of violence" (verse 5)*. From his name we know that the Simon in John 1:42 was a very volatile and unstable man—fierce and full of anger—and Jesus changed his name to Cephas, which means "rock" or "very stable."

In this one act of changing Simon's name, Jesus promised to change his hot tempered, angry, vindictive spirit—over the course of his life—to a stable, loving, compassionate spirit. I've experienced this myself which I will share in the coming days.

LIVING WATER FOR TODAY:

*But we all, with unveiled face, beholding as in a mirror the glory of the Lord, **are being transformed into the same image from glory to glory**, just as from the Lord, the Spirit.*—2 Corinthians 3:18

For today, know that like Peter God has chosen you, yet you are still made of dust *(Psalm 103:14)*. You may still struggle with many fleshly things but He is faithfully changing you *day by day!* Praise the Lord!

This portion of God's word related to Peter is very personal and precious to me. While we will spend several more days looking at Peter's life, I had to pause here to give you a personal testimony of how profoundly God has changed my life over the last 40 years. My experiences are not the same as Peter's and your experiences will not be the same as mine, but the common theme in all of our experiences is the faithful, day-by-day, working of God in each of our lives *(Philippians 2:13, 1:6)*.

That same God who changed Simon's name to Cephas/Peter was working in me in the same transformative way. God changed me *from* the obsession for making more and more money by any means possible (for the first 40 years of my life) *to* just wanting to share God's good news with others today. He changed me *from* a man who did not want too much God for fear that He would take all the fun out of my life *to* a man whose richest enjoyment is found in Christ today.

I look back and see how God has transformed my attitudes and fears in so many ways. For example, for many years I held in my heart a very dark and palpable fear of dying and not waking up in Heaven. Over the years, He changed that fear to absolute certainty that Heaven is my home. No fear remains! Forty years ago, I couldn't walk into a hospital for more than five minutes before growing faint and compulsively needing to leave. I could not handle it—the fear was too great. Today, hospitals are some of my favorite places to be while visiting people who are hurting and in physical need of comfort.

This is the meaning behind *John 4:14* which is the theme verse for this devotional series: *"But whoever drinks of the water that I will give him shall never thirst; but the water that I will give him will become in him a **well of water springing up to eternal life.**"* This water does not become a blueprint that we try hard to follow or apply. It does not represent a lifestyle that calls for us to do our best to live by. No, there is nothing of our human effort found in this verse, only living water from the Spirit of God that becomes in us a well of water springing up to eternal life. It isn't a one-time event but a daily experience. It is the water that is active, we are but containers—and this living water is changing us day-by-day!

JANUARY 26

Simon Peter then, having a sword, drew it and struck the high priest's slave, and cut off his right ear; and the slave's name was Malchus.
—JOHN 18:10

Let's return again to the life of Peter. By the time we come to this verse, Peter has been a follower of Jesus for several years. Scripture makes it clear that he loves the Lord and is a fervent disciple. Yet (true to his fleshly "Simon" nature) after years with Jesus he still reacts angrily at times. This fleshly part of Peter is on full display when some religious leaders confront Jesus, Peter draws his sword and whacks off the ear of the high priest's slave. Obviously, even though Jesus had changed his name, Peter was still very volatile!

How I love God's word—it is so practical! Picture yourself as an observer present and watching this scene play out. You might think, *Wait a minute! God has changed this man's life, gave him a new name, promised to transform him from within, so why is he still wielding his sword? Doesn't he understand that God is totally in control of this situation?*

As a practical matter, we really don't need Peter's example to understand this dynamic because we can see the same inclinations of our flesh in our own lives on a daily basis. We may not draw a sword, but we certainly can get angry or offended at someone whom we feel is disrespecting or trying to provoke us. We may not whack off somebody's ear, but we can be tempted to give that person a piece of our mind.

The point of this verse is not to make us try to be better than Peter, but to demonstrate that we are *exactly like Peter*. It further demonstrates that God has called each of His children and placed them on His ever-brightening path of the righteous *(Proverbs 4:18)*. Every Christian is on this path. God is at work in every believer's life *(Philippians 2:13)*.

LIVING WATER FOR TODAY:

*But the path of the righteous is like the light of dawn, **that shines brighter and brighter until the full day**.*—PROVERBS 4:18

For today, rest in the assurance that God has placed *you* on His *ever-brightening path of understanding*, and God will continue to grow *you* precisely according to His will *(Philippians 1:6)*.

JANUARY 27

And Jesus said to him, "Truly I say to you [referring to Peter]*, that this very night, before a rooster crows twice, **you yourself will deny Me three times**."*

—MARK 14:30

We are not done with Peter. We now have the infamous story of when Peter denied Jesus three times after he had boasted that he would follow the Lord to his death. Today's verse gives us the response Jesus made to Peter, "*before a rooster crows twice, **you yourself will deny Me three times**.*"

Peter was a believer and his boasting obviously reflected deeply held human loyalty and commitment to the Lord. God changed his name, but this same God essentially told Peter, "Look, I appreciate what you are telling me out of your feelings of allegiance to me, and you may feel you are being completely honest, but I'm telling you what I know, because I know you thoroughly through and through, this night won't end before you deny me three times."

What is the insight for us to see from this verse? Although Peter had an undeniable attraction to Christ, he also had his miserable flesh (which failed him often). This is not to condone or give license to our flesh in any way, but it does minister comfort to us right where we live every day. There is not a day goes by that I don't wish God would zap out of me some ugly thing from *my* flesh—anger, impatience, selfishness, an immoral thought—you name it. But that is not God's plan or His timing. His plan is to work in us throughout our lives *(Philippians 2:13, 1:6)* and "zap" our entire flesh only when He resurrects us from this perishable body to an imperishable body *(1 Corinthians 15:42).*

LIVING WATER FOR TODAY:

For it is God who is at work in you, both to will and to work for His good pleasure.—PHILIPPIANS 2:13

For today, simply trust in God's timing for your growth in Him and His growth in others. This simple truth will free you from judging others for what you perceive as manifestations of their flesh, for God is at work in them (just as He is in you) *to will and to do His good pleasure.* This is a glorious freedom. *Praise the Lord!*

WHY DO SOME CHRISTIANS NEVER SEEM TO CHANGE?

You might be wondering if Jesus always changes lives, then why do we know some Christians who don't show any change? Of course, we know that we should not be judging them, but sometimes we do, because we are human. By God's mercy, He has compassion on us because we are but dust. I am asked this question from time to time and here is my answer:

First, we need to remember that we cannot know for certain who is (and is not) a true believer. We don't have the ability to know the true heart of anybody. *Only God does.*

Second, we do not know what God is doing inside a person's life before it starts showing on the outside. The scope of God's work through the misery and damage of a person's life can take time. The person may be living a more fleshly life like the Corinthians were in *1 Corinthians 3* but that did not diminish the fact that Paul referred to them as saints.

Third, we don't know how God is using a person's rebellious years. This really describes the first 40 years of my life. I didn't want too much God, but patiently over decades of time, God brought me to the end of myself and to a point where I wanted to experience God's true life more than anything else. I am not alone in this rebellious way. We cannot see into that process as God can.

Fourth, we don't know where any believer is on God's ever brightening path. Proverbs 4:18 teaches us, *"But the path of the righteous is like the light of dawn, **that shines brighter and brighter until the full day.**"* None of us have God's ability to diagnose another person's "x" location exactly on that ever-brightening path and say definitively where they are.

God has told us that He is at work progressively in every true believer's life and that is why it is not for us to judge anyone. He knows where He has each of His children and He is well able to complete what He has started in them. We can be assured, as Paul was when he wrote, *"For I am confident of this very thing, that He who began a good work in you will perfect it until the day of Christ Jesus"* (Philippians 1:6).

January 28

*While they were eating, He took some bread, and after a blessing He broke it, and gave it to them, and said, "Take it; this is My body." ²³And when He had taken a cup and given thanks, He gave it to them, and they all drank from it. ²⁴And He said to them, "This is **My blood of the covenant**, which is poured out for many."*

—Mark 14:22-24

These verses are familiar to most Christians in the context of what we celebrate as the Lord's Supper. But they are also vitally important for another comforting reason. They are the immediate context for Peter's boasting, *"Even though all may fall away, yet I will not" (Mark 14:29)* and Jesus' response that Peter would deny Him **three times**.

This to me is one of the dearest and most enlightening sections of God's word that I have discovered in my 40 years of study. Jesus is saying through this demonstration that we don't know how weak we really are, but He does. Peter could stand there knowing that Jesus was the Christ, having seen all the miracles He performed, and declare that he would follow Jesus even to death. But Jesus knew Peter could not follow, even with his best intentions. He simply did not have the power to do it. *Neither do we!*

This context gives new meaning to the Lord's Supper. Jesus is pouring out His body and blood for us so He could freely give us of His righteousness. He was not giving us righteousness based on how we act, nor whether we can keep our word that we will never deny Him. Jesus sacrificed his body and blood for us because He knew how weak we are. He knew our flesh would lose its patience a million times during our lives and be selfish and full of pride. By pouring Himself out on the cross, He became for us the righteousness that we could never accomplish for ourselves *(1 Corinthians 1:30).*

LIVING WATER FOR TODAY:

And when He had given thanks, He broke it and said, "This is My body, which is for you; do this in remembrance of Me." ²⁵In the same way He took the cup also after supper, saying, "This cup is the new covenant in My blood; do this, as often as you drink it, in remembrance of Me."—1 Corinthians 11:24-25

For today, remember what Christ has done *for you*; and recognize that like Peter, you cannot live the Christian life even with the best of intentions. Only Christ's sacrifice on the cross makes you righteous before God. *Praise Him again and again!*

January 29

*The **Lord turned and looked at Peter**. And Peter remembered the word of the Lord, how He had told him, "Before a rooster crows today, you will deny Me three times."*
—Luke 22:61

Here is an example where the English language does not carry the richness of meaning contained in the original Greek. Without a word study of the word "looked" it is easy to substitute our own human assumptions of what *we* might do in a similar circumstance. If it were us instead of Jesus, we would have "looked with disappointment," or anger, or in a manner that communicated "I told you! Where's your boasting now, Peter?" All of this would lead us to a gross misunderstanding of God's word.

The word "looked" comes from the Greek word ἐμβλέπω (emplepō), which means to look with love and compassion at Peter, not with anger or disappointment. Why would Jesus look at Peter any other way? He knew that Peter's flesh would fail, no matter how determined he was to follow Jesus. He also knew of His coming death, and how it would remove all of Peter's sins (and ours) as far as the east is from the west *(January 22-23)*. What a glorious word "looked" is! We are getting a deeper glimpse into what John means when he tells us that God deals with all of us out of grace heaped upon grace *(January 17-18)*.

I heard this verse taught for 40 years as an example to suggest that hopefully we would never deny Christ in the same way as Peter. But this story is not about our wishful thinking that we will have more faith and willpower than Peter. It is a story that tells us we are exactly *like* Peter. God changed his name and began a good work in him but he still had an immense amount of flesh active in his life. God knew it all. This story is really about God's great mercy and grace-upon-grace that He bestows on us!

Living Water for Today:

*You then, my child, **be strengthened by the grace**
that is in Christ Jesus.*—2 Timothy 2:1 ESV

For today, do not be discouraged or spend time looking at the activity of your flesh but turn your sight to face Christ who is always looking upon you with compassion and love *(Psalm 40:11)*, as He did Peter. He is your total salvation *this very day (1 Thessalonians 5:9)!*

JANUARY 30

The next day He purposed to go into Galilee, and He found Philip. And Jesus said to him, "Follow Me." ⁴⁴Now Philip was from Bethsaida, of the city of Andrew and Peter. ⁴⁵Philip found Nathanael and said to him, "We have found Him of whom Moses in the Law and also the Prophets wrote—Jesus of Nazareth, the son of Joseph." ⁴⁶Nathanael said to him, "Can any good thing come out of Nazareth?" Philip said to him, "Come and see."

—JOHN 1:43-46

These verses demonstrate how Jesus always reveals Himself in a way that *causes us* to believe in Him. I use the phrase "causes us" rather than "gives us a choice" because there is no indication from these verses that the faith created in Philip and Nathanael upon meeting Jesus had anything to do with them. The faith demonstrated by both of them was obviously a life-saving gift from God. When Philip encountered Jesus, he was not given a choice but a command. Jesus didn't say, "Would you like to believe in Me?" but rather: *"Follow Me."* Philip didn't respond, "let me think about it," but immediately found Nathanael and said *"We have found Him of whom Moses in the Law and also the Prophets wrote."* As a result of Jesus' command, Philip believed.

Likewise, when Philip sought out Nathanael, he didn't try to convince him of anything. When Nathanael wondered, not in a negative way, what could possibly come out of a poor, small, insignificant little town like Nazareth, Philip's simple answer was *"Come and see."* Philip's own experience told him that Jesus would reveal who He is and His glory to Nathanael. It is not up to us to figure it out. God will handle all the details. How comforting this is as we share Christ with others. There is no pressure on us to convince anyone of anything. Our response is simply: *Come and See!*

LIVING WATER FOR TODAY:

*For by grace you have been saved through faith; and **that not of yourselves, it is the gift of God;** ⁹not as a result of works, so that no one may boast.*—EPHESIANS 2:8-9

For today, contemplate your own experience in coming to believe in Jesus. Did you have to weigh and balance reams of evidence before you made your decision? Or upon confronting Jesus face to face, did you already believe without a decision on your part at all? Praise God for His gift of faith!

January 31

Jesus saw Nathanael coming to Him, and said of him, "Behold, an Israelite indeed, in whom there is no deceit!" ⁴⁸Nathanael said to Him, "How do You know me?" Jesus answered and said to him, "Before Philip called you, when you were under the fig tree, I saw you." ⁴⁹Nathanael answered Him, "Rabbi, You are the Son of God; You are the King of Israel." ⁵⁰Jesus answered and said to him, "Because I said to you that I saw you under the fig tree, do you believe? You will see greater things than these."
—John 1:47-50

In *verse 47* Jesus declared that Nathanael was an Israelite in whom there was no deceit. That means that Nathanael had no ulterior motive—he was sincerely looking for the Messiah. In *verse 48* Nathanael asks, "How do you know me?" Jesus told him that He saw Nathanael while he was still under the fig tree. Nathanael's response was one of belief.

Although the above verses are from the NASB translation, *verse 50* in the NIV translation is more accurate: *Jesus said, "You believe* [this is a statement of fact] *because I told you I saw you under the fig tree. You will see greater things than that."* Jesus' response was a statement of fact not a question.

Nathanael was chosen by God, just as we are. By making His statement, Jesus revealed Himself to Nathanael in such a way that it *caused him* to believe in Jesus as the Christ (the Messiah). God penetrated Nathanael with those words. Today, that is exactly our experience. There is no boast we can make for ourselves. We don't deserve any more credit than our neighbor who does not believe. God gets all the glory for His great mercy bestowed upon us. Tomorrow, we will see this in the Apostle Paul's own testimony.

Living Water for Today:

So that, just as it is written, "Let him who boasts, boast in the Lord."—1 Corinthians 1:31

For today, consider Nathanael's experience and compare it to your own. Nathanael already believed and was seeking the Messiah. There was nothing for him to do once he met Jesus. None of us have anything to boast about. Praise the Lord! It is all God's marvelous doing out of the great richness of His mercy toward us *(Ephesians 2:4-5).*

FEBRUARY 1

But when God, who had set me apart even from my mother's womb and called me through His grace, was pleased[16]*to reveal His Son in me so that I might preach Him among the Gentiles, I did not immediately consult with flesh and blood.*
—GALATIANS 1:15-16

I will never forget the first time I came across these verses and realized that this is Paul's personal testimony of how he experienced his salvation. He first says, *"but when God, who set me apart from my mother's womb."* Paul recognized that God was interested in him while he was still in his mother's womb! This is the same Paul who spent much of his adult life killing and persecuting Christians; yet, *God set him apart before his birth.*

Paul next declares that God *"called me through His grace."* If anyone would recognize that God's calling was based on God's grace (unmerited favor) rather than "good deeds" it would be Paul. As just mentioned, all of Paul's "good deeds" focused on killing and persecuting God's children. Not a particularly good resume to earn favor from God!

From today's perspective, we would expect Paul to next tell us how he prayed a four-step prayer to accept Christ into his heart. I'm not being critical of the prayers we pray today, but mention them to give insight into Paul's actual words found in scripture. He said, *"But when God ... was pleased to reveal His Son in me."* He didn't say "when I decided to accept Jesus as my personal savior." He said *"when God was pleased to reveal His Son in me."* Do you see the difference? I can't think of a single person who would have been more opposed to the concept of "Jesus as Savior" than Paul. But according to Paul's personal testimony, it wasn't up to him, but entirely up to what pleased God.

LIVING WATER FOR TODAY:

For if while we were enemies we were reconciled to God through the death of His Son, much more, having been reconciled, we shall be saved by His life.—ROMANS 5:10

For today, feel the weight of your human effort in trying to please God fall completely off of you. It is all God's work and none of yours. He has called you from your mother's womb and set you apart by His grace. And when it pleased Him, He revealed His Son *in you* (which constitutes your salvation, *Colossians 1:27*). Like Paul you *were* an enemy of God, but He saw you only as His child. *Praise Him—again, and again!*

LIVING WATER FROM JOHN 1:35-51

January 24	God provides Christian witnesses who point people to Christ.
January 25	Jesus is continually transforming us from our fleshly nature into the glory of the Lord.
January 26	Christ has placed us on His ever-brightening path of understanding.
January 27	For it is God who is continually and effectively at work in us, both to will and to work for His good pleasure.
January 28	Jesus poured out His body and blood so we can freely receive His righteousness.
January 29	Christ is always looking at us with compassion and love as He did Peter who denied Him three times.
January 30	Jesus reveals Himself in a way that causes us to believe in Him; our response to others is "Come and see!"
January 31	God gets all the glory for His great mercy in bestowing belief upon us in Christ.
February 1	God sets us apart from our mother's womb and calls us through His grace.

PRAYER

*Dear God, I praise You that You are speaking commands
into my life and I hold life-saving faith in my heart because
of Your speaking. Father, I am just like Peter, full of fleshly
attitudes and actions, but You are hourly and daily at work
in me, transforming me into what pleases You.
Thank You for placing me on Your path of the righteous.
Amen & Amen.*

JESUS CARES ABOUT THE SMALL THINGS IN OUR LIFE

———

JOHN 2:1-11

A SPECIAL WORD TO THE READER...

We now come to a section in John's gospel *(John 2 through 11)* where John shares a series of miracles performed by Jesus. I have often heard that these miracles are shared by John to prove that Jesus is God (and that is certainly true), but that is not the whole story.

To understand these miracles at a personal level, it is helpful to view them in the broader context of the entire biblical narrative. From Genesis to Revelation there is one unified message: **It is a story of man's total depravity, inadequacy, ineptness, and faithlessness, AND God's patience, love, redemptive power, and new life.** Every page of the Old Testament points to Christ; and the New Testament reveals Christ as God's salvation plan for us whom He has chosen. The miracles in John provide one illustration after another of this theme: Our utter depravity and God's great mercy; our profound sinfulness and God's abiding grace; our self-centered and empty hopelessness and Jesus' total sacrifice to rescue us from darkness and fill us with something we could never produce, earn, or deserve on our own.

In this context, we are going to see that all these miracles illustrate many glorious truths about Jesus and His involvement in our lives. We will see, from the very first miracle, how Jesus turning water into wine is about ***God putting His New Covenant Life—"Eternal Life"—into Us***. It is a living parable of how much He cares about even the smallest details in our life, filling us to the brim with His love, joy, peace, patience, and every other fruit of the Spirit every day. While our best effort can only fill our pot with water (although we often feel empty even of that), Jesus fills us to the brim with His best wine (His divine life).

As we work through this progression of miracle narratives, may the Lord shine His light on the full meaning *directed to you personally* within each of them. Collectively, they contain a message that will forever alter your life and set you free to continually praise Him as you experience His glorious freedom gifted to you by God.

FEBRUARY 2

*On the third day there was a wedding in Cana of Galilee, and the mother of Jesus was there; ²and both **Jesus and His disciples were invited to the wedding.***

—John 2:1-2

As we view this first miracle in terms of a message to us personally, we must consider what it means for Jesus to be the "wine" in our life. Also, what is the significance of Him converting water into wine? To answer these questions, we should look to the immediate context in which the miracle occurs. By inspiration of the Holy Spirit, John chose a modest wedding between an ordinary couple without apparent fame or fortune. In other words, they were people just like you and me. The personal take away of the "wine" is several fold: (i) It first demonstrates that Jesus puts His own Life (which includes His love, joy, peace, patience, and every fruit of the Spirit) into you and me as empty pots; (ii) it reveals that by filling us to the brim with His life He is present with us in all the everyday events we experience throughout our lives (no matter how small the detail of the event); and (iii) it confirms that He is active—not passive—ready and willing to intervene on our behalf according to His perfect will.

At this wedding—just as in our own lives despite our intentions or planning—the "wine" runs dry. At the very least, this represents an embarrassing situation, but Jesus cared for this newly married couple and intervened. John chose this miracle to assure us that Jesus is involved in all situations in our life—even in the smallest ones. Jesus turned the *running out of wine* into the *best wine possible!* And whether we recognize it or not He is accomplishing this miracle in our lives every day *(Romans 8:28)*.

LIVING WATER FOR TODAY:

*In the same way He took the cup also after supper, saying, "**This cup is the new covenant in My blood**; do this, as often as you drink it, in remembrance of Me."*—1 Corinthians 11:25

For today, consider what hope this is for your life. The new covenant wine represents all that Christ means to you: your forgiveness, your guilt-free life, your wisdom for each day, your hope in any situation, your confidence that you are never alone, and that God's perfect will is prevailing (on your behalf) each day even amidst your failures *(Philippians 2:13). Praise Him!*

FEBRUARY 3

*And in your godliness, brotherly kindness, and in your brotherly kindness, love. ⁸For if these qualities are yours and are increasing, they render you neither useless nor unfruitful in the **true knowledge of our Lord Jesus Christ**. ⁹For he who lacks these qualities is blind or short-sighted, **having forgotten his purification from his former sins**.*

—2 PETER 1:7-9

Several years ago, after repeated requests, I compiled what I felt to be the ten selections of scripture that most significantly impacted my life. After considerable thought, I published these top ten portions in a little book called *Knowing the God Who Chose You*. This section from *2 Peter* was one of those selected. After today's devotional, they may become equally precious to you.

Peter tells us that he who lacks certain qualities, like kindness and love, has forgotten something important. Can you see the parallel between this verse and running out of wine in the first miracle *(February 2)*? Just like the miracle, Peter doesn't exhort us to *try harder* to be kind, loving, or forgiving. He tells us to **remember** what Jesus has done! During the wedding, Jesus produced an abundance of wine. Peter tells us to **remember** the new covenant that Jesus has ushered in through His death on the cross and the shedding of His blood for our *"purification from...former sins."*

I tried for many years to develop the qualities Peter is talking about through my own effort. The whole experience was like trying to apply a Band-Aid in the shower. You keep trying and it keeps sliding off. God never said, to try harder. He said to **remember**. The power is in **remembering** God's new covenant. Remembering the wine (Christ's shed blood) causes us to remember all that Christ has done for us, which in turn, miraculously supplies that same unconditional love and kindness to us for others.

LIVING WATER FOR TODAY:

*Remember the word which Moses the servant of the LORD commanded you, saying, "The **LORD your God gives you rest** and will give you this land."*—JOSHUA 1:13

For today, consider this Old Testament verse; recognize that from Genesis to Revelation it is *always* God who is the One who gives goodness, kindness, love, rest, etc. *It is never something you have to earn* but is *always* derived from God's new covenant for you.

THE POWER OF REMEMBERING WHAT CHRIST HAS ACCOMPLISHED FOR US!

I don't know if you have ever tried this, but if you haven't, I suggest writing yourself a note this week to practice the simple task of *remembering*. After the Lord taught me this, it changed my life. It is miraculously powerful. When I am struggling to show unconditional kindness to a person who I know is talking negatively about me behind my back (or when I learn that someone did something hurtful to me) and it disrupts my peace and calm within, I can testify to you that there is miracle-working power in *remembering*.

Just imagine that you are with the disciples in the upper room that last evening before Jesus goes to the cross. The Lord is speaking and passes around a cup with wine in it. He tells you that the cup represents a new covenant from God that He is about to accomplish on your behalf. Finally, He tells you, as you live your life going forward, to *remember* this new covenant. This command causes you to remember the Father's words that *He has forgotten every sin that you have committed or ever will commit (January 22)*. You continue to dwell on the Father's words and recall that He, a holy and righteous God, *holds nothing against you* and He has made you *completely righteous in His eyes*, as righteous as His Son Jesus.

This is what Jesus accomplished for us on the cross. He didn't ask us to "pay for it" in any way. *It is all free of charge!* There is nothing more we can ever do to make God happier, or to please Him more, than what His Son has already done. God accomplished it all through the loving sacrifice of His Son for us. And throughout our lives His Spirit of love, beyond what we could ever imagine, continues transforming us from "sinner" to "saint," and from "full-of-guilt" to "no-guilt-at-all." Peter tells us in *2 Peter 1:7-9* that every time we are struggling with a lack of unconditional love, or a spirit of unforgiveness, it is the power within the act of *remembering* that can deliver us.

I cannot tell you how many times I have been jogging in the morning, or driving to or from work, when I begin to struggle with an attitude toward somebody or something. When God causes me to *remember* what He has accomplished *for me*, it buckles my knees in my heart to Him. It evaporates my fleshly feelings and attitudes; and reestablishes a right spirit within me toward that person I was just angry with. *PTL!*

FEBRUARY 4

When the wine ran out, the mother of Jesus said to Him, "They have no wine." ⁴And Jesus said to her, "Woman, what does that have to do with us? My hour has not yet come." ⁵His mother said to the servants, "Whatever He says to you, do it."

—JOHN 2:3-5

Mary was Jesus' human mother who raised Him from a baby, she knew Him well. She already knew that He would act when faced with a need, so she did not try to convince Him of anything. She simply presented the need to Him: "They have no wine." Jesus responded that His time had not yet come to usher in the new covenant. Mary may not have understood what Jesus meant by that statement but one thing she knew with certainty: *Jesus would act to meet the human needs of this married couple.*

As I said in a previous devotional *(February 2)*, had I been John I would have picked a much bigger and more spectacular miracle to begin my section on miracles: Make the sun go dark, move a mountain, stop a river from flowing, raise someone from the dead. All of these are miracles mentioned in scripture. But John, led by the Holy Spirit, chose to emphasize the exact opposite—Jesus is willing to become involved in the smallest of detail in our lives; right down to providing wine for a wedding, and not just wine but the best wine, to prevent two people from being deeply embarrassed before their guests. This is my testimony. God is intricately involved in our lives in just this way. He is caring for all the little details out of His perfect love and mercy for us.

LIVING WATER FOR TODAY:

The LORD is my shepherd, I shall not want. ²He makes me lie down in green pastures; He leads me beside quiet waters. ³He restores my soul; He guides me in the paths of righteousness for His name's sake. ⁴Even though I walk through the valley of the shadow of death, I fear no evil, for You are with me; Your rod and Your staff, they comfort me.—PSALM 23: 1-4

For today, consider the "calls to action" that King David used in his Psalm 23. Note that the Psalm is written in present tense and *personal*: The Lord IS *my* shepherd! He knows when *I* need to lie down and rest; He knows where to lead *me* in peace and guide *me* in righteousness; He knows when *my* soul needs restoring and comfort. Our great Shepherd, on a 24/7 present-tense basis, is caring for every aspect of your life. *PTL!*

FEBRUARY 5

Who is the man who fears the LORD? **He will instruct him in the way he should choose.**
*¹³His soul will abide in prosperity, and his descendants will inherit the land. ¹⁴The secret of the
LORD is for those who fear Him, and* **He will make them know** *His covenant* [or His will].
—PSALM 25:12-14

In modern-day English usage the word "fear" carries a negative connotation. This is
not the scriptural meaning of someone *"who fears the LORD."* "Fear" in this context
means *one who believes in and reveres (or respects) the Lord.* In short, it is referring to
all believers.

As the Lord progressively brings us into the reality of these verses, they become
sweeter and more precious to us. We begin to experience the everyday stresses, which
we previously struggled with, being lifted off our shoulders. Stress from financial or
job difficulties; stress from personal family matters associated with spouse or kids;
stress from medical challenges; or uninvited drama from associates and friends. All
such stress disappears. Why? *Because all stress comes from our flesh, not from God.* These
verses promise that God *WILL* instruct us in what to say, what to do, and what path
to take. God *WILL* make us to know His will in any given situation. What is the
result of this reality as it plays out in our lives? All the stress for us to "figure it out" or
"get it right" is removed. It is now God's responsibility to *instruct us* and *make us know*
what to say and the path to take. He promises to do that.

In the page that follows, I will address a common question: *How does God make
us know?* The answer is life-changing.

LIVING WATER FOR TODAY:

*Therefore humble yourselves under the mighty hand of God,
that He may exalt you at the proper time* [that is, His help
will come at just the right time], *⁷***casting all your anxiety on
Him,** *because He cares for you.* —1 PETER 5:6-7

For today, recognize that God is the Almighty-Creator-God, and you are His created.
This is humbling and allows you the freedom to cast *all* your anxiety and stress on Him,
knowing that He cares for *all* things in your life, no matter how small. He will guide
your path and make you to know His will. To *"exalt you at the proper time"* means that
in His timing (not yours), He will bring the help you need at just the right time.

How Does God Make Us Know?

Yesterday's devotional scripture declared that God will *instruct us* and *make us know* His will. *How does He do this?*

The key to understanding the answer to this question is to first face an uncompromising truth about ourselves. It is a truth found in both Old *(Psalm 14:1-3, 53:1-3)* and New Testaments *(Romans 3:10-12)*. Simply put, *Romans 3:10* reads, *"There is none righteous, not even one"*; *Romans 3:11* states bluntly that *"There is none who seeks for God"*; and *Romans 3:12* declares, *"There is none who does good, there is not even one."* We may think that we are better than this, but scripture is emphatic: *NOT EVEN ONE!*

Recognizing this truth brings us to a place where we can understand how God leads, instructs, and makes us know His will every day. Left to ourselves, we would *never* seek God. Thus, we can be certain that when we DO have a thought about God, read scripture, pray, or have thoughts of doing something good for someone; all these thoughts and resulting actions *must* be sourced from God. They could *never* be sourced from us.

Here is how this works. God draws us to read, *"Be anxious for nothing"* *(Philippians 4:6)*; *"Be still and know that I am God"* *(Psalm 46:10, NIV)*; *"Pray without ceasing"* *(I Thessalonians 5:17); "Now to Him who is able to do far more abundantly beyond all that we ask or think, according to the power that works within us" (Ephesians 3:20).*

Verses like these build a foundation of faith in us to trust God. The Holy Spirit then continues to teach us, shape our thinking, influence us throughout the day (often using these same verses). We may believe a thought or idea came from us, but it is really God guiding and making us know His will *moment by moment*. If we are feeling anxious or lacking peace about something, we can be confident that this is the Holy Spirit directing us to know that our current plan is NOT from God but from our flesh.

FEBRUARY 6

*Now there were **six** stone waterpots set there for the Jewish custom of purification, containing twenty or thirty gallons each. Jesus said to them, "**Fill the waterpots with water.**" So they filled them **up to the brim**.*

—JOHN 2:6-7

To appreciate these verses and their personal message to us, we need some Jewish cultural context. Jewish custom in Jesus' day required each wedding guest to wash their hands before eating. This was not only for the obvious hygienic purposes we still practice today, but it also symbolized spiritual cleansing to the Jews. With that in mind, imagine the number of guests that were attending this wedding—so many that six stone waterpots each holding between twenty to thirty gallons (totaling 120-180 gallons of water) was needed to perform this ritual cleansing. These pots were not there by accident, brought into the wedding only to stand empty. They suggest a large amount of water had already been used to perform this ceremonial cleansing of the wedding guest. With that many guests, no wonder they ran out of wine!

The number "six" is symbolic of "humanity" in scripture. Have you ever felt like your life closely resembled those six empty pots? I know mine has. I had the "financial success" pot, the "business" pot, the "wife" pot, the "kids" pot, the "peace" pot, and the "what people think of me" pot, all nicely organized for those looking at me from afar, but I knew they were all dry as bones in a desert. The harder I worked at trying to fill those pots the drier they got. The very first miracle that John wants us to know about is truly good news. He tells us that it is not up to us to do anything to fill "our" pots. It is Jesus who fills every aspect of our lives with His [living water] *"up to the brim"* (and miraculously, turns that water into a celebration of new life). *PTL!*

LIVING WATER FOR TODAY:

*And **He will be the stability of your times, a wealth of salvation, wisdom and knowledge;** the fear* [faith] *of the LORD is his treasure.*—ISAIAH 33:6

For today, take a moment to think back and consider all the "pots" in your life. Have any been broken or empty in times past? Isaiah promises that God is the stability for your marriage pot, family pot, social pot, work pot, etc., filling them all with the wealth of salvation, wisdom, and knowledge of Him in everything you do. *He is your treasure!*

February 7

*When the headwaiter tasted the water which had become wine, and did not know where it came from (but the servants who had drawn the water knew), the headwaiter called the bridegroom, ¹⁰and said to him, "Every man serves the good wine first, and when the people have drunk freely, then he serves the poorer wine; **but you have kept the good wine until now.**"*

—John 2:9-10

John tells us that Jesus provided the *"good wine"* last, which means He provided the best wine last. Today and tomorrow I want to share four thoughts as to what the good (or best) wine means to you and me.

First, it means (and I love this), that we can never improve on what God transforms our life into. He has converted us from sinners (water) to saints (wine); from being full of failure, darkness, and sin, to being completely redeemed, sanctified, and made righteous in Christ *(1 Corinthians 1:30)*. These things cannot be improved upon by us adding any amount of our own efforts. There is nothing more we can do to please God. He has *FILLED* us with His *best* wine—*CHRIST!*

Second, the best wine means there is nothing compared to what Jesus brings to our life. This is what Jesus brought to the wedding. He didn't hold back and produce only cheap wine; He produced the *best* wine. Everything about Jesus is the best. No doubt the bridegroom, as the headwaiter suggested, did offer the very best wine that he could afford at the beginning of his wedding, but the wine that Jesus produced was better yet.

Living Water for Today:

*And in the hidden part **You will make me know** wisdom.*

—Psalm 51:6b

For today, abide in God's repeated promises to you from scripture—that **HE will make you know** what you need to know today. Your source of guidance is not in self-help books or the internet. He is your guide. He is the best wine. He will *make you know* what you need to know, and when you need to know it. He will fill all your pots to the brim with His New Covenant wine—bringing you wisdom, joy, and peace as He directs your path. Pray that the Lord will enlighten you to understand: He has done it all—He is all you need! You are but the container holding this priceless treasure: *"Christ in you" (Colossians 1:27). PTL!*

FEBRUARY 8

*When the headwaiter tasted the water which had become wine, and did not know where it came from (but the servants who had drawn the water knew), the headwaiter called the bridegroom, ¹⁰and said to him, "Every man serves the good wine first, and when the people have drunk freely, then he serves the poorer wine; **but you have kept the good wine until now.**"*
—JOHN 2:9-10

Continuing from yesterday the four thoughts as to what the wine means to you and me:

Third, this first miracle is a picture of our entire Christian life. It demonstrates that we experience our Christian life in just the same miraculous way as Jesus turning water into wine. We cannot produce any of God's new-wine life ourselves, any more than we can convert water into wine. So when our flesh starts whispering that there is some "good" in us, or we can cooperate and "help" God make us even better, I pray that we all will now realize the absurdity of such thoughts. May the Lord continually remind us of this wedding miracle and that He is the *only One* who can transform water into wine. If you still think there is some *"good"* in you to offer God, prayerfully reread *Psalm 14:1-3, 53:1-3* and *Romans 3:10-12.*

Fourth, this first miracle demonstrates that in life there are certain things that happen which are beyond our human ability to control or change. The bridegroom at the wedding ran out of wine. Apparently, no amount of pre-wedding planning helped him avoid this embarrassment. Every week I have people come to me sharing horrific circumstances that defy human solutions. It is in those times when the Lord reminds me of this wedding story and His first miracle. He renews my faith that only He has the power to change water into wine. And some things (possibly *many* things) in our life must be left to Him to transform from burden to blessing.

LIVING WATER FOR TODAY:

How foolish can you be? After starting your new lives in the Spirit, why are you now trying to become perfect by your own human effort? —GALATIANS 3:3 NLT

For today, rejoice that your Savior Jesus does transform water into wine. So, there is no amount of fear, anger, discouragement, guilt, loneliness, addiction, unforgiving spirit in your life that Jesus cannot convert into His new wine: *an abundantly joyous life for you!*

FEBRUARY 9

*"These things I have spoken to you so that **My joy may be in you**, and that **your joy may be made full.**"*

—JOHN 15:11

W e often hustle and bustle about searching for ways to bring happiness into our lives. The best we can usually manage is a few moments or hours of heightened excitement, but never really anything we would call *fullness of joy*: A child is born; a graduation or wedding day; a hole-in-one (with witnesses); or a shopping spree with friends are all examples of this temporal fun. But the joy Jesus is referring to in this verse is lasting; it abides, it does not come and go. In those final hours with His disciples, He inaugurated the Lord's Supper, revealing that His shed blood would usher in a New Covenant (relationship) between God and Man. He used wine as a symbol to teach this. In today's conversation He also expanded this covenantal concept by linking it to a vineyard (and the principle of abiding in the vine) so that His children would be made full of joy.

Take a careful look at today's verse. Jesus may have spoken parables to the religious leaders, but He speaks plainly to His disciples. This verse explains with exacting precision the purpose and motivation behind why Jesus is speaking to them; and it reveals a powerful "cause and effect" dynamic which brings clarity to how joy is established in our lives. Jesus is speaking to them: *"SO THAT **My joy** may be in you, AND THAT **your joy** may be made full."* How does Jesus' eternal joy get into us? Through His spoken words! And His joy, in turn, transforms and multiplies our joy as we abide in Him as a branch in the vine. It is God's speaking that does the work and produces the joy, not anything we do. We are merely vessels to contain His eternal joy. As we rest in Him, He fills us to the brim with His spoken word, and that produces abiding joy!

LIVING WATER FOR TODAY:

*"I am the vine, you are the branches; **he who abides in Me and I in him, he bears much fruit, for apart from Me you can do nothing.**"* —JOHN 15:5

For today, cease from your striving and rest in the word of God, spoken to you—which is living and operative *(Hebrews 4:12)* and always accomplishing what it was sent to do *(Isaiah 55:10-11)*. And as you abide in Him, trust that He is producing abundant fruit in your life, guiding you, and making you to know His will, just as He has promised.

LIVING WATER FROM JOHN 2:1-11

February 2	Jesus is actively working in us, willing to intervene on our behalf, according to His perfect will.
February 3	The power in remembering God's new covenant reminds us of all that Christ has done for us.
February 4	Almighty God is intricately involved in caring for all the details of our lives out of His perfect love and mercy for us.
February 5	God promises to instruct us and make us know His will; as He does this, the stressful things we often feel fall away.
February 6	Jesus fills our lives to the brim with living water, and miraculously turns that water into a celebration of new life in Christ.
February 7	We can never improve on what God transforms our life into; He has filled us with His "best wine"—Christ!
February 8	There is no amount of difficulty—fear, discouragement, guilt, etc., that Jesus cannot convert into an abundantly joyous life for us.
February 9	Jesus multiplies our joy as we abide in Him as a branch in the vine.

PRAYER:

Dear God, Your Son Jesus is the Miracle Worker who is turning my "empty pot" of a life into one that is full with His best wine. He continues day by day to transform aspects of my life that remain full of worries and struggles into New Covenant wine that fills me to the brim with joy and peace. I pray that you will continue to open my eyes to see how my whole life as a Christian is nothing more than a continuation of this first miracle at the wedding. Strengthen my faith to recognize that every detail concerning You, every thought of You, every desire to read my Bible, every prayer I utter, every good thing I do for others, is a gift from You as You draw me relentlessly to Yourself. I pray that You will increase the hunger in my heart for your word. Build within me the foundation upon which You guide me and make me to know Your will in my life day by day, hour by hour, and moment by moment.

I PRAISE YOU!

Amen.

JESUS DISAPPROVES OF PROFITING ON WHAT HE GIVES FREE

JOHN 2:12-25

A SPECIAL WORD TO THE READER...

We are studying through the *Gospel of John* in this daily devotional. But what does the word "gospel" really mean? You have likely heard that "gospel" means "good news," and this is certainly true. But who's good news is it? Is it what we would consider good news from our local newspaper or the internet? No. It is *God's good news!* Have you ever stopped for a moment to grasp the true meaning of this phrase?

If *all* good comes from God *(James 1:17)*, if He is the essence of goodness (which He is); if He is *all* righteous, *all* fair, *all* just, *all* loving, *all* giving, *all* peace, then God revealing His *good news* is beyond difficult for the human mind to comprehend. We can hardly get our heads wrapped around the breadth and depth of God's *good news*, even at the most superficial level. We can only begin to glimpse His immense goodness by the light He shines on the scripture He has given us. Thanks be to God for giving us the *Gospel of John*, which progressively reveals ever-deeper aspects of the goodness of God!

In the coming days, John reveals to us a series of increasingly profound dimensions of God's *good news*. For example, many Christians are taught that they can lose their salvation, or that if they conduct themselves in a certain way it may be evidence that they were never "saved" in the first place. John is about to tell us something different and much more glorious. We know that God loved us so much that He sent His Son to rescue us from the kingdom of darkness and redeem us into the family of God; we may not know that His love was so great that He also did not leave the welfare of our eternal security in our human hands. Part of the awesome *good news* of God is that He retained the responsibility for our eternal security *in His own hands* so we would be completely and irrevocably secure. You read that right! He gave us, those who are undeserving in every respect, His eternal life that we cannot possibly lose because He is the keeper of it! How good is THAT *good news?*

This is but one example of a series of *good news* events that John will share with us in the coming days to teach us the depth and pervasive power of God's goodness for us!

FEBRUARY 10

*After this He went down to Capernaum, He and His mother and His brothers and His disciples; and they stayed there a few days. ¹³The Passover of the Jews was near, and **Jesus went up to Jerusalem.***

—JOHN 2:12-13

We just considered the first miracle performed by Jesus in the *Gospel of John*, where out of His compassion for a couple at their wedding party, He turned ordinary water into the best wine. Now John tells us about an event that may appear to be a bit out of context. After all, what does Jesus chasing a bunch of crooks out of the temple have to do with anything? Many scholars interpret the story as addressing Jesus' authority and zeal concerning His Father's house (which is true), but it reveals much more. John is sharing additional details about Jesus' compassion, like in the first miracle. This time, the Lord's compassion flows to those who are being ripped off by people who would steal from them in the name of God.

These first two verses begin to set the context for the verses that follow. Jesus, His mother, brothers, and disciples have just traveled 16 miles from Cana (where the first miracle took place) to Capernaum. There were no cars, buses, taxis, trains, Ubers, or anything else in those days. They strapped on their sandals and walked it. It is not surprising that they stayed in Capernaum for a few days. But then John tells us that Jesus goes up to Jerusalem, a distance of 78 miles on foot! How many of us would walk 78 miles to attend a religious ceremony? That shows how significant the Passover was to God and to those worshipping Him. It was particularly important to Jesus because the Passover was a picture that pointed to His own sacrifice for us.

LIVING WATER FOR TODAY:

*I pray that the eyes of your heart may be enlightened, so that you will know what is the hope of His calling, **what are the riches of the glory of His inheritance in the saints.***—EPHESIANS 1:18

For today, contemplate that God considers Himself rich with *you!* He sacrificed His Son to give you eternal life *(John 3:16)*; He clothed you with His righteousness *(Isaiah 61:10)*, and He calls you a saint *(1 Corinthians 1:2)*; and Jesus willingly offered up His life to rescue *you* from this present evil age *(Galatians 1:4). Praise Him!*

FEBRUARY 11

*And He found in the temple **those who were selling** oxen and sheep and doves, and the **money changers** seated at their tables.*

—JOHN 2:14

The Passover mentioned in *verse 13* was an annual feast day located on the temple grounds in Jerusalem. Jewish people came from all over to celebrate God freeing them from Pharaoh's slavery in Egypt. Everyone attending was required to make a sacrifice. If they didn't bring one, they had to buy it within the temple grounds at an extremely marked-up price (because those selling had a corner on the market).

What made things even more egregious was the fact that people coming to honor God through sacrifice could not buy a sheep, calf, or dove to make that sacrifice with just ordinary money. Oh no! They had to exchange their money for temple currency. Again, this was done at an extremely inflated exchange rate.

Further, these sacrificial animals and the currency exchange were originally intended to be a convenience for all those traveling long distances to visit the temple. Profiteering, however, crept in as the sellers' and money changers' love of money drove them to increasingly charge as much as they could get away with. Those people coming to sacrifice were stuck. They had only one place to purchase a sacrificial animal and only one currency to do it with. They had to pay whatever was being demanded by the sellers and money changers—a double blow all in the name of God!

Finally, if we are to understand the full context of these verses, we must note that there is no way any of this could take place inside the temple courtyard without the consent of the religious leaders who ran the temple. It is likely that they were benefiting in some way by condoning the robbing of the average (and poor) people coming to honor God.

LIVING WATER FOR TODAY:

*Jesus entered the temple and began to drive out those who were selling, *[46]*saying to them, "It is written, 'AND MY HOUSE SHALL BE A HOUSE OF PRAYER,' but you have made it a ROBBERS' DEN."* —LUKE 19:45-46

For today, contemplate the impact of the Lord's actions on your behalf; God's entire plan, from start to finish, is free and without cost to you *because His Son paid it all.*

FEBRUARY 12

And He made a scourge of cords, and drove them all out of the temple, with the sheep and the oxen; and He poured out the coins of the money changers and overturned their tables; ¹⁶and to those who were selling the doves He said, "Take these things away; stop making My Father's house a place of business."

—JOHN 2:15-16

For much of my life I used these verses of Jesus driving out the sellers of animals and money changers from the temple as a proof-text to justify my own anger. I would say, *"Well, Jesus got angry in the temple, so I can too."*

Before we explore the question of anger, however, I want to highlight the "hidden" miracle that John reveals here. Consider this: *If Jesus were just an ordinary man could He have accomplished this feat?* The temple courtyard would have held hundreds, if not thousands, of greedy, money-hungry crooks lining their pockets on Passover day—the busiest day of the year for visitors to come to the temple for sacrifice and worship. These crooks would not have tolerated just anyone taking away their money-making schemes. Anyone who tried would have been seized and tossed out! But Jesus was not ordinary! He was the Son of God who miraculously spoke His will into every crook's heart, making them run from the temple like a stampede of rats fleeing a sinking ship.

This brings me wonderful peace of mind when I remember these verses. *God always accomplishes ALL that He wills to accomplish (Isaiah 46:10).* We can be at peace about our loved ones because Jesus always accomplishes His good pleasure concerning them (and us)! *"But things don't look so good, Daryl,"* you may say. Tell me, have you created anything *(Job 38:4)?* Have you ever spoken the word, *"Let there be light,"* and did even one star appear *(Genesis 1:3)?* God has! He has told us not to be anxious about anything *(Philippians 4:6)* because it is all under His sovereign love and care.

LIVING WATER FOR TODAY:

Declaring the end from the beginning, and from ancient times things which have not been done, saying, "My purpose will be established, and I will accomplish all My good pleasure."—ISAIAH 46:10

For today, abide in this incredible promise, *"I will accomplish all My good pleasure,"* and recognize it as God's soothing balm over every anxious thought or worry that you are concerned with today.

February 13

And He made a scourge of cords, and drove them all out of the temple, with the sheep and the oxen; and He poured out the coins of the money changers and overturned their tables; ¹⁶and to those who were selling the doves He said, "Take these things away; stop making My Father's house a place of business." ¹⁷His disciples remembered that it was written, "ZEAL FOR YOUR HOUSE WILL CONSUME ME."

—John 2:15-17

D o you use these verses to justify your anger? Today, consider for yourself whether Jesus got angry. While these verses do not actually say that Jesus got angry, that never stopped me from justifying my own anger by arguing that He did. Now, as I write this devotional, I must be honest: I find no mention of the word "anger." I checked more than 20 translations and NOT ONE translates what Jesus did as anger. Even the Amplified version does not go that far.

What scripture talks about in these verses is Jesus' ZEAL for His Father's house. My dictionary refers to "zeal" as fervor for a person or endeavor, enthusiasm, diligence, or ardor. Ardor refers to intense devotion or passion. The Greek word for zeal in scripture is ζῆλος (zēlos) which is most often translated "jealousy" or "zeal". When Paul refers to a "godly jealousy" (2 Corinthians 11:2) he uses the derivative ζῆλοω (zēloo), which is most often translated "earnestly desire," "desire earnestly," or "eagerly seek."

Regardless of whether you believe Jesus got angry, there is one major difference that distinguishes His "anger" from ours. I will explore more deeply this difference in the page that follows. While we get angry at people and circumstances that offend us, Jesus got "angry" (if He did) at people who disrespected His Father. One is called "fleshly anger" and the other "righteous anger."

Living Water for Today:

*For zeal for Your house has consumed me, and the **reproaches of those who reproach You have fallen on me.** —Psalm 69:9*

For today, be comforted in knowing that as passionate as Jesus was to defend His Father's house, He is equally impassioned to protect and care for you as a child of God throughout every moment of every day, *including today! PTL!*

CONNECTING THE THEOLOGICAL DOTS

I was speaking at a Christian business conference some years ago on the topic of anger. One attendee raised his hand and wanted to argue: "Well, Jesus got mad in the temple," he said, "and besides, Daryl, God gave us our emotions—one being anger—so it must be okay for us to get angry from time to time." I knew *exactly* where this man was coming from because I had used this same "logic" to justify my own anger for decades.

To understand "anger" from God's perspective, let's connect the dots throughout scripture, which we know will never contradict itself. *Ephesians 4:31 declares, "Let all bitterness and wrath **and anger** and clamor and slander be put away from you, along with all malice." Colossians 3:8 reads, "But now you also, put them all aside: **anger**, wrath, malice, slander, and abusive speech from your mouth."* And *James 1:20 states, "For the **anger of man** does not achieve the righteousness of God."*

So then, anger never achieves God's true will, or His true peace, contentment, or joy. How are we to reconcile these three scriptural admonitions (among many from God's word) with Jesus' actions in the temple (even if we classify those actions as anger)? A careful look at scripture clarifies this distinction. The anger of man in *James 1:20* refers to our human fleshly anger. This fleshly anger never achieves the righteousness of God. It is the anger we experience when we feel that some form of injustice has been *done to us*, or *we feel* mistreated, offended, or when *we* don't get our own way.

Jesus' actions by contrast (even if out of anger), were a response to people disrespecting His Father. It was *never* about Jesus. Once I understood this distinction, it didn't take to recognize the source of my own anger. I was angry at people who offended ME, God! The latter is referred to as righteous indignation or righteous anger.

Here is why *not justifying* our anger is important. Any sin of our flesh that is alive us keeps us miserable. Believe me, I speak with extensive experience on this topic! he irony is that often the people (or circumstance) we are angry at aren't even aware of it; yet that fleshly anger *robs us* of God's peace and contentment. To be clear, you can't defeat your anger, *the flesh will never defeat the flesh*. Only God can, as you pray to Him.

PRAYER

Lord, I'm just clay. I'm repeating to You what You have revealed to me in Romans 9:21. You've told me that I am clay. I have no power to do anything within myself, no more power to fix or shape myself than clay has to shape itself. You are the How-Great-Thou-Art Potter and Lord. I am on my knees in my heart before You. I cannot fix my own anger. Yet, You have shown me that anger festers within me. [†] You are the How-Great-Thou-Art God, who just spoke the words, "Let there be light" (Genesis 1:3) and the whole universe of light sprang into existence. You are far more powerful than my anger. I'm trusting You Lord to hear my prayer. I'm asking You to overcome the anger that dwells in me, remove it from me with Your forgiving Spirit and compassion.

In Jesus name, Amen.

[†] Add to your prayer at this point specific anger that you may have eating at you in your life. Offer it all up to God who will shape your life as a Potter does His clay and remove that anger from you. You can trust that He will replace it with His own love, joy, peace, and contentment.

FEBRUARY 14

And to those who were selling the doves He said, "Take these things away; stop making My Father's house a place of business." [17]His disciples remembered that it was written, "ZEAL FOR YOUR HOUSE WILL CONSUME ME."

—JOHN 2:16-17

In *verse 15*, Jesus drives out the sheep and oxen along with their sellers. In *verse 16*, He commands the sellers of doves to remove them. Jesus didn't overturn the dove's cages and set the doves free. No, whether sheep, oxen, or doves, the sellers remained in possession of the things they were selling. Jesus was not infringing on their right of ownership but only the profiteering on a legitimate religious activity. For these sellers (and religious leaders who allowed it) the sale of these animals was no longer an act of compassion to support those worshippers traveling long distances to the temple. It had degenerated into nothing more than a business contrived to make money.

Many commentaries highlight the fact that Jesus throwing these crooks out of the temple was an act of cleansing the temple (and that is true). It also suggests that Jesus disapproves vehemently of people making money on **what He gives free**. He said, *"stop making My Father's house a place of business."* This could be paraphrased: *"stop making the gospel a commodity,"* or *"stop using the gospel to line your pockets."*

Remember what the Passover signified. Pharaoh refused to free the children of Israel from slavery. Moses told Pharaoh that God would kill the first-born child throughout the land, except for those who applied the blood of a lamb to the door post of their households. This event became the basis for the Passover the Jews were celebrating in the temple when Jesus visited. It was a demonstration of God's mercy and grace to the children of Israel; and pointed to the future sacrifice of Jesus on the cross as our Passover Lamb today. All of this was *free* to the people. God paid the price for it all!

LIVING WATER FOR TODAY:

Clean out the old leaven so that you may be a new lump, just as you are in fact unleavened. **For Christ our Passover also has been sacrificed.**—1 CORINTHIANS 5:7

For today, rejoice that Christ, by His act of pure love, mercy, and grace (without any cost to you), has cleansed you, and is continuously cleansing you, as the temple of God.

WOULD JESUS WEAR A ROLEX?

Ray Stevens once wrote and performed a humorous song that cut right to the heart of this issue. It is worth your time to look it up on YouTube and listen to it in its entirety. It goes like this:

Woke up this mornin'
Turned on my T.V. set.
There in livin' color was somethin' I can't forget.

This man was preachin' at me, yeah, layin on the charm
Askin' me for twenty with ten thousand on his arm.

He wore designer clothes and a big smile on his face
Sellin' me salvation while they sang Amazin' Grace.

Askin' me for money when he had all the signs of wealth
I almost wrote a check out, yeah, but then I asked myself:

> Would He wear a pinky ring?
> Would He drive a fancy car?
> Would His wife wear furs and diamonds?
> Would His dressin' room have a star?

If He came back tomorrow, well there's somethin' I'd like to know
Would Jesus wear a Rolex on His television show?

Would Jesus be political if He came back to earth?
Have His second home in Palms Springs, yeah, but try to hide His worth?

Take money from those poor folks when He comes back again
And admit He's talked to all those preachers who say they been talkin' to Him?

> Just ask ya' self, would He wear a pinky ring?
> Would He drive a fancy car?
> Would His wife wear furs and diamonds?
> Would His dressing room have a star?

If He came back tomorrow, well there's somethin' I'd like to know
Could you tell me, would Jesus wear a Rolex?
Would Jesus wear a Rolex?
Would Jesus wear a Rolex on His television show?

FEBRUARY 15

Ho! Every one who thirsts, come to the waters; and you who have no money come, buy and eat. Come, buy wine and milk without money and without cost.

—ISAIAH 55:1

When I see someone on television, an evangelist or Bible teacher, who wants us to buy a prayer cloth so he or she can pray for us, or they ask for the giving of a certain amount of money as a condition for fellowshipping with them, I see no difference between that practice and those temple profiteers in *John 2:15-16*. Today's verse in Isaiah makes it clear that God's grace is contrary to that business mentality. When any believer is made to feel guilty because they don't give enough to whatever cause, it is time to pray to God to cleanse the business out of that organization.

This in no way suggests that pastors and full-time workers for the Lord should not be paid a fair and adequate wage for their service. The Apostle Paul is clear on this point *(1 Timothy 5:17-18; 1 Corinthians 9:7-11)*. But understanding that God's good news is *totally free (Romans 6:23)* evaporates all the guilt and fears that Christians are subjected to by modern day profiteers. It never guilts us. It never says we are not doing enough. It never burdens us. It makes us feel lighter and lighter!

Scripture, Old and New, tells us unequivocally that everything Jesus gives us is FREE!

- His forgiveness and eternal life are FREE!
- His righteousness, sanctification, and daily wisdom are FREE!
- His peace and inner-abundant joy daily are FREE!
- His freedom from our painful self is FREE!
- His moment-by-moment progressive molding of our clay is FREE!

LIVING WATER FOR TODAY:

The afflicted and needy are seeking water, but there is none, and their tongue is parched with thirst; ***I, the LORD, will answer them Myself,*** *as the God of Israel I will not forsake them.*—ISAIAH 41:17

For today*,* do you feel afflicted and needy? Are you parched with thirst? Without cost, the Lord promises to personally answer your prayers, for He will never forsake you! He will meet whatever need you have—*FREE!*

FEBRUARY 16

*The Jews then said to Him, "What sign do You show us as your authority for doing these things?" ¹⁹Jesus answered them, "Destroy this temple, and in three days I will raise it up." ²⁰The Jews then said, "It took forty-six years to build this temple, and will You raise it up in three days?" ²¹**But He was speaking of the temple of His body.***

—JOHN 2:18-21

With an understanding from yesterday that God's *good news* is offered to us *free of charge* solely out of God's mercy and grace, the dialogue contained in *John 2:18-25* comes into sharper focus. We will look at these verses over the next three days.

Jesus has driven the crooks from the temple and the Jews are demanding by what authority He did these things. From their perspective, the only "authority" that would justify this action would be a sign proving that He was God. Jesus gave them the sign they asked for, but they did not understand it at the time. In essence, Jesus told them *"I am the One who has authority over life and death. When you think you have put me to death, I will rise up again in three days."* How incredible and powerful is *THAT* authority!

Verse 21 is a wonderful word-picture and promise for us today. Jesus has just overturned the operations of the money changers and driven out the sellers of things that distract from the true worship of God. Paul tells us in *1 Corinthians 3:16* that we are the temple of God. Often, we can feel our "temple" filling with sinful actions, worries, doubts, and thoughts of selfishness and anger (to name a few). These are all "robbers," that steal away our joy, peace, and contentment in worshipping God. But praise God! Jesus remains in His temple (in us), *daily driving these thoughts out of us (Philippians 2:13)!*

LIVING WATER FOR TODAY:

*Do you not know that **you are a temple of God** and that the Spirit of God dwells in you? You are from God, little children, and have overcome them; because greater is He who is in you than he who is in the world.* —1 CORINTHIANS 3:16; 1 JOHN 4:4

For today, know this with assurance; no matter how cluttered your human temple may feel with sinful thoughts and worries that want to rob you of God's joy and peace, Jesus is the Greater Temple within you; active daily in your temple driving out those things that rob you of His peace and contentment in the true worship of God. *PTL!*

February 17

*So when He was raised from the dead, His disciples remembered that He said this; **and they believed** the Scripture and the word which Jesus had spoken. ²³Now when He was in Jerusalem at the Passover, during the feast, **many believed** in His name, observing His signs which He was doing.*

—John 2:22-23

Today and tomorrow John shares with us a truth that is so liberating and life-changing that you may want a box of Kleenex nearby. In these verses, John tells us something critically important about "believing" and "faith." Two groups of people "believed" in these verses. Jesus' disciples remembered what Jesus had predicted about destroying His bodily temple and rising again in three days, and many other Jews believed in His name by observing the signs He was doing. Look carefully at the basis of belief for both groups: (i) belief in scripture, (ii) the words which Jesus spoke, (iii) belief in Jesus' name, and (iv) observation of Jesus performing signs and miracles. All that sounds legitimate doesn't it? In fact, it sounds like the very criteria we use today in our churches to discern whether someone has genuinely prayed a prayer of salvation based on a proper belief. The problem is, which we will see tomorrow, Jesus was not buying it. *Oops!*

This has modern day commentaries scrambling for ways to explain this conundrum. One commentary says that the word "believed" in these verses means that the people believed Jesus was a great miracle worker, but not that He was the Savior. Another commentary says that the people believed Jesus had the favor of God, but they did not believe in all His claims and commands. This, of course, is all supposition (particularly as it relates to the disciples). There is a simpler explanation that we will see tomorrow. I will give you a hint: No amount of human belief *we* can muster is *saving* belief. Only the belief *gifted to us by God*, saves us.

Living Water for Today:

*For by grace you have been **saved through faith; and that not of yourselves, it is the gift of God**; ⁹not as a result of works, so that no one may boast.*—Ephesians 2:8-9

For today, rejoice that while all your human "faith" and hard work to please God will not save you (and gives you nothing to boast in), God has not left you bereft of hope for He has *gifted to you eternal, solid, stable, never-changing faith* that DOES save you. *PTL!*

FEBRUARY 18

But Jesus, on His part, was not entrusting Himself to them, for He knew all men, ²⁵and because He did not need anyone to testify concerning man, for He Himself knew what was in man.

—JOHN 2:24-25

Yesterday, we read about Jesus' disciples and many Jews "believing" in Him, all for apparently good reasons that were focused on Jesus. In fact, scripture gives no reason to doubt that all their belief was completely genuine. The problem is it was nothing more than *human belief*—fickle, capricious, and ever-changing.

Today's verses explain the puzzle posed from yesterday. Jesus did not trust *their* belief because He knew all men. He didn't need a letter of recommendation for those who believed. He knew that human belief no matter how genuine and sincere it is, is like smoke in the wind. Here is how *The Living Bible* puts it: *"But Jesus didn't trust them, for he knew mankind to the core. No one needed to tell him how changeable human nature is!"*

Remember Peter in *John 13:37-38?* He sincerely believed that he would lay down his life for Jesus. Jesus, in a loving and compassionate way, let Peter in on a little secret. I'll paraphrase: *"You Peter, will deny Me three times this very night before the rooster crows."* Peter obviously loved the Lord. Yet, he flipped 180 degrees in a matter of hours. This ever-changing quality of human belief is why Jesus would not trust these believers. It was not because they did not believe in the right things, as many commentaries suggest, but because they were using *human belief* rather than *God-given belief* to trust in Jesus. As we saw yesterday in *Ephesians 2:8-9*, only the belief that is given to us by God, which is not from us so we can't lose it or boast in it, is the only faith that saves. What a glorious freedom this is! Are you reaching for a Kleenex? How great is the grace of God? How great is the *good news* of the gospel? He has done it all for us! None of it depends on us!

LIVING WATER FOR TODAY:

For now we are all children of God through faith in Jesus Christ. —GALATIANS 3:26 TLB

For today, rejoice in the glorious truth that your salvation does not depend on your faith; but God has secured your eternal salvation once and for all by giving you faith to believe in His Son Jesus —*which can never by lost or proven inadequate! PTL!*

LIVING WATER FROM JOHN 2:12-25

February 10	Jesus, our Passover Lamb, traveled over 78 miles on foot to attend the Passover feast; the Passover foreshadowed His sacrifice for all humanity.
February 11	God's temple, intended to be a house of prayer, was being used as a "robbers' den."
February 12	The powerful words of Jesus drove out the money changers who were using His Father's house for a place of business.
February 13	Jesus is as passionate to care for us every moment of every day as He was to defend His Father's house.
February 14	Jesus disapproved of people profiting on what He offered freely—a place to come and worship God.
February 15	God offers everyone who thirsts to come freely to the living waters.
February 16	Our bodies are a temple of God, and His Spirit continues to drive out the things that rob us of His joy and peace.
February 17	Being saved through faith is the gift of God—eternal, solid, stable, never-changing faith.
February 18	God secured our eternal salvation by giving us faith to believe in Jesus; none of it depends on us.

PRAYER

Father, I am on my knees in my heart to You.
I have no words to express the profound joy and relief I
feel in knowing from scripture that my eternal salvation
does not depend on my fickle, ever-changing human belief
to keep me saved. You, dear God, have saved me from
myself! You have placed in me faith to believe in Your Son
Jesus. Now, with the utmost confidence,
I can proclaim with assurance that I am eternally
saved. I now know with absolute certainty that my life,
in eternity, will be spent in Your presence in glory.
Dear God, I am filled to overflowing with praise
and worship to you. In Jesus name,
Amen.

BORN A SECOND TIME!

———

JOHN 3:1-16

FEBRUARY 19

*Now there was a man of the Pharisees, named Nicodemus, a ruler of the Jews; ²this man came to Jesus by night and said to Him, "Rabbi, we know that You have come from God as a teacher; for no one can do these signs that You do unless God is with him." ³Jesus answered and said to him, "Truly, truly, I say to you, **unless one is born again he cannot see the kingdom of God."***

—JOHN 3:1-3

Nicodemus was a religious man and well-respected leader of the Jews. He honored the scriptures as he understood them and addressed Jesus with respect ("Rabbi" means teacher). He readily acknowledged his belief that: (i) Jesus came from God, (ii) the actions Jesus performed were supernatural signs, and (iii) that God was with Him. *Verse two* tells us that Nicodemus came to Jesus by night, apparently to avoid other religious leaders finding out that he was seeking Jesus personally.

Yet, according to *verse three*, Jesus ignored Nicodemus's opening words, as complimentary as they were, and spoke directly to the issue that Nicodemus most needed to hear: his lost condition. The beliefs Nicodemus expressed to Jesus in his opening remarks *were not enough to save him*. Jesus gave him the answer to the question that Nicodemus didn't know how to ask: *Nicodemus, you must be born again.*

Over the next several days we will explore what it means to be *born again*. For today, let us consider another phrase from these verses: *"the kingdom of God."* The *kingdom of God* is not a geographic destination, like Houston, Texas, or Paris, France—someplace that we finally arrive at (like Heaven) when we die. The *kingdom of God* refers to the realm of *God's quality of life*, and the experiencing of this life not just someday in eternity, but moment by moment right now! Jesus is telling Nicodemus that experiencing God's life (His eternal life) begins the moment we are born again into the *kingdom of God*, in the same way that a baby begins to experience physical life the moment he or she is born.

LIVING WATER FOR TODAY:

See how great a love the Father has bestowed on us, that we would be called children of God; and such we are.—1 JOHN 3:1A

For today, as a child of God, delight yourself in the kingdom of God's quality of life that He is revealing in you more and more each day.

FEBRUARY 20

*Jesus answered and said to him, "Truly, truly, I say to you, unless one is born again he cannot see the kingdom of God." ⁴Nicodemus said to Him, "How can a man be born when he is old? He cannot enter a second time into his mother's womb and be born, can he?" ⁵Jesus answered, "Truly, truly, I say to you, **unless one is born of water and the Spirit** he cannot enter into the kingdom of God."*

—JOHN 3:3-5

J esus tells us in *verse three* that we are "Christians" *solely* because we are "born again." This may be an inconvenient truth for some, but that is what Jesus tells us. We are not Christians because we were baptized or belong to a particular church. We are not Christians because we are religious, or based on the good things we do and the bad things we do not do. Neither are we Christians saved by grace because of how many people we witness to or "lead" to the Lord. Scripture is very simple and clear: *We are either born again or NOT born again*, nothing else matters regarding our eternal destiny.

Being presented with this truth, Nicodemus thinks exactly as we would think with our finite human minds: *How can we possibly crawl back into our mother's womb and be born again?* Nicodemus only had the physical realm (or kingdom) to serve as his "reality." Jesus responds emphatically, *"Truly, truly"* (meaning, *listen to this carefully, it is important)* unless you have two births (that of water *and* Spirit) you cannot enter God's kingdom, or know God personally, or experience His everlasting life.

Many Bible commentaries engage in much discussion about the hidden meaning of "water" in *verse five*: "*unless one is born of water and the Spirit*." But the context is simple and straightforward. Jesus is telling Nicodemus that he needs more than just a physical birth; he also needs a spiritual birth. There is nothing in these verses more complicated than that.

LIVING WATER FOR TODAY:

*If **Christ is in you**, though the body is dead because of sin, yet the spirit is alive because of righteousness.* —ROMANS 8:10

For today, meditate on the statement: *Christ is in you!* Your flesh carries the death of sin, but your spirit is alive because of Christ's righteousness in you. God's quality of life is springing up in you through the Holy Spirit who is at work in you *(Philippians 2:13).*

FEBRUARY 21

*"That which is born of the **flesh is flesh**, and that which is born of the **Spirit is spirit.**"*
—JOHN 3:6

It is easy to forget that the "chapter" and "verse" designations we see in modern Bibles were not part of the original text. They were inserted in the 16th century to provide an easier way to reference scripture. While this may be helpful, such artificial divisions sometimes carve into pieces a conversation that should be understood in context as a cohesive whole. So it is in this conversation between Jesus and Nicodemus. Jesus tells Nicodemus he needs a second birth to enter the kingdom of God; Nicodemus continues to plead his ignorance; Jesus then describes the difference between the two births by first classifying them as *water* and *spirit*, and then telling Nicodemus: *"That which is born of the **flesh is flesh**, and that which is born of the **Spirit is spirit.**"*

Jesus is telling Nicodemus that we are first born of the flesh (which means we are born with a physical body), but we also must be born of the Spirit to enter the kingdom of God. That makes sense doesn't it? When a new baby is born, don't we often hear the details later that the mother's "water broke" at such and such a time and her baby was born shortly thereafter? The water that "broke" is the amniotic fluid that sustained us until we were born. Jesus is referring to this fluid when He refers to *water (verse five)* and immediately links it to *"that which is born of the flesh is flesh" (verse six)*; or that which is born of the human body is a human body.

When considering the entire conversation, the central point Jesus is making is not about the "water" or "flesh" in these verses concerning the first birth; but about the need for Nicodemus (and us) to have a *second* birth: a spiritual birth.

LIVING WATER FOR TODAY:

*"For the **promise is for you and your children** and for all who are far off, as many as the **Lord our God will call to Himself.**"* —ACTS 2:39

For today, contemplate that God is calling you (and your family) as His children. He sent His Spirit to give new birth to your spirit. You didn't earn it or deserve it, but He called you to Himself anyway—a call that can *never be stayed, delayed, or revoked! PTL!*

FEBRUARY 22

*"**Do not be amazed** that I said to you, 'You must be born again.'"*

—JOHN 3:7

Isn't this comment interesting? Jesus obviously did not think the need to be "born again" was anything out of the ordinary. He treated it in a matter-of-fact way. He did not say you must be born again ... *and ... and ... and* (as though there were a list of things to do). He named only this one-time event (of being born again) as determinative of whether a person will enter the kingdom of God.

Pause for a moment to consider the powerful implications of Jesus' statement. We have all been born once in the flesh; and for those God calls to enter His kingdom, we have been born a *second time by the Spirit*. Thus, our entire Christian life is based *solely on this second birth*. There is no such thing as being "sort of born again," or "possibly born of the Spirit," or "used-to-be born of the Spirit." We are either born a second time by the Spirit of God or we are not! What are the implications of this truth?

- Are there "better" or "worse" Christians in God's kingdom?
- Are there "superior" or "inferior" Christians in God's kingdom?
- Are there "more worthy" and "less worthy" Christians in God's kingdom?
- Does it depend on whether a person is baptized, attends church, or tithes?
- Does it depend on how much we witness or how many we lead to the Lord?
- Does it depend on how we live (or don't live) our lives?
- Does it have *anything* to do with us at all? (*See February 24 for more discussion*).

The answer is an emphatic "NO!" to all these questions. How this truth has stripped me of so many fleshly, negative, and judgmental attitudes about other Christians!

LIVING WATER FOR TODAY:

*For through the grace given to me I say to everyone among you not to think more highly of himself than he ought to think; but to think so as to have sound judgment, as **God has allotted to each a measure of faith**.*—ROMANS 12:3

For today, celebrate that God has allotted to you the same measure of faith He has given to each of His children; there is not one Christian better, superior, or more worthy than you (nor none worse, inferior, or less worthy). *Praise God!*

FEBRUARY 23

"The wind blows where it wishes and you hear the sound of it, but do not know where it comes from and where it is going; so is everyone who is born of the Spirit."
—JOHN 3:8

Jesus has told Nicodemus that he must be born again, and Nicodemus has expressed his puzzlement regarding *how* this could be. Jesus now explains *how* a person becomes born again. This is one of the most thrilling and freeing verses in all of scripture. Jesus begins His explanation by saying: *"The wind blows where it wishes."* What an incredible way to start this explanation! What does the wind have to do with being born again?

If we were answering Nicodemus from today's point of view, we would tell him that *he must make a decision. He* must pray a salvation prayer, or *he* must be baptized, or declare his faith before an assembly of witnesses. All our modern-day responses *focus on Nicodemus* and the decision—we think—*he* must make to be saved. But this is not what Jesus answered. Jesus told Nicodemus it was the "wind" who decides the *when* and *where* of a person's new birth. Nicodemus would be able to feel the results of the wind's actions, but not to control it. To say this another way, *Nicodemus' new birth had nothing to do with anything he did!* But what does the wind have to do with a spiritual new birth?

It just so happens that the Greek word for wind is πνεῦμα (pneuma), the exact same word for spirit! Do you think God had something to do with that coincidence? Jesus is teaching us how we become born again of the Spirit. He likens the movement of God's Spirit to the movement of the wind. Are you the one who decides whether the wind blows or not? No! The Spirit of God moves upon those He chooses to bring into new life. You can do nothing to prevent or inhibit the Spirit's movement in your life. *Praise the Lord!*

LIVING WATER FOR TODAY:

John [the Baptist] *answered and said, "A man can receive nothing unless it has been given him from heaven."*—JOHN 3:27

For today, rejoice that your eternal salvation depends solely on God's choosing, and has nothing for you to do, contribute to, or boast in. *The Spirit decides whom He chooses,* and He chose you as evidenced by His wind/Spirit in you. *PTL!*

FEBRUARY 24

*"The wind blows where it wishes and **you** hear the sound of it, but do not know where it comes from and where it is going; **so is everyone who is born of the Spirit.**"*
—JOHN 3:8

I live in the mountains where there are lots of tall trees. When the wind blows, I can hear it whistling through those trees; and in strong winds, it sounds like a freight train moving through the forest. From a distance I can see the limbs sway and bend with the wind's passing. Do I see the wind? No. I only see the *effect* of the wind. Jesus told Nicodemus that this is exactly how it is with everyone who is born of the Spirit.

I pray that God will guide our understanding of this verse as though Jesus is speaking to us personally. Jesus is telling Nicodemus (and us) that our born-again experience in life has nothing to do with us. It has as much to do with us as we have to do with directing the wind. This is so comforting and freeing! The movement of the Spirit of God is a great mystery to us. We cannot see Him. We cannot tell Him what to do or facilitate or inhibit His movements. At His choosing, He gives us the faith to believe.

And the Spirit doesn't stop with our new birth. He leads us into a deeper trust that God is righteous and totally just. He loves all of us equally, including our children and unsaved relatives (and far more than we have the capacity to do ourselves). He tells us that His ways are unsearchable, so we need not try to understand them. It is all according to His timing. The wind blows where it wishes, and we don't know where it comes from or where it is going. The Spirit of God moves where He wishes and we do not see Him because we are not God. We haven't created anything while He has created *everything* and is moving and working to accomplish His good purpose—His eternal plan which includes us. He is the Creator-God who is sovereign over all things, *including us being born of the Spirit.*

LIVING WATER FOR TODAY:

*Therefore if anyone is **in Christ**, he is **a new creature;** the old things passed away; behold, new things have come.*
—2 CORINTHIANS 5:17

For today, celebrate that God has chosen you and placed you *in Christ*. He has done it all and made you a new creation in Him. *PTL!*

FEBRUARY 25

*"The wind blows where it wishes and you hear the sound of it, but do not know where it comes from and where it is going; so is everyone who is **born** of the Spirit."*

—JOHN 3:8

Sometimes, *one* word can flood us with volumes of meaning and insight. So it is with one word from this verse. Jesus uses the word *born* to describe our human experience of being given eternal life by the Spirit of God. He could have described this process in any number of ways, but chose to sum it all up in one word: *Born.* What message is Jesus conveying to us through this particular word?

In truth, this is yet another way of stating the same lesson from yesterday—that we have no control over the wind's movement (or the Spirit of God's decisions). When Jesus uses the term *born*, as in born again, He is conveying this same truth. Our born-again experience—where we enjoy a salvation full of God's quality of life, both today and eternally—has nothing to do with us or any decision we make. Our physical birth is not something we decide to do for ourselves; it is something that happens to us. The same is true with our spiritual birth. Jesus chose His words carefully for this verse.

Read how *The Living Bible* translates this verse: *"Just as you can hear the wind but can't tell where it comes from or where it will go next, so it is with the Spirit. We do not know on whom he **will next bestow this life from heaven.**"*

I know you may be struggling with this as I did for many years. But it is believing what God's word says that strips away all the baggage that keeps us weighted down with notions that we have something to do with our salvation. In reality, we don't invite Jesus into our lives; but rather, *when it pleases God*, He reveals Christ in us (*see* Paul's description of his own conversion in *Galatians 1:15-16*). Our salvation is a gift of pure love from God upon us who are totally undeserving. That is grace upon grace! *PTL!*

LIVING WATER FOR TODAY:

*Even when we were dead in our transgressions, [He] made us **alive together with Christ (by grace you have been saved).***—EPHESIANS 2:5

For today, rejoice that God has made you *alive in Christ!* You were dead! The dead can do nothing for themselves. This is amazing grace! Praise God today for His amazing love in which *He loved (and loves) you.*

FEBRUARY 26

*Nicodemus said to Him, **"How can these things be?"** ¹⁰Jesus answered and said to him, "Are you the teacher of Israel and do not understand these things?"*

—JOHN 3:9-10

Nicodemus, upon hearing Jesus previous response, asks yet another *how* question: *"How can these things be?"* In modern English usage, such a question sounds like Nicodemus was uttering a statement of understanding and amazement. But that is not the meaning of his question. From his pragmatic experience, Nicodemus was really asking: *"How do I experience this?"* Or, *"What part do I play in this process?"* Remember, Nicodemus was an astute religious leader of the Jewish people. He had earned this position of leadership through a personal, life-long commitment to religious education and adherence to the commandments given by God to His people through Moses. He was used to having *a role to play* regarding the things of God throughout his entire life. The Law required *him* to do (or not do) certain things; and based on *his actions*, God would respond by either blessing or punishing *him* for what *he* did (or did not do).

But now, Jesus was telling him that he had *no part to play* in being born again. Nicodemus had to be shocked by what Jesus was telling him. Talk about revolutionary! He, no doubt, listened carefully to Jesus' statement about the wind and the Spirit (and would instantly understand the connection). He was keenly attuned to figure out how *he* fit into the process of being born again. But there was no misunderstanding what Jesus said: Nicodemus had *nothing* to do with being born again. It was exclusively the work of the Holy Spirit. Just like the wind, the Holy Spirit blows where He wills and grants this grace upon those He chooses to grant it. God is in control of all of it.

Little did Nicodemus know, the Holy Spirit was already at work drawing him to Jesus.

LIVING WATER FOR TODAY:

"For I know the plans that I have for you," declares the LORD, *"plans for welfare and not for calamity **to give you a future and a hope."*** —JEREMIAH 29:11

For today, regardless how you may feel in the present, God has given you a new spiritual birth. Be confident in God's plan for you: A plan full of a glorious future and hope. *PTL!*

FEBRUARY 27

*"Truly, truly, I say to you, **we** speak of what **we** know and testify of what **we** have seen, and you do not accept our testimony. ¹²If I told you earthly things and you do not believe, how will you believe if I tell you heavenly things? ¹³No one has ascended into heaven, but He who descended from heaven: the Son of Man."*

—JOHN 3:11-13

In these verses, Jesus continues to press home to Nicodemus that, on his own, he can't stir up enough human belief to gain a second spiritual birth. All his religious training, education, leadership experience, and human wisdom are worthless when it comes to a new birth by the Spirit of God. This, undoubtedly, was not easy for Nicodemus to hear.

In *verse 11* Jesus does something interesting. He uses the collective word "we" repeatedly. Most Bible scholars believe He is referring to the Trinity by these references: God the Father, Son, and Holy Spirit. Jesus is telling Nicodemus that even though the Triune God tells him this truth, he is still incapable of believing it on his own. Why? Because his "spiritual organ" is deadened and needs to be *made alive* again through a new birth. Until then, his whole being is dead to understanding spiritual things.

This is why every person—who God has *not* given faith to believe in Jesus—thinks that what we teach and believe is foolishness *(1 Corinthians 1:18)*. There is a growing belief in America that any interest in worshiping God, or any reference to scripture, is a waste of time and takes away from having a productive life. These are those who live in darkness. You can get in their face and argue with them. It does no good. You can try twisting their arm, but it doesn't help. You are talking to darkness. Jesus is making the point that humans, without God's Spirit blowing faith into them, are incapable of believing in Christ. They are spiritually dead. They cannot understand spiritual truth.

LIVING WATER FOR TODAY:

*For the word of the cross is **foolishness to those who are perishing**, but to us **who are being saved** it is the power of God.*—1 CORINTHIANS 1:18

For today, test your faith to see if it is from God. Do you think that Christ's death on the cross is nothing but foolishness and a waste of time? Or is it the power of God for your salvation? If you believe the latter, you are one of those *who are being saved by God!* There is *never* a reason to doubt your salvation for as long as you live! *PTL!*

A PERSONAL TESTIMONY

NOT ALL BELIEF IS SAVING BELIEF!

I have been to India several times over the years as part of missionary outreach. India is a country with a landmass one-third the size of the United States, but with three times the population (over one billion people). On my first visit there I spent a month touring many villages throughout the country. It was a profoundly sobering experience. The people in village after village are exceedingly poor.

One thing was prevalent, however, in spite of the deep poverty. In every village I visited there would be an approximate 4x6 platform made from a crude mix of concrete and straw and raised 14 to 18 inches above the ground. Placed upon it, crafted by the villagers' own hands, usually out of concrete, were small statuettes representing the three predominate gods of their Hindu religion. These gods were believed to provide water for crops, fertility in bearing children, and healing of the sick.

Every morning, the villagers would bring whatever bits of rice, bananas, chapatti (a sort of thin pancake) to lay on the platform at the feet of their gods. They would then bow down and ring a bell, as though they were waking the gods up to eat. As my interpreter and I watched, the villager would eventually turn and leave. The moment they were gone, the crows, rats, and other creatures would dash onto the platform and snatch the offered food.

I did not wish to be disrespectful or judgmental of anyone else's religion (after all, I am no better than any of them), but I was intensely curious. I could not grasp how anyone would think that what they had made with their own hands could be a god worthy of worship. I pulled my interpreter quietly aside and asked. He said that Hindus believe that anything they choose to put their faith in becomes a god. While I had his attention, I had noticed maybe 15-18 smaller clumps of concrete spaced around the perimeter of the 4x6 platform that held the three major gods. I asked what those were. He said those are the gods they created to guard the three main gods on the platform. It was a complex belief system.

When I got back home I learned that the interpreter was not technically correct in his explanation of Hindu beliefs. To be more exact, I was told, the Hindus believe that whatever object they believe in as a god, that god then comes and inhabits the object they believe in. In practice, the interpreter was right. The object became the god for worship.

FEBRUARY 28

*"As Moses lifted up the serpent in the wilderness, even so must the Son of Man be lifted up ¹⁵so that **whoever believes will in Him have eternal life.**"*
—JOHN 3:14-15

After God miraculously rescued the children of Israel from 40 years of slavery in Egypt *(Numbers 21)* we read that the Israelites were growing impatient with the journey from Egypt to the Promised Land. They regularly complained about the "miserable food" (manna) God provided them each day along the way *(Numbers 21:4-5)*. They repeatedly expressed their wish that Moses and God had left them back in Egypt. This time God used their complaints as an opportunity to foretell about His Son Jesus, who would come to save His people from eternal death.

Scripture tells us that God sent poisonous snakes among the people and many were bitten and died. How quickly the attitudes of the Israelites changed! They were soon crying out to God for mercy; and God gave Moses the cure. Moses was to make a snake out of bronze and hang it up on a pole for all to see. God promised to all who were bitten, that they need only look upon the brass serpent to be healed. No need to do or say anything. No complex rituals, no lengthy prayers, no sacrifices of any kind. They need only look upon the brass serpent to be saved from a poisonous death.

It is difficult to hold back tears when recognizing that this event in *Numbers 21* is symbolic of Jesus (the Son of Man) being lifted-up on the cross, and Him bringing salvation and healing to those who simply look upon (believe in) Him. *Verse 15* repeats the recurring theme we have seen throughout John: whoever *believes* in Him has eternal life. In both *Numbers* and *John* there is nothing added to that saving belief!

LIVING WATER FOR TODAY:

*And the testimony is this, that **God has given us eternal life**, and this life is in His Son. ¹²**He who has the Son has the life**; he who does not have the Son of God does not have the life.* —1 JOHN 5:11-12

For today, rejoice—then rejoice again! God has *given you* eternal life. It is nothing you earned or labored to achieve. You didn't even ask for it! God *freely* revealed His eternal life in you when it pleased Him *(Galatians 1:15-16)*. Again, I say, rejoice!

FEBRUARY 29 (LEAP-YEAR BONUS)

*Looking unto Jesus, the **author and finisher of our faith.***

—HEBREWS 12:2A (NKJV)

On this leap day, let's take the opportunity to explore the issue of faith more fully. I realize that you may be wondering, *if my faith comes from God, then what about those times when I have doubts, or when my faith isn't strong because of worry, or whatever?* Today's verse gives us insight into a powerful freedom-truth. Not only does this verse say that Jesus *authors* our faith in the first place, but in the *NASB* it states that He also *perfects* it. What does "perfecter of faith" mean? It means two things:

First, Jesus is the One who increases our faith in an experiential way each day, *"who gives life to the dead and calls into being that which does not exist" (Romans 4:17)*. This applies not only to our faith, but to every aspect of our Christian life. Are you struggling with a spirit of unforgiveness or impatience? Are you fearful, frustrated, anxious, or depressed? Don't try to force change in your situation or dredge up more patience or forgiveness out of your own self-effort. *Focus on the How-Great-Thou-Art Almighty God—turn to Him.* Ask Him to manifest His Spirit of forgiveness and patience in you. He will call into being that which does not exist in your life.

Second, Jesus *IS* the perfect faith that God sees *in* us. What God sees is reality. Just as God sees Christ as our righteousness, our perfect patience, our perfect forgiving spirit, and our perfect morality, He also sees Christ as our perfect faith. Ephesians 2:8 refers to ***this*** faith and tells us that it was given to us by God. This is why our faith (as God sees it) is always strong. *Christ never falters within us to keep His faith.* I may be feeling weak today or vulnerable, but God sees my faith strong because *Christ is my perfect faith.*

LIVING WATER FOR TODAY:

When the Gentiles heard this, they began rejoicing and glorifying the word of the Lord; and as many as had been appointed to eternal life believed.—ACTS 13:48

For today, know that you believe (the gospel) because God has *"appointed"* you to eternal life! God chose **you** to be saved. *Rejoice and give glory to God!*

March 1

*"For God so loved the world, that He gave His only begotten Son, that **whoever believes in Him shall not perish, but have eternal life.**"*

—John 3:16

Today we read the most recognized and familiar verse in all of scripture. Everything we need to know about God's good-news gospel is included in this one verse. God loved us and demonstrated that love by sending His Son Jesus as a *gift* of eternal life to us: "Whoever believes in Him will not perish, but have eternal life." That's it! It's that simple. Why? Because God does it all on our behalf. He even gives us the faith to believe.

Many Christians like to use this verse as a *recruiting verse for unbelievers*, for the purpose of presenting them with the gospel. To this end, we often see *"JOHN 3:16"* on signs alongside freeways, in the end zones at football games, and mingled among the galleries at golf tournaments. It is simple and concise. I certainly would never criticize the use of this verse in such a manner; but from the context of Jesus' discussion with Nicodemus, the verse is actually intended by John to be a *confirming verse for believers* to test whether God has given them a spiritual new birth.

From John's perspective, *John 3:13-16 IS* the testimony referred to by Jesus in *verse 11*: *"we speak of what we know and testify of what we have seen."* The testimony Jesus is referring to is His own *eyewitness testimony*. He can speak with authority about heavenly things because He is the One who has *"descended from heaven: the Son of Man."* What is this testimony Jesus tells Nicodemus? God so loved the world (or loved the world in this way) that He gave His only begotten Son Jesus to be lifted up on a cross (like the brass serpent in the wilderness) so that whosoever looks upon Him and believes shall not perish but have everlasting (eternal) life. For Nicodemus, a man who had spent his entire life working for God, this testimony was nothing short of revolutionary.

Living Water for Today:

*These things I have written to you who believe in the name of the Son of God, **so that you may know that you have eternal life.**—*1 John 5:13

For today, no matter how you feel about yourself, *rest* in your belief that Jesus is your Savior. God wants you to KNOW that you have eternal life—*as a free gift from Him!*

CONSIDER THIS:

How to Know You Are Born a Second Time

How can each of us **KNOW** we are born again? That the Holy Spirit has chosen to blow God's grace on us? Here are three ways for you to clearly know:

First, *John 3:19-20* tells us that the unbeliever hates the light and does not come to the light for fear his or her deeds will be exposed. The unbeliever loves darkness rather than the light. The first way to know if you have been a recipient of God's spiritual new birth is to ask yourself if you have a greater affinity and attraction to God or to a life without God in it at all. **If you prefer God**, that is absolute evidence that you are born again.

Second, in *2 Corinthians 13:5* Paul encourages us to test ourselves to see whether we are in the faith: that Jesus Christ is in us. **Do you have promptings of His Spirit in you**, drawing you to pray, speak to someone, or read His word? Have you been comforted by something you read in scripture? No unbeliever ever draws comfort from the words of scripture. The unbeliever thinks scripture is foolishness and crazy. Do you ever ask the Lord to help you in a stressful situation, like when you are angry at a relative and you pray that God will remove the anger and replace it with His compassion for that relative? Even if you only have the thought, it is confirmation that you are born again. Only the Spirit of God puts those promptings, thoughts, or prayers in you. Those thoughts never come from your flesh.

Third, *1 Corinthians 1:18* tells us that the word of the cross, Christ coming to be our sacrifice sent by God to die in our place, is foolishness to those who are perishing (referring to all unbelievers). By contrast, to those who are being saved it is the power of God. Which is it for you? If Christ's death on the cross is foolishness to you, then you are not born again. **If you believe Christ's death and resurrection are all part of God's plan to save us, then you are absolutely, 100% for sure, born again.**

John is writing his gospel that you may rejoice, and never doubt your salvation!

LIVING WATER FROM JOHN 3:1-16

February 19	As a child of God's kingdom, we experience His life daily.
February 20	Our spirit is alive because of Christ's righteousness in us.
February 21	We must be born of the Spirit (a second birth) to enter the kingdom of God.
February 22	For those God calls, He allots a measure of faith.
February 23	The Spirit of God chooses to give us new life.
February 24	The Spirit of God gives us the faith to believe and leads us into a deeper trust that God is righteous and just.
February 25	Being born of the Spirit has bestowed on us life from heaven.
February 26	God gives us a new spiritual birth—a glorious hope.
February 27	The Holy Spirit enlightens us to believe in Christ and understand heavenly things.
February 28	Whoever believes in the Son of Man has eternal life.
February 29	Jesus, the author and perfecter of our faith, increases our faith in an experiential way each day.
March 1	Out of His great love, God gave His only begotten Son and whoever believes in Him has eternal life.

PRAYER

*Dear Heavenly Father: Thank You for Your Son Jesus!
I readily acknowledge that sin still dwells in my flesh and
that sin creates doubt in my mind as to whether I am truly
and eternally saved. But deeper than my flesh is a believing
heart of faith, which You have revealed in me, that believes
in Your Son as my Savior to save me from those sins.
I praise You that You have not left me to worry and fret
over my eternal destiny with You. You have given me belief
in Your Son Jesus. I am drawn to things concerning You.
I feel Your leading at times in my life. All of which is
absolute evidence, according to Your infallible word, that
I have been born again by Your Holy Spirit and have
eternal life in Your Son Jesus. What is left for me to say or
do but praise You! In Jesus precious name, I pray. Amen.*

My Living Water Thoughts

_____

_____

_____

_____

_____

_____

_____

_____

_____

_____

_____

_____

_____

_____

_____

_____

_____

_____

_____

_____

_____

_____

_____

_____

_____

_____

_____

_____

GOD IS DIRECTING OUR STEPS

———

JOHN 3:17-36

MARCH 2

"For God did not send the Son into the world to judge the world, but that the world might be saved through Him. ¹⁸He who believes in Him is not judged; he who does not believe has been judged already, because he has not believed in the name of the only begotten Son of God."

—JOHN 3:17-18

I n these verses, Jesus continues to drive home to Nicodemus that *belief* is the critical indicator whether a person has been born again by the Spirit of God. I have shared on previous days that John refers to *belief* scores of times as the sole basis for salvation. Here are three more references to this fact in these two verses.

Jesus tells Nicodemus (and us) that God did not send Him (Jesus) to judge the world, but to save it. Just as the brass serpent was raised up in the wilderness; so too, God sent His own Son to be lifted up (on a cross) to save the world from certain death. In the wilderness, God spoke, people believed and looked upon the serpent, and were healed. The same is true today. To know with certainty that God has chosen you for salvation requires the answer to only ONE question—do you *believe* that Jesus is God's gift to save you? *Belief* is like a reagent that changes color in a chemistry experiment in the presence of something else. If the Spirit of God has chosen to give you God's new life, the "reagent" of *belief* appears in your life and you will never be judged. If you do not believe, you are *already* under a death sentence because of your lack of belief.

Many believers get anxious when they read a verse with the word *judgment* in it. They often think of some future judgment day. But this judgment is joyous good news! It is a judgment that has *already* taken place. The word *judgment* here means that God has already *determined* how He will save His people. The Holy Spirit moves (like the wind), entering those chosen by God to be His children, resulting in life-saving *belief* in that person. Jesus has crystalized into one word, the essence (and evidence) of the entire born-again experience for Nicodemus (and us): that word, again, is *belief.*

LIVING WATER FOR TODAY:

*"Come to Me, all who are weary and heavy-laden, and **I will give you rest.**"*—MATTHEW 11:28

For today, rest in God's word that you will *never* suffer judgment because you *believe* in His Son—who is God's true righteousness and sanctification *in you (1 Corinthians 1:30).*

MARCH 3

*"This is the judgment, that the Light has come into the world, and men loved the darkness rather than the Light, for their deeds were evil. ²⁰For everyone who does evil hates the Light, and **does not come to the Light** for fear that his deeds will be exposed. ²¹But he who practices the truth **comes to the Light**, so that his deeds may be manifested as having been wrought in God."*

—JOHN 3:19-21

J esus now tells Nicodemus exactly what God's judgment (or conclusion) is: despite sending Jesus, who is referred to by one of His proper names *Light*, humanity still loved (or preferred) their own selfish, immoral, deceitful ways over the things of God. *Roman 3:12* tells us that there is NONE who does good, *not even one!* The natural state of *every* human is to remain in darkness and live as they choose without God. All things related to God: all spiritual things, saving grace, righteousness, true life, goodness, and love are all rejected by man in darkness. Based on this determination by God, He sent His Spirit to blow where He wills and to grant *new birth* to those He chooses.

Jesus is teaching Nicodemus that there are *only* two groups of people in this world. Those who do evil deeds, which are the *acts of unbelief*. And those who practice the truth, which are the *acts of belief*. There are those who live their lives with no thought or desire for God; and there are others who are attracted to the things of God regardless how sinful they may think themselves to be. From our human perspective, since we still have sin alive in our flesh, we immediately get anxious about the *evil deeds* mentioned here, thinking that they refer to *our* personal sins. The joyous **good news** is that the *evil deeds* in this verse are not referring to our sinful acts but the evil acts of *unbelief*. Since no one comes to the Light as a result of their own choosing, this act of coming to the Light is, in reality, solely the result of God working in us.

LIVING WATER FOR TODAY:

Then Jesus again spoke to them, saying, "I am the Light of the world; he who follows Me will not walk in the darkness, but will have the Light of life."—JOHN 8:12

For today, let your heart swell with thanksgiving, for the Light of the world (Jesus) has chosen to dwell in you; you cannot walk in darkness. You walk each day in the Light of God's Spirit, prompting you to pray, read His word, and fellowship with believers.

John 3:21 is a verse that can engender worry and guilt or freedom and rejoicing in us, depending on how it is understood. It reads, *"But he who practices the truth comes to the Light, so that his deeds may be manifested as having been wrought in God."* If we read the verse as an exhortation *for us* to "practice the truth" and "come to the Light," then everything gets worrisome. Are we practicing *enough* truth or coming to the Light *often enough* to manifest ourselves as wrought in God? This worry only leads to a life full of anxiety and doubt because our flesh will always fall short of God's righteous performance standard.

But notice that both the phrase *"practices the truth"* and *"comes to the Light"* are expressed as present-tense actions while the phrase *"manifested as having been wrought in God"* is in the past tense. Jesus is telling Nicodemus (and us) that our present-tense experiences are the **result** of something God has already wrought (or accomplished) in us. The phrase *"practices the truth"* does not mean we are always acting like bastions of truth without sin. Far from it! The Spirit is always at war with our flesh *(Galatians 5:16)*. Even the Apostle Paul struggled with his flesh *(Romans 7:18)*. John 3:20-21, when taken together, reveal those who have (and have not) received salvation. *Verse 21* provides evidence from our present-day experiences that we are eternally saved. If our *prevailing* desire is an attraction to God (the Light), then we are manifesting what God has already worked in us (or wrought in us). Every believer has God working in them 24/7 *(Philippians 2:13)*, creating this attraction to the Light. It is this *practice of desiring God* which the phrase *"practices the truth"* is referring. Again, we see that it is God, not us, who saves us. This fills our hearts with praise and rejoicing (not worry and doubt)!

Ask yourself: *Is the primary desire in my life one of yearning for righteousness or a lust for sinfulness?* Since *Romans 3:12* tells us that none of us desire righteousness by our own initiative, those who *practice the truth*, that is, desire righteousness, are reflecting the Holy Spirit's compelling influential work in their lives. John shares this same idea in *1 John 1:6-7* when he says, as we *"walk in the Light,"* as God Himself is in the Light ... the blood of Jesus cleanses us from all sin. Yet again, the cleansing comes first, resulting in our walking in the Light. *John 3:21* is yet more evidence of *God's glorious salvation for us!*

MARCH 4

*After these things Jesus and His disciples came into the land of Judea, and **there He***
***was spending time with them** and baptizing. ²³John also was baptizing in Aenon near*
Salim, because there was much water there; and people were coming and were being
baptized—²⁴for John had not yet been thrown into prison.

—JOHN 3:22-24

I n these verses we move on from Nicodemus. John tells us that Jesus and His disciples have come into Judea, and He is spending time with them. In modern ver-
nacular, Jesus was "hanging out" with his disciples, no doubt teaching, exhorting, and
guiding them. It warms my heart to realize that under God's new covenant, this is
exactly what Jesus is doing with us today. He is the indwelling Christ, spending time
with (and in) us; and through His spoken and written word, He is writing His teachings, exhortations, and guidance onto the tablets of our hearts *(2 Corinthians 3:3);*
creating (over the course of our lives) an imprint that changes us. We become a reflection of what His word says.

While Jesus spent time with His disciples, they were busy baptizing those who
were coming to Jesus. *Verse 22* may be taken to suggest that it was Jesus who was doing
the baptizing, but John, in *John 4:2*, makes it clear that it was Jesus' disciples, not Jesus,
who were baptizing. We are not told whether all of Jesus' disciples were baptizing at
the same time, or they were doing so in shifts, but either way, it suggests that large
crowds were coming to Jesus. This sets the scene for the events that follow.

A word about baptism is insightful here. Many Christians believe that baptism
is a uniquely Christian sacrament. However, the purification rites of Jewish law and
tradition is an ancient ritual of ceremonial washing with water by immersion (which
many Jews still practice today). The ritual represented a person's confession of sin and
their recognition of the need for the cleansing power of God's forgiveness. This context gives us deeper insight into the hearts of those coming to Jesus.

LIVING WATER FOR TODAY:

For from Him and through Him and to Him are all
things. *To Him be the glory forever. Amen.* —ROMANS 11:36

For today*,* give God the glory; lift up your heart to Him in praise and thanksgiving for
He is the source of all good things and the sole means by which you experience them!

MARCH 5

Therefore there arose a discussion on the part of John's disciples with a Jew about purification. *[26]And they came to John and said to him, "Rabbi, He who was with you beyond the Jordan, to whom you have testified, behold, **He is baptizing and all are coming to Him.**"*

—JOHN 3:25-26

Let's put this scene in context. John the Baptist and his followers have been baptizing crowds coming to them for some time. These crowds were large enough to draw the attention of the Jewish leaders in Jerusalem. These leaders sent messengers to John asking who he was—whether he was the Christ, Elijah, or the prophet *(John 1:19-21)*. John answered that he was none of these, but only a voice crying in the wilderness *(John 1:23)*. To John's followers, they were obviously part of something *very* special.

Now look again at today's verses. The crowds coming to John have dwindled to the point where a Jew, probably someone coming to be baptized and observing the greater size of the crowds going to Jesus, approached John's followers and likely asked whether John's rite of purification was as good (or effective) as Jesus' baptism. John's followers came to John decrying the fact that *"He* (Jesus) *is baptizing and **all are coming to Him.**"*

While we will explore John's answer over the next few days, it is fair to observe in general terms that John was not at all concerned about the shift in the crowd size or his diminishing role; in fact, he was filled with joy about it *(see March 7)*. John knew that God was directing him to do exactly what he was doing and that was all that mattered. Ask yourself what you would have thought if you were that Jew observing these events? We would probably think that John must have lost his gift or that he must not be serving God the way God wants him to. But John knew that God directs what we do each day; and as we will see, this brought comfort to John and filled him with joy.

LIVING WATER FOR TODAY:

Since the Lord is directing our steps, *why try to understand everything that happens along the way?* —PROVERBS 20:24 TLB

For today, why question, worry, or stress over things that you do not yet understand? Be comforted that God is directing everything in your life today, and every yesterday and future day. A priceless comfort! *PTL!*

MARCH 6

*John answered and said, "**A man can receive nothing unless it has been given him from heaven.**"*

—JOHN 3:27

J ohn the Baptist cuts immediately to the crux of his follower's confusion. He said, "*A man can receive **nothing** unless it has been given him from heaven.*" The Living Bible puts it this way, "*God in heaven appoints each man's work.*" How clear is that? Where is the confusion? John tells his followers not to feel bad for him, because God is the One who has appointed to John the work he does. Why should John care whether he no longer has the same size crowds; or that someone else has a bigger ministry with larger crowds? It means nothing to him because he had nothing to do with it in the first place. He is merely acting as the human agent for God, carrying out what God has given him to do. It is not his work, or for his glory, but God's. For John, it isn't how much he is doing for God, but entirely about God doing the appointing of each man's work.

There is another interesting dimension to John's answer. According to John, God not only determines *what each of us does*, but also *the result* of what we do. For John, God gave him both the ministry of going out as the forerunner for Jesus and baptizing those who came to him; but also the result of larger (then smaller) crowds to baptize. God was in total control of it all. Isn't that amazing? John never claimed to be anything and never desired to be the center of attention (like his example of the bridegroom). He desired only to hear the bridegroom's voice. This is what filled John with joy.

LIVING WATER FOR TODAY:

*Every good thing given and every perfect gift is from **above**, coming down from the Father of lights, with whom there is no variation or shifting shadow.* —JAMES 1:17

For today, abide in the peace of knowing that God is both appointing the work that He desires for you to do today, and the results you will experience from that work. Take comfort in the fact that He is in total control of everything about you. *PTL!*

A close Christian friend approached me some time ago (with good intentions) about joining another church in our community. He said, "Daryl, the Lord is really blessing us in this new church. We are growing by leaps and bounds. You need to come be a part of it." While listening to my friend, God brought to my mind John's comments to his followers. The number of people attending any particular church has nothing to do with how much God is blessing. God appoints and directs each of us individually.

I know another dear brother and his wife who organize two to four trips to Israel every year. The logistics of such an endeavor is massive. I greatly admire and love them for introducing thousands of people to the Holy Land and God's people, but I don't wish to be in their shoes. I feel no guilt for not joining them in this ministry. God has appointed this work for them to do, not me. As for me, right now today, God has me studying His word in my office, writing this devotional, praying for three families, sending two verses via text messaging to two people that I know are in need. Before God, there is nothing to compare between these two works. Each is doing what God has appointed.

Do you pastor a congregation of thousands or lead a Bible study of five? Do you organize the feeding of hundreds in your community or care for just one grandchild during the day? How much value does God put on that child? What if we are teaching five junior high schoolers on Sunday, or praying for several people a day at home, are you, like John the Baptist, at peace with what God has appointed you to do?

God has a master plan, and He has each of us plugged into it. If we are speaking to thousands, that is no credit to us. God appointed it and has brought the numbers. It has nothing to do with us. God has plugged us in here and there because He knows the needs He intends to meet. For example, how important is prayer? It is the most important thing on earth! I have people come to me and say they don't think they do much for God. I ask whether God ever draws them to pray. They often answer, "Yes, I pray a couple of hours a day." I greatly admire them for such work. *They are real prayer warriors*—an amazing gift!

It is so comforting to know that God is the One who appoints each of us to His work and produces the results from that work as He desires. *Praise the Lord!*

MARCH 7

"You yourselves are my witnesses that I said, 'I am not the Christ,' but, 'I have been sent ahead of Him.' ²⁹*He who has the bride is the bridegroom; but the friend of the bridegroom, who stands and hears him, rejoices greatly because of the bridegroom's voice. So this joy of mine has been made full."*

—JOHN 3:28-29

John continues to answer his followers by telling them that his joy has been made full. This is truly glorious when you consider the context. Yes, the numbers coming to John for baptism have dwindled to almost nothing, yet he declares to his followers that he is full of joy. If he were baptizing thousands upon thousands, his joy could not be greater than it was for him at that moment. John reveals why he is full of joy in these verses.

He first asks his followers to remember his earlier declaration to the fact that he never claimed to be anybody significant. He said, *"I am not the Christ,"* but, *"I have been sent ahead of Him."* John then refers to a marriage custom of his day that his followers would be familiar; and refers to himself as the *friend of the bridegroom.* While he is neither the bride nor the groom, yet he is blessed with great joy to hear the groom's comments to his bride. In this same way, John tells his followers that he is full of joy because he hears Jesus' words to His bride, which according to *Ephesians 5:27,* includes you and me.

John's joy is made full, not by his baptizing one, ten, 100, or 1,000 people. His joy is full just by hearing Jesus' words! For his part, he didn't need to be baptizing anybody. He didn't need to be center stage, or on any stage at all. By hearing Jesus' words alone, whether he did anything else, that was the source of John's joy. May the Lord write His words on our hearts to grow our understanding, that like John, it is the same with us today. *His word is our joy!*

LIVING WATER FOR TODAY:

*So that He might sanctify her, having cleansed her by the **washing of water with the word,** ²⁷that He might present to Himself the church in all her glory, having no spot or wrinkle or any such thing; but that she would be holy and blameless.* —EPHESIANS 5:26-27

For today, fret not what more you can do for God; but join with John in hearing Jesus' words that wash you and fill you to the brim with abundant joy! *PTL!*

March 8

*"He who comes from above is above all, he who is of the earth is from the earth and speaks of the earth. He who comes from heaven is above all. ³²What He has seen and heard, of that He testifies; and no one receives His testimony. ³³He who has received His testimony has set his seal to this, that **God is true.**"*

—John 3:31-33

Those still following John were obviously missing something important. Remember, some of Jesus' first disciples came from John's followers because of John's declaration—*"Behold, the Lamb of God" (John 1:36-37)*. Andrew, Peter's brother, was one of these early converts *(John 1:40)*. Jesus' identity was not a secret to John's followers, yet some still did not grasp the worth of that identity. If they did, there would be no question why Jesus' crowds were larger than those coming to John. A debate over the rite of purification was a ludicrous distraction from *who* was standing in their midst!

Nevertheless, John patiently went over all of it again with them, that Jesus is the One who has come down from Heaven and is above all things. That John, by contrast, is from earth. There is simply no comparison between the two. Jesus speaks of heavenly things that He has seen and heard, while John speaks of earthly things only.

We have seen this before. Jesus is the Light coming into the world (and to His own), but they would not **receive** Him *(John 1:9-12)*. He came down from heaven, speaking what He knew, but Nicodemus would not **accept** *(John 3:11)* or **believe** *(John 3:12)*. Jesus came as an eyewitness of what He had seen and heard, but no one **receives** this testimony *(John 3:32)*. This brings us to *John 3:33*: *"He who has **received** His testimony has set his seal to this, that **God is true.**"* To "set a seal" means to certify. A person certifying declares that he or she is personally assured that the facts being certified are true. In this context, those who *received* Jesus' testimony were personally assured (according to the *Amplified Bible*) that it was divine truth that God cannot lie. This kind of belief comes only from God!

Living Water for Today:

And He did so to make known the riches of His glory upon vessels of mercy, which He prepared beforehand for glory, ²⁴even us. —Romans 9:23-24a

For today, rejoice greatly that you are a *vessel of God's mercy*, not based on what you do, *but simply because you were chosen by God for glory, to contain a saving belief that God is true!*

MARCH 9

*"For He whom God has sent speaks the words of God; for **He gives the Spirit without measure.** ³⁵The Father loves the Son and has given all things into His hand. ³⁶**He who believes in the Son has eternal life**; but he who does not obey the Son will not see life, but the wrath of God abides on him."*

—JOHN 3:34-36

John continues to repeat themes to his followers that we have seen before. In these verses he tells them that God gives the Spirit without measure. What do we know about the Spirit? He is like the wind blowing where He wills *(John 3:8)*. No one tries to measure the wind. It is too immense to measure! So too, God has given the Spirit without measure to move where He wills to bring eternal life to whom He chooses. There is no place on the surface of the earth that doesn't have an abundance of wind. Take comfort that there is enough Spirit/wind to blow upon your children, relatives, and coworkers. No one is separated from, or forgotten by, the Spirit of God!

John also returns once again to emphasize the life-saving connection between eternal life and belief. Belief is not the cause, but the manifestation, that a person experiences when they have been chosen by the Spirit of God to be a vessel of mercy to contain God's eternal life. Many interpret *verse 36* in the opposite manner, as a cause-and-effect verse that *first* calls for a decision on our part to believe in Jesus *before* God will grant eternal life to us. However, as we have seen in previous verses throughout this gospel, the Spirit of God is the One who blows where He wills, choosing to give a person eternal life, resulting in their belief in God's gift: Jesus! This is further confirmed in *verse 36* by noticing that the opposite of *he who believes* is not *he who disbelieves*, but *he who does not obey*. This is not referring to God offering eternal life to those who will not accept His Son, but rather, of man's natural condition of rebellion against God as explained in *Romans 3:10-18 ("There is none righteous, not even one")*.

LIVING WATER FOR TODAY:

*Now **He who prepared us for this very purpose** [eternal life] **is God**, who gave to us the **Spirit as a pledge**.*—2 CORINTHIANS 5:5

For today, revel in the amazing work of the Spirit of God; it is God who prepared you for His eternal life, and gave you His Spirit to forever seal His pledge **to you**. *PTL!*

MARCH 10

"He must increase, but I must decrease."

—JOHN 3:30

Today's verse summarizes John the Baptist's entire answer to his followers: *He must increase, but I must decrease.* What is he telling them? I imagine him saying, "Look, those of you who are questioning how many we are baptizing compared to Jesus' disciples, or whether our rite of purification is as effective as Jesus' baptism, or those of you who are worried that I am losing my crowd, or that it doesn't look like I am doing very much anymore for God; when you boil it all down, *"He must increase but I must decrease."* The Living Bible reads, *"He must become greater and greater, and I must become less and less."*

When we read John's full answer to his followers it is clear that he is a man who doesn't want to receive recognition. He doesn't want any applause for himself. He was not striving for a bigger gold crown for winning more souls to the Lord or baptizing more people. He didn't want any credit for anything. For John, it was all about Christ's life (and His coming death and resurrection)—accomplishing eternal life for all of us—why would we argue over who is doing what? Christ's death and resurrection is everything!

God is caring for everything that concerns us, to the point that we don't need to worry about a thing. We can truly say together with John, *"He must increase, but I must decrease."* Whenever we are thinking (in the future) that we need to be doing more, all we need do is go back and read John's answer to his followers *(John 3:22-36)*, that God is directing all of our steps every day, and directing the results that occur. It will bring us to the same place, on our knees in our hearts before God, with the prayer: *"Dear God, your Son must increase in me, and I, my ugly flesh, must decrease."*

LIVING WATER FOR TODAY:

> *Be anxious for nothing,* but in everything by prayer and supplication with thanksgiving let your requests be made known to God. *⁷And the peace of God, which surpasses all comprehension, will guard your hearts and your minds in Christ Jesus.*—PHILIPPIANS 4:6-7

For today, you need not worry about *anything* because God is in complete control over everything in your life. As you turn to Him, you will experience anew His peace guarding your heart and mind.

Jesus' talk with Nicodemus *(John 3:1-21)* and John's answer to his followers *(John 3:22-36)* wonderfully illustrate Paul's demand for an answer from the Galatians: *"Are you so foolish? Having begun by the Spirit, are you now being perfected by the flesh?"(Galatians 3:3)*.

The Spirit of God with resurrection power moves like the wind, choosing those He wills to resurrect from spiritual death. Jesus told Nicodemus, using the wind as an example, that this is by **God's will alone.** He alone chooses to quicken those who are spiritually dead with life-giving faith. Scripture is clear, direct from Jesus' own mouth, that the initiation of our salvation *has nothing to do with us and everything to do with God.* John 1:12-13 confirms this: *"But as many as received Him, to them He gave the right to become children of God, even to those who believe in His name, *[13]***who were born, not of blood nor of the will of the flesh nor of the will of man, but of God"** (see January 14 and 15).

Our human flesh, however, continues to tease, tantalize, and torment us with the notion that *we need* to initiate some spiritual qualities within ourselves, or add to the ongoing work of God by living our lives in a certain way. To put it in the way it was presented to me in church, *"God saved us by faith, but it is up to us to live for Him."*

The glorious truth, however, is this: the same Almighty Spirit of God, with the same resurrection power that blew upon us and brought us life-saving belief, is the SAME vibrant active power that continues to grow our spiritual life each day *(Philippians 1:6)!* God's Spirit (wind power) has not faded from our lives, leaving us to struggle with becoming better Christians ourselves. This is what John refers to when he says his joy is made full by hearing the Bridegroom's (Jesus') voice *(March 7)*.

There are some who worry that such freedom gives license to sin. But that can never be true according to Paul's declaration in *Philippians 2:13: "For it is God who is at work in you* [24/7, present tense], *both to will and to work for His good pleasure."* Scripture clearly and repeatedly tells us that the Holy Spirit's power which gave us faith to believe, continues to shape our lives for God's glory and our good. Any teaching that *we* are not doing enough for God, or *we need* to improve our Christian life in some way, is not the Christianity we see in scripture. *PTL!*

LIVING WATER FROM JOHN 3:17-36

March 2	He who believes in the Son of God is not judged.
March 3	The act of coming to the Light is solely the result of God working in us.
March 4	We become a reflection of what God's word says as the indwelling Christ spends time transforming us.
March 5	Just as God directed John the Baptist to baptize for a period of time, God is also directing what we do each day.
March 6	God in heaven appoints each person's work and produces the results He desires.
March 7	Jesus' words fill us to the brim with abundant joy.
March 8	Whoever receives Jesus' testimony believes what He says is true.
March 9	Jesus, whom God sent, speaks the words of God, and gives the Spirit without measure.
March 10	God must become greater and greater, and we must become less and less.

PRAYER

Dear God, how wonderful is Your word which tells me that I can receive nothing unless it has been given to me from You. What a relief this is, to know the source of everything that comes into my life. I am freed from my own expectations and anxieties of what I should be doing to minister in Your name. Your word has promised me that You have plugged me into Your eternal purpose and will give me the exact work you would have for me to do. Like John the Baptist, my joy will be made full, as I hear Your word and am content in doing Your work for Your glory; not my work for my glory. Dear God, touch my heart, search it for any darkness or evil thing, for I yearn for Your Son Jesus to increase in me, and my fallen, ugly flesh to decrease. Amen.

_____

_____

_____

_____

_____

_____

_____

_____

_____

_____

_____

_____

_____

_____

_____

_____

_____

_____

_____

_____

_____

_____

_____

_____

_____

_____

_____

_____

JESUS
PASSED BY YOU
AND ME
"AT THE WELL"!

JOHN 4:1-18

March 11

Therefore when the Lord knew that the Pharisees had heard that Jesus was making and baptizing more disciples than John ²(although Jesus Himself was not baptizing, but His disciples were), ³He left Judea and went away again into Galilee.
—John 4:1-3

While Queen Alexandra of Jerusalem appointed the Pharisaic leaders, in approximately 141-67 BC, to be the formal administrators of all public affairs, *John 3:38* tells us that the *Father loves the Son and has **given all things into His hand**.* Thus, *John 4:1* begins with the word *therefore*, to emphasize that what Jesus does next flows from His God-given authority. The Pharisees were already worried enough to send messengers to question John *(John 1:19-27)*. They learned that someone they did not yet know is (present tense) among them, the thong of whose sandals John did not feel worthy to untie *(John 1:26-27)*. Now, the Pharisees learn that Jesus is drawing crowds larger than John's. This fact would make them more nervous and put their governing authority in doubt.

Jesus, knowing that: (i) He would be seen as a threat to the Pharisee's authority, and (ii) that the time had not yet come for a confrontation with them (which would result in His crucifixion), He left Judea for Galilee. He would not allow the Pharisees to question or confront Him yet. Jesus was always attuned to God's timing! Not only did He leave in time to avoid a confrontation with the Pharisees, but also left precisely at the right time to cross paths with a solitary woman by a certain well in Samaria.

In light of our previous discussion regarding doing the Lord's work *(March 6 & 7, and page 122)*, I cannot help but think of the Lord's disciples in *verse two*. One minute they are actively baptizing large crowds coming to Jesus, then in the next, are just walking with Him on their way to Galilee. So, we see again, that it is not the particular work that counts, but spending time in the presence of Jesus, who is directing our path each day*!*

Living Water for Today:

*The LORD has established His throne in the heavens, and **His sovereignty rules over all**.*—Psalm 103:19

For today, take comfort in the absolute sovereignty of God over all things in your life, including your spiritual growth, your children, relatives, work, and our government— everything! God's perfect good is prevailing on your behalf each day! *PTL!*

MARCH 12

*And **He had to pass** through Samaria.*

—JOHN 4:4

Notice the words "***He had to pass** through Samaria.*" The *King James Bible* reads. "*And He **must needs** go through Samaria.*" Does this mean there was only one passable road to get from where He was in Aenon (John 3:23) to Galilee? Not at all! It was common for Judean Israelites (like Jesus) to cross the Jordan River and skirt around Samaria entirely because of the hostility between these two Jewish factions. While both Judeans and Samaritans were Jewish (they worshipped the same God and adhered to their respective forms of Torah) in truth, they held deep animosity for each other. Their distrust for each other is similar to modern day tensions between the Sunni and Shia factions within the Muslim faith—each thinking they are the pure followers, and the other is impure and corrupt.

So Jesus *"must needs"* had nothing to do with convenience of roads, shortcuts, personal safety, or favorable geography. It had everything to do with God's divine will for Him to go through Samaria at that very moment in time to accomplish God's purpose. It was God's plan, before the creation of the world and before any person inhabited Samaria, that Jesus *must needs* pass through Samaria that morning. *None of God's will ever fails!*

This story should make us all drop to our knees and praise God because Jesus, before the creation of the world, said "I *must needs* pass by Daryl," and "I *must needs* pass by [add your name]." It is all part of God's divine plan. It had nothing to do with us. The Samaritan woman didn't get up that morning and make a decision to meet God by the well. That decision was entirely made by God. When *we* were dead in our trespasses and sins, God said, "*I **must needs** pass by each of my chosen and make them alive in Christ.*"

LIVING WATER FOR TODAY:

*But **God, being rich in mercy**, because of His great love with which He loved us, ⁵even when we were dead in our transgressions, made us alive together with Christ (by grace you have been saved).*—EPHESIANS 2:4-5

For Today, thank God! He chose to pass by you, and He will forever continue to be *rich in mercy* toward you. Thank Him again that *He never will treat you according to what you deserve but only out of His immense love, grace, and kindness!*

MARCH 13

*So **He came to a city of Samaria called Sychar**, near the parcel of ground that Jacob gave to his son Joseph; ⁶and Jacob's well was there. So Jesus, being wearied from His journey, was sitting thus by the well. It was about the sixth hour.*

—JOHN 4:5-6

In *Genesis 33:18-20* we read of the initial purchase of this land by Jacob. Located at the base of Mount Gerizim, it was the holiest place of worship for the Samaritans (as much as Jerusalem, with its Mount Zion, was for the Jews). It was full of rich heritage and significance, and the mount of YHWH's (Yahweh, The Lord's) covenantal blessing *(Deuteronomy 27:12)*.

Given the distance between Aenon and Sychar, Jesus was at least into his second full day of traveling on foot and was now taking a rest at Jacob's well. Scripture tells us it was about the sixth hour, or around noon in modern timekeeping. As we will learn in *verse eight (March 14)*, in spite of the fact that Samaria was not the most friendly or safest of places to travel for a Jew, *all* of his disciples left Jesus alone, at least some going to buy food. We are not told how this happened, but it is fair to conclude that it was God's will that Jesus be alone as this solitary Samaritan woman approached the well.

What an encouraging realization this is when we consider our own salvation or that of our children, loved ones, relatives, and friends. God *must needs* pass by this Samarian woman, and in doing so, He cared for every nuanced detail of that meeting—the time, place, topic, and those who were near. Nothing is happenstance with God!

LIVING WATER FOR TODAY:

*For whatever is **born of God** overcomes the world; and **this is the victory that has overcome the world—our faith.***—1 JOHN 5:4

For today, rejoice that you have been born of God, who has produced faith in you. That faith—given to you by God—*is the victory* over the world. It is not a tool, weapon, sword, or shield you must use to fight temptation in the world, but it *is the victory*, already accomplished, without effort on your part to resist or fight anything. That faith/belief that God is Sovereign, He is your Savior, your comfort in all things, your daily living water—and in His presence is your eternal home—that faith is your victory!

MARCH 14

There came a woman of Samaria to draw water. Jesus said to her, "Give Me a drink."
⁸For His disciples had gone away into the city to buy food.

—JOHN 4:7-8

Scripture is intentionally vague about who this woman was, *perhaps because she represents all of us.* No name was ever given. She never appears again in any of the gospels beyond this inclusion, but God *must needs* meet with her on that noon hour.

Many commentaries assume that she was a woman of ill-repute, and an outcast from her community. One commentary goes so far as to refer to her as a prostitute (although there was no social custom in biblical times suggesting that "prostitutes" routinely married their customers). If these assumptions are correct, however, it is easy to see why she would come to the well to draw water at a time when all the other "reputable" women from the city had come to draw water and were now gone.

It may also be possible, as one noted Messianic-Christian theologian has pointed out, that she may have been a woman suffering from severe depression, having outlived a number of husbands in her life (which was not unheard of in those days) and was now living with a male relative (or another man short of marriage) for survival. As anyone who has suffered from a deep, despondent depression will tell you, they could readily understand why the woman would wish to avoid the chit-chat socializing that goes on among the women during these early morning gatherings to collect water for the day.

Whichever woman she was, we can worship God, knowing that it made no difference to Jesus. He knew every detail of her life and still *must needs* come to her that day. Now, what is comforting to us is that her story is *our* story. She had nothing to redeem her to God, no sterling character traits or noble accomplishments to earn God's favor. Yet God still chose to touch her that day. *Praise God for His love, mercy, and amazing grace for us!*

LIVING WATER FOR TODAY:

*Among whom **you also are the called of Jesus Christ**.*

—ROMANS 1:6

For today, like the Samaritan woman, realize anew that you didn't decide one day to meet God, or earn His favor; but rather, Jesus *must needs* pass by you, and He called **YOU** to Himself! *PTL!*

MARCH 15

*Therefore the Samaritan woman said to Him, "How is it that You, being a Jew, ask me for a drink since I am a Samaritan woman?" (**For Jews have no dealings with Samaritans.**)*
—JOHN 4:9

You can feel the contempt radiating from this woman's words in her first response to Jesus. She presumably recognized Him as a Judean Jew by the clothing he wore, and she hurled her perception of Jewish arrogance at Him like a lance. She was a product of deeply ingrained prejudices of her times, and the passion and tension between Jews and Samaritans boiled up within her as a living and palpable accusation against Him.

Did her bitter attitude turn Jesus aside? Not in the least. He still *must needs* cross her path that day and meet her exactly where she was amidst her own prejudices and resistance. To those who interpret that she was a woman of ill-repute, she was undoubtedly the lowest of the low, yet Jesus still met with her. If she was a sadly depressed woman, Jesus touched her in that depression. As we will see in the coming days, *Jesus' words progressively comforted her* and drew her out of herself to the point where she testified boldly of Him to the community where she lived.

I often grab for a tissue whenever I try to grasp the level of grace that Jesus displayed to this Samaritan woman (and to us). People often think that God couldn't possibly still love them because they have made too big a mess of their lives. Jesus, however, tells us *He must needs cross our path!* Do you feel downtrodden? He *must needs!* Do you feel chained to some addiction? He *must needs!* Are you lonely or deeply depressed from the loss of a loved one? Do you feel you've made too many bad choices? The wondrous good news is it has *NEVER* been about our conduct, but only that Jesus *must needs! PTL!*

LIVING WATER FOR TODAY:

*Just as a father has compassion on his children, so the LORD has compassion on those who fear Him. For He Himself knows our frame; **He is mindful that we are but dust.**—PSALM 103:13-14*

For today, notice Jesus' immense compassion for the Samaritan woman and realize His compassion for you is the same. Jesus Himself knows that you are just dust. He expects nothing more from you. *He brings all that is truly good to your life.* Take comfort in this!

MARCH 16

*Jesus answered and said to her, "**If you knew the gift of God**, and who it is who says to you, 'Give Me a drink,' you would have asked Him, and **He would have given you living water.**"*

—JOHN 4:10

Jesus knew everything about this woman, so we can confidently infer what she did (and did not) know based on what Jesus said to her. He said, "**If you knew the gift of God, and who it is who says to you, 'Give Me a drink,'....**" **If you knew** the gift of God, you would have asked. **If you knew** who it is who talks to you, you would have asked. This means, and it buckles my knees in worship to God as I write this, that the Samaritan woman *did not know* who Jesus was, and was in no way looking for the eternal life He was offering her as this conversation begins. Similar to Nicodemus in the previous chapter, she had no spiritual discernment. But praise God! Before she woke up that morning, Jesus had been walking over a day to reach her. Our salvation is not based on what we know or do, but solely on what the Spirit of God chooses to do—to blow upon her (and us), filling her with life-giving water.

How many times have we seen this same theme repeated in scripture? Salvation does not come from our actions, or us deciding to seek God, or accept Jesus. Scripture likens us in our natural, unsaved state *(1 Corinthians 2:14)* to being dead *(Ephesians 2:4-5)*, as dead as Lazarus was for so many days in the tomb. As a dead person, what could we do for ourselves? *Nothing!* Dead is dead, powerless, and empty of all life! Only by the Spirit of God blowing upon us and God's speaking resurrection power into us—not us trying to believe or apply—but again, God speaking His resurrection word into us, do we receive new life in Christ. Without God initiating this action, we would remain hopelessly and eternally enslaved in death.

LIVING WATER FOR TODAY:

*But the **natural man does not accept the things of the Spirit of God, for they are foolishness to him;** and he cannot understand them, because **they are spiritually appraised.**—1 CORINTHIANS 2:14*

For today, rejoice that the things of God are not foolishness to you! By God's mercy His Spirit has chosen you and abides in you, bringing you spiritual discernment. *PTL!*

MARCH 17

*She said to Him, "Sir, **You have nothing to draw with** and the well is deep; where then do You get that living water? [12]You are not greater than our father Jacob, are You, who gave us the well, and drank of it himself and his sons and his cattle?"*
—JOHN 4:11-12

The Samaritan woman quickly recognizes that this is no ordinary man, and moves to address Him as "Sir" (or Lord), yet she still lacks any spiritual discernment of who He really is, so she is left asking human-type questions. *"Sir, You have nothing to draw with and the well is deep* [meaning too deep for you, whoever you are]." If this doesn't demonstrate that she had no idea who Jesus was, I don't know what could be clearer. She is talking to the How-Great-Thou-Art Almighty God, who simply spoke four words, *"Let there be Light"* and the sun, moon, planets, and billions of galaxies containing hundreds of millions of stars sprung into being—and she is jabbering that He doesn't have the means to draw water? Or whether He thought Himself greater than Jacob who built the well and drank from it? Building a well versus creating a universe, that is pretty funny when you think about it. This demonstrates how foreign, spiritually discerned truths are to the natural, unsaved mind.

For some, it is hard to come to grips with the spiritually discerned truth that our salvation is *all* from God, *AS IS* our spiritual growth and sanctification throughout our life. This narrative would have been a perfect place to insert a verse or two that suggested the Samaritan woman did something to earn Jesus' respect resulting in her salvation. For example, the well itself likely had the means to draw water, she could have offered that to Him. Or when He asked for some water to drink she could have actually given Him some rather than barraging Him with an onslaught of human questions. But she did none of these things. Scripture records nothing she did to earn favor from God. It was entirely a matter of God's own *must needs!*

LIVING WATER FOR TODAY:

*This was in accordance with the eternal purpose which He carried out in Christ Jesus our Lord, [12]in whom **we have boldness and confident access through faith in Him.**—*EPHESIANS 3:11-12

For today, rest in God's eternal purpose which He (God) carried out in Christ Jesus, and the fact that you can access with boldness and confidence through faith in Him. *PTL!*

A PERSONAL TESTIMONY

GOD KNOWS THE BEGINNING FROM THE END

The human questions posed by the Samaritan woman to Jesus really caught my attention. Here is a woman talking to God, the Creator of everything. Obviously, she does not recognize Him, or she would be on her face before Him rather than hitting Him with such mundane questions from her human perspective. At first, I dismissed her questions entirely, thinking they weren't important. Then God touched my heart to recognize that we all do the very same thing—all the time. Let me give you an example.

Scripture encourages us to *"Be anxious for nothing" (Philippians 4:6a)*, and to live by faith, not by sight *(2 Corinthians 5:7)*. The same God who spoke to the Samaritan woman; who created everything by speaking four words and the planets, moon, stars, and the universe itself appeared *(Genesis 1:1,3)*, who tells us that we are His children *(Acts 17:28)* and that He is our How-Great-Thou-Art Shepherd *(John 10:11)*; this God tells us not to be anxious over anything but live by faith. Do we respond by "faithing" in what scripture says, and worshipping and praising God? That is often not my experience. Many times I respond, like the Samaritan woman, with a cascade of questions flooding my mind with every conceivable human concern? Have you experienced that when you get anxious?

The Samaritan woman did not recognize the value and power of the person she was talking to, and she raised concerns that subtly put Jesus' capacity and abilities in doubt: "You have no rope," ... "the well is [too] deep," ... "do you think you are greater than our father Jacob?" Just like the Samaritan woman, our questions reflect doubt in the power and capabilities of our God. They always reflect our finite, fleshly, human perspective.

Here is what we forget: God knows the beginning AND the ending. When He says, *"Be anxious for nothing,"* he is not telling us to think good thoughts and hope for the best. He already *KNOWS* how it (whatever concerns us) ends, and from His perspective, He tells us that there is nothing to be anxious about. *Proverbs 20:24 TLB* says, **"Since the Lord is directing our steps, why try to understand everything that happens along the way?"** God knows the beginning from the end and is directing our steps all along the way. While our flesh often struggles against this wonderful freedom, and we get anxious and ask about this and that, *we remain sheep in the hands of our Great Shepherd*, caring for us 24/7! *PTL!*

MARCH 18

Jesus answered and said to her, "Everyone who drinks of this water will thirst again;
¹⁴but whoever drinks of the water that I will give him shall never thirst; but the water
*that I will give him **will become in him** a well of water springing up to eternal life."*
—JOHN 4:13-14

The Samaritan woman has just told Jesus He has no means to draw water, inferring that the well is too deep. Jesus answers her by setting up a comparison between the water in that man-made well and the living water God gives to those He chooses. After a few hours, those who drink water from the well will be thirsty again. They will return to draw more water, only to get thirsty once more. By contrast, Jesus said: *"but whoever drinks of the water that I will give him shall never thirst"*; what a miraculous contrast!

Almost every word of Jesus' next statement explodes off the page as we read them: *"but the water that I will give him **will become**,"* not *may* become or *should* become or *could* become (*if* the person lives right) but ***will become***. This is Almighty God telling this woman a spiritual fact. There is no hopeful thinking here, no hyperbole, just Jesus telling it like it is. This water will become *in him*, not *to* him, *for* him, or *with* him, but *in him* **a well of water,** not a cup, glass, or pot of water, but a reservoir of water—a well comparable to the well that Jacob built for generations upon generations of an entire city to drink—*springing up*, not something a person has to work to haul out of a well (like the Samaritan woman) but water that is living and active (which springs into action to bring the one who drinks it) *to eternal life* (God's quality of life in that person).

The Christian life is all about what God produces inside of us. He didn't say it was water for those who ask for it (or helped Him); it was water *He would give*. We can't make it bubble up in us, and more importantly, *we can't prevent it from bubbling up in us!*

LIVING WATER FOR TODAY:

Nor is He served by human hands, as though He need-
ed anything, *since He Himself gives to all people life and*
breath and all things. —ACTS 17:25

For today, recognize in your heart that your God doesn't need anything from you, but out of His great love and mercy grants you your life, breath, and all things He knows are good for you. *PTL!*

CONNECTING THE THEOLOGICAL DOTS

I know some will struggle, as I did for half my adult life, with the notion that both our initial salvation as well as all our spiritual growth throughout our entire Christian life is entirely the result of God's working in us. We can neither speed it along nor slow it down. God doesn't cause our troubles and hardships, but uses them all for our good *(Romans 8:28)*. In all things, God is faithful to do the transforming work in us. I would never wish to convince you of anything, only God can touch your heart in such matters. But I can share a few more verses with you, from many in scripture, that may support you in seeking assurance from God that *He has done it all—He is all you need!*

1 Corinthians 1:30-31. Follow this closely: *"But by His doing* (that is God's doing, not our doing, not joint-partnership-type doing, but all God's doing) *you are in Christ Jesus, who became* (past tense, meaning it is an accomplished fact) *to us **wisdom** from God, and **righteousness** and **sanctification**, and **redemption**, ³¹so that, just as it is written, 'LET HIM WHO BOASTS, BOAST IN THE LORD.'"* Paul makes it clear that none of us have anything to boast about when it comes to any of those four vital growth experiences as they relate to us. It is all from God. Our boast is: *Christ is our wisdom, righteousness, sanctification, and redemption. It is nothing we have earned, it has all been given to us from God!*

Philippians 1:6. This verse tells us the same thing. Paul says: *"For I am confident of this very thing, that He who began a good work in you will perfect it until the day of Christ Jesus."* He didn't say God began a good work in us but then expects us to do our part to finish it, or at least help Him perfect it in some way. No, Paul said God began the work and will continue to do the same work to perfect (or finish) our spiritual growth, right up to the moment when Jesus returns at His second coming. This is not our job, but God's.

2 Corinthians 3:18. *"But we all* (referring to all believers), *with unveiled face, beholding as in a mirror the glory of the Lord, are being transformed* (what a statement of fact that is!) *into the same image from glory to glory, just as from the Lord, the Spirit."* This verse reveals an awesome fact about God's working in us: the Spirit in us is presently transforming us into a mirror image of the glory of the Lord, incrementally over our entire life from glory to glory *until we reflect the perfect image of Christ in glory!* Praise God! This is no small task. It is a miracle that only God can accomplish. *He alone deserves the praise and worship for doing it!*

Philippians 2:13. *"For it is God who is* (present tense, ongoing, at this moment), *at work in you, both to will and to work for His good pleasure."* Again, no mention of how we might help. I have mentioned this verse several times already in this devotional because it is worth repeating again and again. Only God is at work bubbling up His living water in us.

Galatians 3:3. *"Are you so foolish? Having begun by the Spirit* (meaning God put His life in us), *are you now being perfected by the flesh?"* Paul calls this notion foolishness. In reality, it is the Spirit who, like the wind, blows God's life into us, and continues that work moment by moment, from glory to glory, until the Lord Jesus returns.

John 7:38. *"He who believes in Me* (referring to all believers), *as the Scripture said, 'From his innermost being will flow rivers* (yes, you read that right: rivers plural) *of living water.'"* From Jesus own mouth, here is a statement of spiritual fact from God: Out of each believer's innermost being will flow multiple rivers of living water. There is no suggestion that a believer can reduce the number of rivers of living water flowing from them or increase the number either. God has simply spoken: *out of every believer, rivers of living water will flow!*

Hebrews 10:14. *"For by one offering* (referring to the sacrifice of Christ on the cross) *He has perfected for all time* (past tense, an accomplished fact) *those who are sanctified"* (not who will be sanctified in the future but who *ARE* sanctified in the present, also an accomplished fact). *The New Living Translation* translates it this way, *"For by that one offering he forever made perfect* (that is our justification, past tense) *those who are being made holy* (this is our sanctification/spiritual growth, being carried out in present tense)."

Personally, nothing is more gloriously freeing than to realize that our spiritual growth and Christian progress is all the work of God. How good is the grace and mercy of God? We can't prevent it from happening, nor improve on its pace. We trust God's timing. How glorious is that? For those of us who feel like we wear a big "L" for loser on our foreheads because we have been divorced several times, or had a number of affairs, or struggle with deep addictions, keep a Kleenex ready as we continue to watch Jesus' *must needs* meeting with this woman. If all proclaimers of God's word understood this, no believer would ever leave any church feeling guilty (for times when their flesh rises-up) or beaten down (with feelings that they are not good enough or doing enough for God). They would leave feeling their knees buckle in praise and worship and thanksgiving to God for His great love and mercies for us!

March 19

The woman said to Him, "Sir, give me this water, so I will not be thirsty nor come all the way here to draw." ¹⁶He said to her, "Go, call your husband and come here."
—John 4:15-16

Some commentaries suggest that the Samaritan woman was now getting sarcastic with Jesus and her comment was an attempt to mock Him. As this theory goes, Jesus strikes back at her snarky attitude by raising a very sensitive topic to put her in her place and on the defensive. But as I prayerfully read this scripture, I sense an entirely different exchange going on here. I find the woman, who continues to address Jesus as Sir (or Lord), being increasingly drawn to what Jesus is saying yet still without spiritual discernment. Of course, she desires living water that will cause her to never thirst, but she sees it only in terms of saving her additional trips to Jacob's well. She still lacked a final piece to the puzzle: the Spirit of God needed to blow upon her and reveal who was speaking to her. Once she understood that revelation, the entire conversation would have an entirely new meaning.

I love the way Jesus chose to gently reveal this last piece of the puzzle to her. To declare Himself to be Almighty God, Creator of the universe would have intimidated and frightened her. What He did was vastly more important to the woman than that. While she is asking Him for this living water, Jesus suddenly switches to the topic of fetching her husband, then returning back to Him. What did her husband have to do with whether Jesus would give her living water? He gently demonstrated in real and personal terms that He knew everything about her life, so He had to be God. Yet, He wanted her in His presence anyway.

Living Water for Today:

Fixing our eyes on Jesus, the author and perfecter of faith, who for the joy set before Him endured the cross, despising the shame, and has sat down at the right hand of the throne of God.—Hebrews 12:2

For today, experience the joy and peace of fixing your eyes on Jesus, who authored and perfected life-saving faith, and He has given that eternal faith to you! *PTL!*

MARCH 20

The woman answered and said, "I have no husband." Jesus said to her, "You have correctly said, 'I have no husband'; ¹⁸for you have had five husbands, and the one whom you now have is not your husband; this you have said truly."

—JOHN 4:17-18

We have all done what the Samaritan woman did in her answer. She shared a narrow bit of truth to keep much more hidden. Was she too ashamed of her past; or did it bring her unbearable pain? In biblical times, women were not allowed to bring an action for divorce so she was either a widower of five husbands, or some condition; perhaps an inability to bear children, was causing multiple men to marry, then divorce her. Either way, the sadness and depression would be deep and abiding. Alternatively, if she was a woman of ill-repute, it would certainly be a part of her life that she preferred to keep secret, particularly from a stranger (who was also a Jew).

Many Christians perceive God as a hard taskmaster, always ready to punish His children. Based on that perception, Jesus should have rebuked the woman and called her out for her "true-lie," but He didn't do that. On the contrary, He praised her for being honest while at the same time revealing all the things that she had tried to hide. Can you imagine her mouth dropping open and eyes going wide as she listened to Him tell her all the details of her hidden life? What a shock to her! Yet, here He was, talking *to her* rather than seeking a woman with an impeccable reputation from the city.

Again, this woman represents each of us. Jesus knows every unrighteous act we have committed, even those we have not yet committed, and He died to save us anyway. *There is nothing we can add to what Christ has already done for us.*

LIVING WATER FOR TODAY:

*So faith comes from hearing, and **hearing by the word of Christ.***—ROMANS 10:17

For today, meditate on the link between faith and God's word. Take any verse God leads you to and read it. Don't worry if you can't understand it, *for the word is living and active (Hebrews 4:12)*, it will cause you to hear what God wants you to hear throughout your day. *Be confident that through His Spirit in you and His word, God is at work strengthening your faith. PTL!*

LIVING WATER FROM JOHN 4:1-18

March 11	God's perfect good is prevailing on our behalf every day.
March 12	God's divine will, made known to Jesus, was that He should go through Samaria, an area hostile to the Judean Israelites.
March 13	Jesus' "must needs" timing to meet the Samaritan woman, knowing every detail of her life, was God's perfect timing.
March 14	In God's perfect time He chose to pass by and call us to Himself.
March 15	The Lord has compassion on His children. He knows our frame—that we are but dust.
March 16	When God speaks His resurrection word into us, we receive His gift of living water—new life in Christ.
March 17	Living water gives us spiritual discernment, boldness, and confidence through faith in Christ.
March 18	Drink of the water Jesus gives—a well of water springing up to eternal life.
March 19	Jesus is the One authoring and perfecting our faith.
March 20	Jesus knowing our every unrighteous act (past, present, and future), still chose to die on our behalf to save us.

PRAYER

Dear God, You know every detail of my life, every sinful act and every selfish or hateful thought that I have ever had or will ever have. You know every sordid detail, yet You loved me. You chose me as Your child! Dear God, I still see so much sin in my life on a daily basis. Like Paul in Romans chapter seven, my flesh is constantly warring against what I most want to do. Please deliver me from the delusion that my flesh will ever be capable of improving itself to the point of pleasing You. Strengthen my faith to keep my eyes focused on You throughout the day. Quicken Your living word within me, that I may grow deeper in understanding that You alone are doing the daily, monthly, yearly transforming work in me. Amen.

THE
MEANING
OF
"BELIEVE"

———

JOHN 4:19-54

MARCH 21

*The woman said to Him, "Sir, I perceive that You are a prophet. ²⁰Our fathers **worshiped** in this mountain, and you people say that in Jerusalem is the place where men ought to **worship**." ²¹Jesus said to her, "Woman, believe Me, an hour is coming when neither in this mountain nor in Jerusalem will you **worship** the Father."*

—JOHN 4:19-21

Have you ever done what the Samaritan woman did when confronted with something embarrassing and uncomfortable? She suddenly changed the subject away from her past husbands and current living situation to a topic of religious doctrine she thought was a safe position. Her estimation of Jesus was clearly growing to one of awe. She was now perceiving Him as a prophet of God and asked Him a question that struck at the heart of the dispute between Judean and Samaritan Jewish factions: *where to worship?*

She had to be stunned (once more) to hear Jesus' answer. Certainly, she expected Him to take a position on *which physical location* (Sychar or Jerusalem) is the proper place to worship. But Jesus answered that a time had now come when physical locations were no longer necessary to worship the Father *because true worshippers worship **in spirit**!*

Consider this glorious freedom-truth! The Jews and Samaritans were squabbling about where they had to go to worship God. One said, "You have to come over here to pray to Him," while the other said, "No, not there; you must come to this mountain to pray." We hear echoes of this same argument today: "Come to our church to pray." Jesus told the Samaritan woman that worshipping God is no longer a matter of geographic location. God has made a means to worship Him *continuously* each moment of every day. And the best news yet? He hasn't left it up to us to worship Him! His indwelling Spirit prompts us to think of Him, pray for others, read His word, and hunger for Him to increase and for us to decrease—all of which is worship to God. *PTL!*

LIVING WATER FOR TODAY:

*For there is no distinction between Jew and Greek; for the same Lord is Lord of all, abounding in riches for **all who call on Him**.*—ROMANS 10:12

For today, rejoice in the fact that God did not leave it up to you to worship Him, but He produces all the worship in you that He desires. He is truly, from within you, abounding in riches as He causes you to continually call on Him. *PTL!*

MARCH 22

*"You **worship** what you do not know; we **worship** what we know, for salvation is from the Jews. ²³But an hour is coming, and now is, when the true **worshipers** will **worship** the Father in spirit and truth; for such people the Father seeks to be His **worshipers**. ²⁴God is spirit, and those who **worship** Him must **worship** in spirit and truth."*

—JOHN 4:22-24

Between yesterday's verses and today's, the words worship/worshippers are mentioned ten times in just six verses. Jesus tells the Samaritan woman (and us) that worshipping God need no longer take place only in geographical locations, like on mountain tops (Mount Gerizim), or in constructed temples (Jerusalem), or in our modern-day church buildings. True worship takes place *in the spirit*! What does this mean? It means that when the Holy Spirit causes us to *believe in Christ*, that is worshipping God. Our faith in Jesus is worshipping God. As the Holy Spirit prompts us to pray, we are worshipping God. As He gives us more desire for Christ to be manifest in our life, that is worshipping God. As we praise Him, we are worshipping God. As God grows His sanctifying life in us, we are worshipping God!

For decades I have had a simple routine of running four miles in the morning. At my current age, this "run" looks more like a half jog/half walk, but I still enjoy getting out into nature for an hour every morning. During that time, I have never set out to make it a time for praying to God, but that is frequently what God draws me to do. In my early years as a Christian, these prayers were laced with guilt and anxiety. I lived in fear of losing my salvation based on my performance—how many church services did I attend, or how much was I tithing or witnessing for Christ. Today, prayers along my daily jog/walk are filled with praise and worship. I am filled with a growing peace and contentment, knowing that God has called us to worship Him in spirit and truth.

LIVING WATER FOR TODAY:

*Being manifested that **you are a letter of Christ**, cared for by us, written not with ink but with the Spirit of the living God, not on tablets of stone but on tablets of human hearts.*—2 CORINTHIANS 3:3

For today, recognize that God has *made you* a letter of Christ, and that the *inspiration of the Spirit of God in your heart is worshipping Him!*

MARCH 23

*The woman said to Him, "I know that Messiah is coming (He who is called Christ); when that One comes, **He will declare all things to us.**" ²⁶Jesus said to her, "I who speak to you am He."*

—JOHN 4:25-26

What a momentous day this is turning out to be for this Samaritan woman! She first shifts the conversation from her past husbands to a doctrinal question regarding where God should be worshipped. When she is stunned by Jesus' revolutionary answer, she once again pivots to a more symbolic conversation about the coming Messiah—who, in her mind, would answer the question of where people should gather to worship. But in moving the conversation from topic to topic, she reveals that she, in truth, *believes* in the coming Messiah, only to be told by Jesus that *He was the One* she believed in! This was no longer an imaginary or symbolic conversation! She was now standing face to face with the very Messiah her heart yearned for. No wonder in that moment her sense of self (whether of sin or depression) dropped away from her.

As much as we can tell from ancient writings, the Samaritan concept of the Messiah in biblical times was that of a Teacher and Prophet (as opposed to the Judean concept of Messiah as King and Priest). This may be why she said when the Messiah comes, "*He will declare all things to us.*" This gives us insight into the approach Jesus took in asking about her husband and then disclosing all things related to her life. Jesus gave her an actual demonstration of the very attribute that she believed the Messiah would possess.

Praise God for this insightful conversation. I can identify with this Samaritan woman on so many levels. Don't we sometimes have a running conversation with God filled with "but what about this, God?" which attempts to raise all manner of excuses or qualifiers? I have done this many times over the years. By God's patient mercy, He always brings the conversation back to the only thing that really matters: "*I who speak to you AM HE.*"

LIVING WATER FOR TODAY:

For "**WHOEVER WILL CALL ON THE NAME OF THE LORD WILL BE SAVED.**"—ROMANS 10:13

For today, don't think of salvation only as a future heavenly event; but in the midst of anxiety or fear you may have right now, *call upon the name of Jesus and be saved (set free)!*

MARCH 24

At this point His disciples came, and they were amazed that He had been speaking with a woman, yet no one said, "What do You seek?" or, "Why do You speak with her?" ²⁸*So* **the woman left her waterpot,** *and went into the city and said to the men,* ²⁹**"Come, see a man who told me all the things that I have done;** *this is not the Christ, is it?"* ³⁰*They went out of the city, and were coming to Him.*

—JOHN 4:27-30

I sn't it interesting how *verse 27* is sandwiched into the overall narrative of the Samaritan woman, as though it was an interruption? It appears that right in the middle of the Lord's conversation with the woman, the disciples return and interrupt His talk with her. But God is *never* interrupted in what He does. The woman's plan for the day had been radically altered, but God's plan for her had not changed. By the time the disciples returned, she had heard what Jesus intended her to hear, and it was now time for her to do what God had next planned: testify concerning Jesus to the community where she lived. Obviously, the encounter with Jesus was so meaningful that she either forgot or purposely left behind her waterpot. God always causes His word to become bigger in our life than our current concerns. We often experience the same thing as the woman at the well. We lay out a plan for the day, then we get an emergency call that a friend is in the hospital and we drop what we are doing to go visit them. Is this an interruption in our day, or is it really what God planned for us all along? *In God's economy, there are no interruptions!*

Regarding the disciples themselves, the Samaritan woman was not the only one steeped in deeply held cultural prejudice. It was common during biblical times for men to ignore women. It is humorous to watch them try to hold to their prejudices while in the presence of Jesus; none of His disciples could choke out a question that revealed their true bias against women. Again, Jesus' life was a constant source of amazement to them.

LIVING WATER FOR TODAY:

Be still, and **know that I am God.**—PSALM 46:10A KJV

For today, meditate on the power of these words. In the midst of your concerns and anxieties ... be still. Know that God is *being* God in your life and is *working* all things together for your good *(Romans 8:28). A wonderful confidence and peace of mind. PTL!*

A PERSONAL TESTIMONY

COME SEE A MAN

Christians sometimes say to me that their family gets offended if they try to talk to them about the Lord. Or they will say that they don't know how to talk to someone about Christ. *John 4* gives us a simple approach to what our testimony should be to others who cross our path in life, such as our unsaved family and friends, co-workers, or other believers. This testimony rarely offends anyone.

The woman at the well left her pot and went into the city. She didn't stand up in front of those she met and tell them: "You are going to hell if you don't come out and see this guy!" She didn't put them on the spot in any fashion, make them feel uncomfortable, ask them a trick question, show them a pamphlet, threaten them, or instill fear into them. *She simply told them what happened to her personally.* She told them that "He told me all the things that I have done." This is exactly what the Samaritans would expect the Messiah to do. There is nothing to be offended at when she only shared what happened to her. It is difficult to argue against personal experience.

We find a similar example when Philip ran to find Nathanael *(John 1:45)*, claiming that they had found Him whom Moses and Prophets wrote—Jesus of Nazareth. Nathanael questioned whether any good thing could come out of Nazareth. Philip didn't argue, or try to explain, he simply encouraged Nathanael to "Come and see" *(John 1:45-46)*.

When we realize that it is God doing the choosing, and the Spirit of God blowing on whom He wishes to give life-saving belief, all the burden and stress on us melts away. It is no longer our job to save or convince anyone of anything. We no longer have any need to argue or debate. If God is drawing them, they will want to know more about Him. We need not have a fancy script all memorized to present. We simply tell them what happened to us.

Remember the blind man who Jesus healed? Jesus healed on the Sabbath, and it caused a huge controversy. They brought the man before the Pharisees, who pressed him about how he received his sight. They then went to his parents, then returned to the healed man and began to question him yet again. I love his answer: *"One thing I do know. I was blind but now I see!" (John 9:25 NIV).*

A SPECIAL WORD TO THE READER...

When writing a daily devotional like this, there are occasions when we come across verses, like the upcoming verses in *John 4:31-36 (March 25-27)*, that are genuinely subject to more than one interpretation. When this happens, I flee to the advice Paul gives us in *Romans 14:1*. *The Message* translates that verse this way: *"Welcome with open arms fellow believers who don't see things the way you do. And don't jump all over them every time they do or say something you don't agree with—even when it seems that they are strong on opinions but weak in the faith department. Remember, they have their own history to deal with. Treat them gently."* Paul's admonition for unity with one another has never been more important than today. In terms of this devotional, I desire only to share, in good conscience, what I believe to be the most accurate interpretation of the word of God. I am not dogmatic, nor do I make any kind of claim to having exclusive truth. For me, God is well able to direct your understanding of His word as much as He does mine. In that I am comforted and confident.

I think I have spent more hours studying *John 4:31-36* through stacks of commentaries and translations than any other section of scripture in my entire life. Yet, I am not a theologian, nor am I attempting to write a comprehensive commentary on the book of John. My prayer to God is always for His leading to write only what is edifying and profitable for you to hear; so that He might work through these daily devotionals to strengthen your faith, and to nourish, encourage, energize, and fill you with abundant and abiding joy as you read His life-changing word each day.

When competing interpretations arise, I will present a short summary of each interpretation, then give you my own sense of what a word, phrase, verse, or section of verses mean, then trust God to guide you in your own prayerful study and understanding of His word. I have no desire to convince you of any specific meaning of a particular section of scripture, because I am convinced that God will use His word to accomplish His purpose in each of us regardless of the interpretation each of us may personally hold.

MARCH 25

*Meanwhile the disciples were urging Him, saying, "Rabbi, eat." ³²But He said to them, "I have food to eat that you do not know about." ³³So the disciples were saying to one another, "No one brought Him anything to eat, did he?" ³⁴Jesus said to them, "**My food is to do the will of Him who sent Me and to accomplish His work.** ³⁵Do you not say, 'There are yet four months, and then comes the harvest'? Behold, I say to you, lift up your eyes and look on the fields, that they are white for harvest.*

—JOHN 4:31-35

Many scholars cite verses like these as evidence of the divine inspiration of the Bible. It is argued that if the Bible were actually written by man (specifically, these very same disciples), given human nature and the male-centric culture dominant in biblical times, they would have described themselves in more favorable light (more perceptive and intelligent), rather than witless incompetents. But here they are, described as the latter, caught up in the shock of Jesus shattering cultural norms by speaking to a woman and whether Jesus has eaten Samaritan food that may not meet Jewish purity requirements.

Imagine this scene. While his disciples were fretting over getting Jesus something to eat, Jesus knew that many from the city were already on their way to see Him. He was feeling "full" of the divine nourishment (energy) that comes from being in alignment with God's will and the fullness of joy *(John the Baptist's testimony, March 7)* that comes from accomplishing His work. While we tend to interpret Jesus' reference to the fields ripe for harvest from a modern-day evangelical perspective, I believe Jesus was actually referring to Himself in His answer to His disciples. It is not beyond imagination to think of Jesus looking off into the distance, seeing the crowd approaching, and saying to His disciples, *"lift up your eyes and look on the fields, that they are white for harvest."* It was Jesus who was doing the work of harvesting those who were coming to Him.

LIVING WATER FOR TODAY:

*Jesus said to them, "**I am the bread of life**; he who comes to Me will not hunger, and **he who believes in Me will never thirst**."*—JOHN 6:35

For today, Jesus draws you to come to Him and believe in Him; and as He does this, He satisfies your deepest hunger and quenches your every thirst! PTL!

MARCH 26

*"**Already** he who reaps **is** receiving wages and **is** gathering fruit for life eternal; so that he who sows and he who reaps may rejoice together. ³⁷For in this case the saying is true, 'One sows and another reaps.'"*

—JOHN 4:36-37

There are two primary thoughts here regarding who Jesus is referring to when He refers to "he who sows" and "he who reaps." The predominant teaching is that Jesus is referring to the prophets (and John the Baptist) and to those in the future who witness, preach, and teach as those who *sow*, and those who "lead someone to the Lord" as those who *reap*. The other understanding holds that the phrase *he who sows* refers to the work of God, and *he who reaps* refers to Jesus, and the Triune God more broadly.

While I share both of these interpretations with you, so you can pray for God's enlightenment and guidance, I am personally persuaded that Jesus in *John 4:34-38* is referring to His own joint work with the Father and Holy Spirit.

I hold this view for three reasons: *First*, Jesus doesn't refer to "he who *will* sow or reap" (future tense) but he who is **already** reaping and receiving wages and **IS** (present tense) gathering fruit for life eternal (I will discuss wages and fruit tomorrow). This description of *sowing, reaping,* and *gathering* fruit for life eternal, and *rejoicing* together can only refer, in my estimation, to the Triune God since He alone was active in the present tense at the time Jesus spoke these words. *Second*, in the *immediate context* of these verses, Jesus is talking about the work that God has sent Him to do, and His need to accomplish that work. That is the "food" Jesus refers to that His disciples know not of. *Third*, we know from scripture that nobody "leads anyone to the Lord." Scripture says that when it pleases God to do so, He draws everyone to Himself and reveals Christ in them *(Galatians 1:15-16)*. We have no part (or credit) in that work of God.

LIVING WATER FOR TODAY:

*Jesus answered and said to them, "**This is the work of God, that you believe** in Him whom He has sent."*—JOHN 6:29

For today, simply trust God's work in you, to daily strengthen the faith He has given you to believe in *His Son Jesus as your Savior, your daily Shepherd, and your EVERYTHING!*

MARCH 27

*"Already he who reaps is **receiving wages** and is **gathering fruit** for life eternal; so that he who sows and he who reaps may rejoice together. [37]For in this case the saying is true, 'One sows and another reaps.' [38]I sent you to reap that for which you have not labored; others have labored and you have entered into their labor."*

—JOHN 4:36-38

I t is clear enough, I think, that whomever Jesus is referring to as "he who reaps" is *already* receiving wages (or receiving the benefit from) the gathering of fruit for life eternal. That is precisely what *John 4:36* plainly says without any "if, and, or but" qualifiers. If Jesus is referring to Himself as the One who is reaping, then the word *wages* and the phrase *gathering fruit for life eternal* are referring to the children of God—that God has given into Jesus' hands *(John 17:6)*—being eternally saved and brought into His kingdom through the work of God, the Holy Spirit, and Jesus. The woman at the well is a good example of this sowing, reaping, and gathering activity of God since she was gathered by Jesus just moments before He spoke these words to His disciples.

Likewise, Jesus' words to His disciples in *John 4:38* do appear to be referring to us, but they must also be interpreted in the context of what Jesus previously said. He said, *"I sent you to reap that for which you have not labored."* This is best interpreted as us reaping the benefit of our new birth in Christ; and having the Spirit of God living in us, directing our path *(Psalm 25:12-14; Proverbs 4:18)* and writing His will on the tablets of our hearts *(2 Corinthians 3:3)*. There is no labor for us to do. It is labor that has *already* been done by others. There is no reaping of other believers for Christ, but only reaping the inward blessing of being born again into the household of the living God.

LIVING WATER FOR TODAY:

*"Look at the birds of the air, that **they do not sow, nor reap nor gather into barns, and yet your heavenly Father feeds them.** Are you not worth much more than they?"*—MATTHEW 6:26

For today, observe the birds of the air as Jesus suggests, do you see any skinny, starving birds? No, you will not. God has called you to reap (experience) the benefit of that which you have not labored; like the birds, you are not called to sow or reap yourself, but only to enter into God's labor of love and caring for you. *"Come to me, all who are weary and heavy-laden, and I will give you REST"* (Matthew 11:28). PTL!

PRAYER

Dear God, every aspect of my life has been crafted by You. You write on my heart moment by moment Your will. You send Your Spirit to guide me. Out of Your love and compassion, You care for every detail of my life. What is there for me to worry and fret about? You have poured out your blessings on me who has not labored for them. You cause me to enter into Your rest. Father, I am left with only praise, worship, and reverence for You. In the name of Your Son Jesus, Amen.

MARCH 28

*From that city many of the Samaritans **believed** in Him because of the word of the woman who testified, "He told me all the things that I have done." ⁴⁰So when the Samaritans came to Jesus, they were asking Him to stay with them; and He stayed there two days. ⁴¹Many more **believed** because of His word; ⁴²and they were saying to the woman, "It is no longer because of what you said that we **believe,** for we have heard for ourselves and **know that this One is indeed the Savior of the world."***

—JOHN 4:39-42

Throughout the entire gospel of John the word "believe" is vital to understanding the text. Probably the most famous verse in all of scripture, *John 3:16,* says, *"For God so loved the world, that He gave His only begotten Son, that whoever **believes** in Him shall not perish, but have eternal life."* Does it say *believe* ... and, and, and something else? No. Does it say believe ... plus, plus, plus do this and that? Again, no. According to the good news gospel of John, there is only one key into eternal life and that key is *belief.*

Do you want to know what *believe* means? It is spelled out simply in today's verses. It is so simple, in fact, that it brings tears to my eyes. In a moment, you too will be reaching for a Kleenex!

By this time, the woman had gone into the city and testified concerning Jesus: that *"He told me all the things that I have done."* Scripture tells us that *many believed* in Him from her testimony *(John 4:39).* Then *John 4:41* tells us that *"many more believed"* because of the words spoken by Jesus Himself. What we have in these verses are three more references to just *believing* in Jesus (this makes 21 references so far in John). Finally, *John 4:42* gives us the precise definition of the belief that leads to eternal life: *"this One* (Jesus) *is indeed the **SAVIOR OF THE WORLD."***

LIVING WATER FOR TODAY:

*But the angel said to them, "Do not be afraid; for behold, I bring you good news of great joy which will be for all the people; for today in the city of David **there has been born for you a Savior,** who is Christ the Lord."*—LUKE 2:10-11

For today, rejoice in this amazing good news! God has sent Jesus to be the Savior of the world. More personally, God has sent Jesus to be YOUR Savior! *PTL!*

A PERSONAL TESTIMONY

What Does Believe Really Mean?

This is a special moment for me as I write this devotional. I am not ashamed to tell you that this wonderful truth regarding the *meaning of belief* has brought me to tears countless times in my adult years. My life was wracked with intense stress as I struggled to understand what it meant to believe. *I can't praise God enough that He has made it so simple.*

I personally get emotional about it because of the background of teaching I had growing up as a young Christian. I don't blame anyone for this teaching, but as a preacher's kid, I was taught I needed to pray a prayer asking Jesus to come into my life, while at the same time committing (the "throne") of my life to Him. And for that to really take hold, I needed to get up in front of a group of Christians and acknowledge that I had made this decision; and then, not as a requisite for salvation, mind you, but as yet further evidence of my new life of commitment to Christ, I needed to get baptized before the congregation. In other words, I needed to believe, then do this and do that and do something else. So much, I felt, depended on me doing it all, and doing it all correctly. My worries were also exacerbated by my youthful fear, deeply residing within me, that God would take all the fun out of my life by sending me to some remote jungle as a missionary. After all, I was a preacher's kid; isn't that what happens to preacher's kids? I wanted a sports car and fun, not a hymnal and a library full of dusty old books about God inherited from my father.

I was certain that my secret desires were negating all my efforts to pray a proper salvation prayer. I could just hear God, who must know all these dark secrets in my heart, say "NO WAY!" as I prayed yet another salvation prayer for the umpteen-hundredth time. No wonder I would wake up in the middle of the night, sometimes drenched in sweat, fearing that if I died at that moment I wouldn't wake up in Heaven. I can't tell you how many times I prayed various prayers of salvation, yet I was never confident that I did it right; with enough sincerity, honesty, or intensity.

Now, praise the Lord, *John 4:42* tells us the wonderful, glorious good news: The meaning and focus of the word *believe* is simply that JESUS IS THE SAVIOR OF THE WORLD (including MY Savior)! It is this belief alone, which God has given us, that is the sole key to eternal life. *There is nothing we need to (or can) add to it! PTL!*

MARCH 29

After two days He went forth from there into Galilee. [44]*For Jesus Himself testified that a prophet has no honor in his own country.* [45]*So when He came to Galilee, the Galileans received Him, having seen all the things that He did in Jerusalem at the feast; for they themselves also went to the feast.*

—JOHN 4:43-45

There is much speculation why Jesus *must needs* go through Samaria *(March 12).* This speculation often infers that the meeting with the woman at the well was nothing more than serendipitous circumstance. Today's verses, however, suggest that the *primary* reason Jesus walked at least a day-and-a-half from Aenon near Salim to Sychar was specifically to meet the woman, and by extension, the entire city of Sychar. I say this because after meeting her, He spent two days with them (those coming to Him from the city), then returned north again into Galilee. Scripture gives no other explanation for this sudden detour—that *Jesus must needs go through Samaria*—other than to reap (save) both the woman at the well, and those who came to Him (and believed) from the city.

What a comforting insight this is concerning our Lord Jesus. No effort is too much hassle for Him, no journey too long to endure, to gather to Himself those that God had chosen for Him to collect. We need not fear the Lord's tireless perseverance to come by those God has chosen to give to His Son. No child, no relative, or coworker that is chosen by God will be forgotten. Jesus gathers them all! *PTL!*

He returned again to Galilee where the people received and welcomed Him readily, as opposed to the hometown where he was raised in Nazareth where the people met him with anger and hostility *(Matthew 13:54-57; Mark 6:1-4; and Luke 4:23-24).*

LIVING WATER FOR TODAY:

For I am convinced that neither death, nor life, nor angels,
nor principalities, nor things present, nor things to come,
nor powers, [39]*nor height, nor depth, nor any other created*
*thing, will be able to **separate us from the love of God,***
which is in Christ Jesus our Lord. —ROMANS 8:38-39

For today, rest in the powerful truth that *nothing* can separate you from God's love, which is in Christ Jesus your Savior, who walked for days to meet one woman by a well, and always meets you wherever *you* are in *your* life. *Nothing can separate you from Him!*

MARCH 30

*Therefore He came again to Cana of Galilee where He had made the water wine. And there was a royal official whose son was sick at Capernaum. ⁴⁷When he heard that Jesus had come out of Judea into Galilee, he went to Him and was imploring Him to come down and heal his son; for he was at the point of death. ⁴⁸So Jesus said to him, "Unless you people see signs and wonders, you simply will not **believe**." ⁴⁹The royal official said to Him, "Sir, come down before my child dies." ⁵⁰Jesus said to him, **"Go; your son lives."** The man **believed the word that Jesus spoke to him** and started off.*

—JOHN 4:46-50

John continues his rapid-fire eyewitness testimony of those who were coming to Jesus and eventually *believing* in Him. We saw some of John the Baptist's disciples become the first disciples of Jesus *(John 1:37, January 24)*, then Nicodemus (a Jewish religious leader in Judea) who by the end of the gospel is an active believer in Jesus as the Christ *(John 19:39)*, then a solitary woman by the well in Samaria (and all those who believed through her simple, non-offensive testimony), and now a royal official in Galilee, living in Capernaum on the northern coast of the Sea of Galilee. Different people from vastly different backgrounds, yet all with one thing shared in common: *Belief.*

This story is a great illustration of the power of God's word. It is God's words *alone* that have the power to lift us up, comfort, encourage, direct, guide, and heal us. In this case, Jesus said, *"Go; your son lives."* This was not a prophetic utterance of some future event. It was not wishful thinking where Jesus hopes the best for the child. Jesus words are a direct command from the How-Great-Thou-Art Almighty God, spoken as fact. The royal official recognized the power and authority in that command—and *believed.*

LIVING WATER FOR TODAY:

*For this reason we also constantly thank God that when you received the word of God which you heard from us, you accepted it not as the word of men, but for what it really is, **the word of God, which also performs its work in you who believe.**—1 THESSALONIANS 2:13*

For Today, thank God that His word *alone* contains the power to accomplish *all* that God desires in and for your life. His word is not a list of dos and don'ts for you to try your best to apply; but *the word of God is the power that performs God's work in you! PTL!*

MARCH 31

As he was now going down, his slaves met him, saying that his son was living.
⁵²So he inquired of them the hour when he began to get better. Then they said to him,
"Yesterday at the seventh hour the fever left him." ⁵³So the father knew that it was
at that hour in which Jesus said to him, **"Your son lives"***; and he himself believed*
and his whole household. ⁵⁴This is again **a second sign** *that Jesus performed when*
He had come out of Judea into Galilee.

—John 4:51-54

Jesus spoke a word of command, *"Your son lives,"* and the father *believed* the word command he heard. He immediately departed for home (it was about 1:00 p.m. and the journey was about 12-15 miles). The father was still on the road the following day when his servants approached him from the opposite direction. At that meeting, he heard the confirmation that his son was, indeed, healed at the exact time Jesus spoke His command. Scripture then tells us that *"he himself believed and his whole household."*

This is how it often is with us. Like the royal official, we find ourselves in a crisis and seek out Jesus. He speaks to us through His word (perhaps we read *Romans 8:28 "God causes all things to work together for good to those who love God"*) and all we can do is put our trust in that word. But as time passes, the power in that word, and its efficacy, becomes a reality within us and our faith in Christ is strengthened even more. This is the ongoing and continual process of transformation *that the Lord performs in us each day.*

Here is the best part. Jesus didn't command the father to do *anything* to save his child. Jesus' word accomplished the task *for the father.* Jesus didn't give him some herbs and tell him to go back and make the kid some chicken soup. God doesn't leave any part of our transformation to us. There is no applying, appropriating, working at, or striving for—just listening. *God's word does the transforming work, from glory to glory, in us!*

LIVING WATER FOR TODAY:

But we all, with unveiled face, beholding as in a mirror the
glory of the Lord, ***are being transformed*** *[present tense,*
24/7] ***into the same image from glory to glory****, just as*
from the Lord, the Spirit.—2 CORINTHIANS 3:18

For today, know that while you may still struggle with many fleshly things, God is speaking His word into you, which is changing you *day by day! PTL and Hallelujah!*

LIVING WATER FROM JOHN 4:19-54

March 21	There is no distinction between Jew and Greek, for the same Lord is Lord of all.
March 22	God has called us to worship Him in spirit and truth.
March 23	The woman at the well believed that the Messiah was coming and would explain everything to the Samaritans.
March 24	The Samaritan woman shared to others: "Come, see a man who told me all the things I have done."
March 25	Jesus was doing the work of harvesting those coming to Him from Samaria.
March 26	We are eternally saved and brought into God's kingdom by the work of our Triune God.
March 27	The work of God is sowing, reaping, and gathering His children for eternal life.
March 28	We have heard and believed through God's revelation that Jesus is indeed the Savior of the world.
March 29	Jesus meets us, and nothing can separate us from His love.
March 30	The word of God is the power that performs God's work in us.
March 31	When we pray, the power in God's word strengthens our faith.

PRAYER

*Father, I rejoice in Your tremendous mercy and compassion
toward me, and Your wonderful provisions for me!
You have given me life-saving belief in Your Son as my
Savior, which has quickened my deadened spirit and
made me born-again into new life. You alone have made
the way possible for me to worship you in spirit and truth!
I can only praise and worship You dear God!
Amen.*

IT PLEASED GOD TO SAVE YOU AND ME

JOHN 5:1-24

April 1

*After these things there was a feast of the Jews, and Jesus went up to Jerusalem. ²Now there is in Jerusalem by **the sheep gate a pool, which is called in Hebrew Bethesda, having five porticoes.** ³In these lay a multitude of those who were sick, blind, lame, and withered, [waiting for the moving of the waters; ⁴for an angel of the Lord went down at certain seasons into the pool and stirred up the water; whoever then first, after the stirring up of the water, stepped in was made well from whatever disease with which he was afflicted.]*

—John 5:1-4

What a dramatic scene we encounter as Jesus comes into Jerusalem for a feast of the Jews. He enters Jerusalem by the sheep gate near a pool called Bethesda. Around this pool were built five porticoes, or decks, which we learn are filled with a multitude (or large group) of those who were sick, blind, lame, and crippled. This scene was generally thought to be entirely symbolic because of the rich symbolism it contains, but the recent archeological discovery of this ancient pool with its five porticoes strengthens the historical accuracy of the Bible and of the writer *John*.

Nevertheless, the symbolism is insightful and inspiring. It is believed the sheep gate was used as the entry point for cattle being brought to the Temple for sacrifice. Is it a coincidence that Jesus, God's sacrificial lamb for our sins, used this same gate to enter Jerusalem? And the name of the pool—Bethesda—means "house of mercy" or "house of grace." In just two verses, scripture tells us about Jesus' sacrifice and mercy for us!

The Bethesda pool, with all the decking around it, is a microcosm of the world we live in. A world full of sick, blind, lame, and decayed people. Everyone disabled in some way and in need of someone to help them. This indicates the spiritual need of *every one of us*. Yet, in the center of this sad gathering of humanity, God placed Bethesda: His house of mercy and grace. *PTL!* What a glorious picture of God's magnificent grace!

Living Water for Today:

*But as for me, **by Your abundant lovingkindness**
I will enter Your house.*—Psalm 5:7a

For today, rejoice throughout the day! For God did not leave you to waste away—disabled, blind, and weak in your sins—but He came to you when you most needed Him, to lift you up and bring you into His glorious, joyous, eternal new home! *PTL!*

ILLUSTRATING JOHN 5:3-4

We come to a section of the Bible in brackets: *"... [waiting for the moving of the waters; ⁴for an angel of the Lord went down at certain seasons into the pool and stirred up the water; whoever then first, after the stirring up of the water, stepped in was made well from whatever disease with which he was afflicted.]"* These brackets indicate that these words are not in most ancient manuscripts. Bible commentators speculate on what to do with them. Some say they shouldn't be there at all. Others say they reflect ancient superstitious belief that the moving water healed people. Still others say these words represent exactly what they say—that an angel of God stirred these waters and healed people. I personally have no opinion as to what is correct.

What should we do in such circumstances? Any student of God's word, or any Christian who has attended several churches, will quickly understand that there are many things in scripture that we just don't understand. There are many subjects that churches have even divided over. In fact, in a few days *(April 7)*, we will touch upon one of these sections of scripture because it can't be avoided.

I am over 80 years old, and I have been studying the Bible for 50 years. I still have no explanation as to how two believers, who both have the same God and the same Holy Spirit drawing them to the same Bible, can reach two opposite understandings of a given doctrine or text. For example, some believe they chose God while others believe God chose them. This is a mystery that only God understands. It indicates how influential our individual life experiences can be.

The comforting thing about this conundrum is: God has given us in scripture *everything* we need to know to be eternally saved. We can trust that He will reveal, in His timing, what we do not yet understand. It is like the song "Where the Lost Things Go" in Walt Disney's *Mary Poppins Returns* movie: "You can't lose what you never lost ... [it is] ... waiting there until it is time to show. Spring is like that ... far beneath the snow." It is gloriously freeing to me, when I do not fully understand something from God's word, to trust that He will reveal it to me in His timing. Until then, I place it in the "place where the lost things go!"

APRIL 2

A man was there who had been ill for thirty-eight years. ⁶When Jesus saw him lying there, and knew that he had already been a long time in that condition, He said to him, **"Do you wish to get well?"** *⁷The sick man answered Him, "Sir, I have no man to put me into the pool when the water is stirred up, but while I am coming, another steps down before me." ⁸Jesus said to him,* **"Get up, pick up your pallet and walk."**
—JOHN 5:5-8

Unlike the bracketed words from *April 1*, today's words are unambiguous. We read of a man who has been ill for 38 years. He is incapable of doing anything for himself. There is no indication he was even looking for Jesus. He was just lying there with all the others who were crippled and diseased. This is a sad scene. But Jesus sought him out!

Jesus asked, *"Do you wish to get well?"* Obviously, the man wanted to be healed or he wouldn't be lying by the pool. Jesus' question was not meant to highlight the man's willingness as a precondition to healing; but rather, his complete inability to help himself. When Jesus asked His question, the poor man did *not* answer directly, but gave Jesus an excuse: *"Sir, I have no man to put me into the pool,"* reflecting how despondent and without hope he was. Praise God! Jesus needed no help from anyone but simply spoke a word from the *Creator-God* to him: *"Get up, pick up your pallet* (his bedroll) *and walk."*

How comforting is this! It calms our anxiety in so many ways. We may be concerned about the salvation or actions of a friend or relative. Perhaps we are worried about the direction America is heading politically, economically, socially, or spiritually. We might be praying about those in other countries where no gospel is preached. God is there, however, giving commands to accomplish His purpose according to His good pleasure.

LIVING WATER FOR TODAY:

Declaring the end from the beginning, and from ancient times things which have not been done, saying, **"My purpose will be established, and I will accomplish all My good pleasure."**—ISAIAH 46:10

For today, recognize that God is not inhibited by anything. He doesn't need any help from anyone or from the stirring of waters (circumstances). He will come to you in your need, regardless of what that might be, and speak a word to accomplish ALL His good pleasure *in* you and *for* you. *PTL!*

April 3

Jesus said to him, "Get up, pick up your pallet and walk." ⁹Immediately the man became well, and picked up his pallet and began to walk. Now it was the Sabbath on that day.

—John 5:8-9

Today, let's consider two ideas, each of which will change your life as they did mine.

First, Jesus came to this crippled man and spoke a word from the *Creator-God* to him. Did he thank Jesus for His words, and promise to apply them to his life? No! The words of Jesus *alone*, not any human response, effectuated the complete healing of this crippled man from his lifetime of disability. *This man was not required to apply or understand anything.* The word of God alone contained the power to fully heal him.

Second, given this first observation, pick up your Bible and flip through it. The word of God *you are holding in your hands*, which speaks to hundreds of topics within its pages, contains the same *get-up-and-walk* power as the words Jesus spoke to this crippled man in *John 5:8!* We may be crippled with anger, impatience, stress, anxiety, depression, loneliness, some form of addiction, just to name a few, but God's word has the *get-up-and-walk* power to heal all of these things. No need to read large sections of God's word or the entire Bible straight through. I often write down just a verse or two, and then look at them throughout the day. Even one or two words from a single verse will do. The power of God's word to heal us of all our afflictions is absolutely amazing!

LIVING WATER FOR TODAY:

*For this reason we also constantly thank God that when you **received the word of God** which you heard from us, you accepted it not as the word of men, but for what it really is, the word of God, **which also performs its work in you who believe.**—* 1 THESSALONIANS 2:13

For today, ask God to imprint His word on your heart, transforming you into the very promises and guarantees stated in His word that you are reading. God's word never fails to succeed at what God sends it to accomplish *(Isaiah 55:11)*. Praise the Lord for His enlightening, *life*-giving, comforting, nourishing, healing, always uplifting, and transforming word! Again, I say: *Praise the Lord!*

APRIL 4

So the Jews were saying to the man who was cured, "It is the Sabbath, and it is not permissible for you to carry your pallet." ¹¹ ***But he answered them, "He who made me well was the one who said to me, 'Pick up your pallet and walk.'"*** *¹²They asked him, "Who is the man who said to you, 'Pick up your pallet and walk'?" ¹³But the man who was healed did not know who it was, for Jesus had slipped away while there was a crowd in that place.*

—JOHN 5:10-13

There are times in our lives when we believe we are following what the Lord has directed us to do, yet we receive criticism from others, even from other Christians. This is what happened to this crippled man soon after being healed by Jesus. The Jewish leaders of the day acted like religious policemen. They were adamant that everyone must comport their actions in strict compliance with the Mosaic law (as *they* interpreted it, including all their added traditions), regardless of the circumstances.

What would you do if you were that crippled man? Follow the direct guidance from the person who just fully healed you from 38 years of misery; or ignore that person, so you could remain in harmony and alignment with what the religious people around you were directing you to do? I love the *formerly* crippled man's answer: *"He who made me well was the one who said to me, 'Pick up your pallet and walk.'"*

I know a lady who feels led by the Lord to remain at home on Sundays to care for her husband who deals with a great deal of physical pain, yet she is sometimes criticized by Christians for not going to church. I'm sure those who speak to her this way are well-intentioned, but their opinions are hurtful. This used to bury her in guilt—however, no longer! She now assures them that she is doing what the Lord has directed her to do.

LIVING WATER FOR TODAY:

Man's steps are ordained by the LORD, *How then can man understand his way? ¹⁴For all* ***who are being led by the Spirit of God,*** *these are sons of God.* —PROVERBS 20:24; ROMANS 8:14

For today, know that God *is leading* and influencing your life in ways you are often not even aware of. Praise God that you can trust His leading. You can trust that He will always make you know what He wants you to know *(Psalm 25:12-14). A priceless comfort!*

A PERSONAL TESTIMONY

Trusting the Lord to Guide You

Several years ago I was invited to speak at a Christian camp for a weekend. As part of my introduction, the attendees learned that I was a business owner. At the end of this weekend of messages, a Christian came up to me and said, "Daryl, I'm going to put this to you straight. You are out of God's will running a business. You need to quit that and go into full-time service for the Lord." This comment was no surprise to me, I've been told that more than once over the years. He obviously loved the Lord and meant well in his comments, but he was not the one who said to the crippled man, *"Get up ... and walk."*

The lesson doesn't end there. Sometimes, when I share this experience with another Christian (to encourage them to trust in the Lord's leading), their first response is, "Daryl, you are going to touch far more lives running a business then if you were a pastor somewhere. You need to stay right where you are. I agree with you." When I get this response, since I am not asking them to agree with me, it is clear they also are missing the purpose of my sharing. Nevertheless, I don't try to correct them. I simply thank them for what they have felt to tell me.

I go away from such discussions, however, realizing that God doesn't lead me by how many people I think I'm touching for the Lord. Do you remember John the Baptist *(March 5-7)*, as the numbers of those coming to him to be baptized dwindled? His response was to rejoice that Jesus was increasing while he was decreasing. He was content to be exactly where God wanted him to be. This is something we can all trust God to do for us (His children)—put us *exactly* in the place He wants us to be. There is nothing mystical or magical about trusting God. Scripture tells us that we can trust Him to *make us to know His leading for us (Psalm 25:12-14)*.

When it comes to waiting on the Lord's leading, I often feel like the dumbest sheep in the Lord's flock. I don't mind telling Him that. When I take my early morning run, I find myself talking to Him, "Lord, I'm not telling You anything You don't already know; I am the dumbest of all Your sheep when it comes to sensing Your leading for me, but I am waiting on You. I'm just going to wait until You make Your will for me so peaceful and clear that even Your dumbest sheep can understand it."

April 5

*Afterward Jesus found him in the temple and said to him, "**Behold, you have become well**; do not sin anymore, so that nothing worse happens to you." ¹⁵The man went away, and told the Jews that it was Jesus who had made him well.*

—JOHN 5:14-15

The Greek meaning contained in *verse 14* does not translate easily into English. It is a wonderful verse, full of affirmation and freedom, but requires a careful analysis in the broader context of scripture to understand its rich message. *"Behold, you have become well"* in the *King James Bible* is translated as *"thou art made whole."* The word "whole" in scripture means to be made complete in Christ—or to be saved. So Jesus did more than heal a crippled man, He gave this man new eternal life!

Next, the phrase *"do not sin anymore"* confirms that God has changed this man's life. It is not a command exhorting him not to sin. That is impossible for any of us. The meaning of the phrase is expressed more clearly in another section of scripture written by the same Apostle John: *"No one who is born of God* (referring to believers) ***practices sin, because His seed*** [Jesus] *abides in him; and he cannot sin, because he is born of God."* *(1 John 3:9).* The phrase *"do not sin anymore" (John 5:14)* carries a similar meaning to the phrase in *1 John 3:9: "No one who is born of God **practices sin**,"* meaning they no longer live a lifestyle completely controlled by sin. God's Spirit now is at work in every believer's life to will and to work for His good pleasure *(Philippians 2:13).*

The last phrase, *"so that nothing worse happens to you"* simply means Jesus made this man whole so that he would be free from eternal condemnation.

LIVING WATER FOR TODAY:

*So then, on the one hand I myself with my mind am serving the law of God, but on the other, with my flesh the law of sin. ¹Therefore there is now no condemnation for those who are in Christ Jesus. ²For the law of **the Spirit of life in Christ Jesus has set you free from the law of sin and of death.**—*ROMANS 7:25B-8:2

For today, be thankful along with the Apostle Paul, that even when you desire and hunger for God, you still act at times from your flesh and commit sin, yet God does not condemn you because you are in Christ Jesus. *Praise the Lord!*

APRIL 6

For this reason the Jews were persecuting Jesus, because He was doing these things on the Sabbath. ¹⁷But He answered them, "My Father is working until now, and I Myself am working." ¹⁸For this reason therefore the Jews were seeking all the more to kill Him, because He not only was breaking the Sabbath, but also was calling God His own Father, making Himself equal with God.

—John 5:16-18

All of creation took God six days and He rested on the seventh. God gave man the Sabbath to reflect this same pattern, so that man would work six days and preserve one day to rest and worship God. Jesus tells us that God is *no longer* resting! He is working, as is Jesus, right up to the present. Nothing in scripture prohibits healing on the Sabbath. The Sabbath does not restrict God, nor is He subject to it. The Sabbath also was not intended to restrict helping a neighbor, nor a lame man (who is healed by God) from carrying his bed, nor preparing a meal for someone who is sick or in need. That is how far the Jewish leaders warped and twisted God's word.

In *John 9:1-14* Jesus healed a blind man. In *Luke 13:10-17* He healed a woman afflicted for 18 years. And in *Mark 3:1-12* He healed a man with a deformed hand. All these healings occurred on the Sabbath. Each one infuriated the Jewish leaders to the point they sought to kill Jesus. Why this intense reaction? These Jewish leaders were far more concerned about what Jesus was teaching than the healings He performed. In *John 5:18*, Jesus refers to God as His Father (making Him equal to God). In the Jewish worldview, their entire belief system viewed God as ONE GOD *(Deuteronomy 6:4)*. But Jesus spoke of God the Father *(John 5:17-23)*, Himself as the Son *(John 5:19-23)*, and the *pneuma*/wind/Holy Spirit *(John 3:8)*—AS ONE TRIUNE GOD! *(Matthew 28:19)* This was too much for the Jewish leaders to accept!

LIVING WATER FOR TODAY:

*But God, being rich in mercy, because of His great love with which He loved us, ⁵**even when we were dead in our transgressions, made us alive together with Christ** (by grace you have been saved).*—Ephesians 2:4-5

For today, rejoice that you were *not only a cripple but DEAD* in your transgressions and sins, yet Jesus came to you, raised you from the dead, *and gave you eternal life! PTL!*

WHY ME AND WHY YOU?

Whether you believe that *God chose you*—or *you chose God*. Whether you believe that humanity has *free will* to choose God or not, or don't believe that such *free will* AFFECTING OUR SALVATION exists (claiming that no-where in scripture is such *free will* found or taught). Whether you believe that you prayed a special prayer to invite Jesus Christ into your life, and therefore, had a part to play in your salvation; or you believe that your salvation is entirely the workings of God's mercy and grace to make you alive when you were dead *(Ephesians 2:4-5)*, just as it pleased Him to do so in revealing His Son in the Apostle Paul *(Galatians 1:15-16)*, or to Nicodemus in *John 3:8* (the wind blows where it wills). And finally, whether you believe you can lose your salvation or must work to obtain it.

Regardless of what you believe, here is the glorious "BIG PICTURE" that unifies: However you became a Christian, we can all agree that *whoever believes in Jesus as their Lord and Savior will not perish but have everlasting life (John 3:16)!* We are all brothers and sisters in Christ! How glorious is that? Scripture affirms this core truth hundreds of times. Beyond that core truth, I have no interest in arguing with anyone. If I am asked what I believe, I will share the verses that lead me to believe the way I do, but I will never debate. I readily acknowledge that there is much I do not understand, so I leave the rest with the Lord *(Romans 14:4-8, 17-19, 22)*.

I personally believe scripture teaches that *God has done it all and He is all we need.* That before the foundation of the world *(Ephesians 1:4)* God chose each of us to adoption as sons through Jesus Christ to Himself *(Ephesians 1:5)* and that He, when it pleases Him to do so, reveals His Son in us just like He did to the Apostle Paul *(Galatians 1:15-16)*. And, on an ongoing basis, God is at work in us daily according to His good pleasure *(Philippians 2:13)* throughout our lives to progressively transform us from glory to glory until Christ returns *(Philippians 1:6; 2 Corinthians 3:16)*.

APRIL 7

*Therefore Jesus answered and was saying to them, "Truly, truly, I say to you, the Son can do nothing of Himself, unless it is something He sees the Father doing; for whatever the Father does, these things the Son also does in like manner. ²⁰For the Father loves the Son, and shows Him all things that He Himself is doing; and the Father will show Him greater works than these, so that you will marvel. ²¹**For just as the Father raises the dead and gives them life, even so the Son also gives life to whom He wishes.** ²²For not even the Father judges anyone, but He has given all judgment to the Son, ²³so that all will honor the Son even as they honor the Father. He who does not honor the Son does not honor the Father who sent Him."*
—JOHN 5:19-23

Jesus is presenting Himself in these verses as the agent of God's divine purpose. He is the One that God works through to accomplish His will in giving you and me eternal life and judging those without Christ. *John 5:21* is a good example. The *NIV* translation reads: *"For just as the Father raises the dead and gives them life, **even so the Son gives life to whom he is pleased to give it."***

On *March 12* we read how Jesus "must needs" go through Samaria to touch the life of one woman at a particular well, and at a particular time of day. Now we are reading about Jesus passing through a great number of sick and crippled people lying about the pool of Bethesda, where Jesus is pleased, among all this multitude, to heal *one* very sick man. Neither the woman nor this man were expecting His visit. But it pleased Jesus to do so. These examples illustrate how God's eternal purpose works: when it pleased God to reveal His Son in you and me, He did so. He didn't do it grudgingly. It *PLEASED HIM* to do so. Why you and why me? I don't know, and I don't expect to know until I get to glory. Scripture, however, makes it clear that it is something God is pleased to do.

LIVING WATER FOR TODAY:

*When the disciples heard this, they were very astonished and said, "Then who can be saved?" ²⁶And looking at them Jesus said to them, "**With people this is impossible, but with God all things are possible.**"*—MATTHEW 19:25-26

For today, abide in the knee-buckling joy of this truth—that what was completely impossible for you to achieve for yourself, God was *PLEASED* to do for you—*to choose you, redeem you, sanctify you, and declare YOU righteous "in Christ" (1 Corinthians 1:30)!*

APRIL 8

*"Truly, truly, I say to you, he who hears My word, and believes Him who sent Me, **has eternal life**, and does not come into judgment, but **has passed out of death into life.**"*
—JOHN 5:24

What a truly glorious final verse to this section of scripture! In the original Greek, the two phrases *"has eternal life"* and *"has passed out of death into life"* are in the perfect tense, meaning they are referring to a settled, unchangeable state! This is Jesus speaking here, saying that it pleased God to come by *you and me* and lift us out of a state of eternal death into a permanent, unchangeable life in glory with Him forever. This brings tears of joy to my eyes! Honestly, I don't have enough praise in me to thank God adequately for His immense mercy and grace to me.

Now—I know some Christians never experience this knee-buckling joy because they focus exclusively on what they consider to be a matter of "fairness." What about those God wasn't pleased to save? How is that fair? Man must have a free will and choice in this somewhere. We can't be just automatons! These are all questions we think are important. God does not. God tells us everything we need to know, that when it pleased Him, He revealed His Son *in us!* What profound mercy and grace! For those who would question God, the Apostle Paul gives an answer in *Romans 9:20-24: "Who are you, O man, who answers back to God? ... does not the potter have a right over the clay?"* All I know is this: God is righteous in all His deeds *(Daniel 9:14)*; and Jesus is just in His judgments *(John 5:30)*; and every good thing given, and every perfect gift is from God, the Father of lights, with whom there is no variation or shifting shadow *(James 1:17)*. God has brought me to trust Him to be full of mercy and infinitely fair to every person. I don't need to understand the mind of God beyond that.

LIVING WATER FOR TODAY:

Oh, the depth of the riches both of the wisdom and knowledge of God! How unsearchable are His judgments and unfathomable His ways! [34]*For **WHO HAS KNOWN THE MIND OF THE LORD**, or **WHO BECAME HIS COUNSELOR?**—*ROMANS 11:33-34

For today, have faith in exactly what the word of God says, no more and no less. You cannot know the mind of God. You can trust that God was pleased to seek out **YOU**, raise **YOU** from the dead, and bring **YOU** into eternal life in His presence. *PTL!*

LIVING WATER FROM JOHN 5:1-24

April 1	Jesus, our sacrificial Lamb, entered the sheep gate near a healing pool called Bethesda: a picture of God's mercy for disabled humanity; a microcosm of today's world.
April 2	God's word accomplishes all His good pleasure in and through us and calms our hearts in many ways.
April 3	The word of God contains the power to heal us of our afflictions.
April 4	We are being led by the Spirit of God and can trust His leading.
April 5	Jesus makes us whole and complete—free from eternal condemnation.
April 6	God made us alive together with Christ and is continually working His will in us.
April 7	The Son of God does whatever the Father does; He gives life to whom He is pleased to give it.
April 8	"... he who hears My word, and believes Him who sent Me, has eternal life, and ... has passed out of death into life" *(John 5:24)* is referring to a settled, unchangeable state.

PRAYER

*Father, I confess that as long as I thought I had a part
to play in my salvation, I didn't thank You, praise You,
or worship You enough. But now, dear God, realizing that
my salvation is ALL You, when You were pleased to seek me
out and reveal Your Son in me, I feel I can't praise
and worship to You enough. I desire only to continually
praise and worship You for Your mercy and grace for me!
Amen.*

THANK GOD
FOR
GIVING US
UNDERSTANDING

JOHN 5:25-47

APRIL 9

*"Truly, truly, I say to you, an hour is coming and now is, when the dead will hear the voice of the Son of God, and **those who hear will live.**"*
—JOHN 5:25

The Apostle John tells us in *John 20:31*, that his goal in writing the book was so we *"may believe that Jesus is the Christ, the Son of God; and that believing you may have life in His name."* In the coming days, Jesus explains what it means for us to *"have life in His name."*

Remember from recent days how Jesus brought life to people He met? He healed a crippled man at the pool of Bethesda *(April 2)* by just speaking the words *"pick up your pallet and walk" (John 5:1-9)*. He also healed the royal official's son *(March 30)*, proving again that He had power over death and life simply by speaking the words *"Go; your son lives" (John 4:46-54)*. These examples demonstrate how the words that God speaks affect those who hear them, and *always* accomplish what they say.

In this same fashion God speaks eternal life into us. Yesterday *(April 8)*, Jesus tells us: *"he who hears My word, and **believes Him** who sent Me, **has eternal life**, and does not come into judgment, but **has passed out of death into life**" (John 5:24)*. In to-day's verse, Jesus expands the scope of this promise to include the dead who hear His voice—even they will live. The phrase: *"an hour is coming and now is"* is best thought to refer to this present age, the *church age* (that will terminate with the return of Christ and the resurrection of the dead).

Who are those who "hear His voice"? *Verse 24* tells us that it is those who *believe*. And what causes them to believe? Jesus speaking His word, quickens belief in them. This is the testimony of every Christian: *Jesus speaks His word into us, and we believe!*

LIVING WATER FOR TODAY:

So also is the resurrection of the dead. It is sown a perish-
*able body, it is **raised an imperishable body;** [43] it is sown*
*in dishonor, it is **raised in glory;** it is sown in weakness,*
*it is **raised in power.**—1 CORINTHIANS 15:42-43*

For today, rejoice that you hear God's voice and will live eternally with Him. Whether dead or still alive when He calls, you will be transformed into a new glorified body. No more illness, fear, worry, discouragement—*only perfect health, peace, and joy forever! PTL!*

CONNECTING THE THEOLOGICAL DOTS

Many Christians are captivated by what Jesus has to say in *John 5:25-29* (and what scripture says more broadly) concerning the dead hearing His voice and the existence of a resurrection. These words are the basis of our hope for loved ones who have passed on before us, and if the Lord tarries, for ourselves as well. But such terms as *"resurrection of life"* and *"resurrection of judgment" (John 5:29)* can also be the source of intense struggle for some, fearing that they will find themselves among those in the latter ("judgment") group rather than those called to eternal life.

To those who struggle with worry, remember this one unchangeable truth about scripture: **GOD'S GOSPEL IS *ALWAYS* GOOD NEWS FOR US!** When understood correctly, without any *"ifs, ands, or buts"* added to it, scripture never puts us under judgment, condemnation, worry, or guilt. It always delivers good news for our eternal salvation, and daily nourishment, encouragement, and guidance in Christ! Here are more verses on this topic:

1 Corinthians 15:51-53. *"Behold, I tell you a mystery; we will not all sleep, but we will all be changed, ⁵²in a moment, in the twinkling of an eye, at the last trumpet; for the trumpet will sound, and the dead will be raised imperishable, and we will be changed. ⁵³For this perishable must put on the imperishable, and this mortal must put on immortality."*

1 Thessalonians 4:16-18. *"For the Lord Himself will descend from heaven with a shout, with the voice of the archangel and with the trumpet of God, and the dead in Christ will rise first. ¹⁷Then we who are alive and remain will be caught up together with them in the clouds to meet the Lord in the air, and so we shall always be with the Lord. ¹⁸Therefore comfort one another with these words."*

1 Corinthians 15:42-44. *"So also is the resurrection of the dead. It is sown a perishable body, it is **raised an imperishable body**; ⁴³it is sown in dishonor, it is **raised in glory**; it is sown in weakness, it is **raised in power**; ⁴⁴it is sown a natural body, **it is raised a spiritual body**. If there is a natural body, there is also a spiritual body."*

The *spiritual body* mentioned here is not intangible, but tangible and real. For those interested beyond what can be presented in this daily devotional, go to the GRACE UPON GRACE FOUNDATION website (www.gugf.org), and click on: Bible studies, 1 Corinthians, and lesson 37 for an entire lesson on this topic.

APRIL 10

*"For just as the Father has life in Himself, even so **He gave to the Son also to have life in Himself**,"*

—JOHN 5:26

Jesus tells us that both He and the Father have life in themselves. This means they can give life to whomever they wish because THEY ARE LIFE! They are not dependent on anyone else agreeing or cooperating with them. They are not restrained by a requirement that we initiate our requests to them before they can act. A perfect example of this can be seen in Jesus speaking to Lazarus who had been dead and buried in a tomb for four days prior to Jesus' arrival *(John 11:39)*. When Jesus ordered the stone to Lazarus' tomb removed, Martha (Lazarus' sister) worried that there would surely be a stench because of the many days Lazarus had been dead and decaying in the tomb.

Now—does Lazarus sound like a person in any condition to help himself? Did Jesus stand outside the tomb waiting for Lazarus to call out to Him for salvation or life? No. Scripture could not be more explicit regarding the condition of Lazarus and the source of the life that Jesus brought to him that day. Jesus said, *"Lazarus, come forth"* *(John 11:43)* and Lazarus came forth. No one could argue that Lazarus had anything to do with his resurrection *(and neither do we have anything to do with the life God gives to us)*.

Praise God! He has no beginning and no end. He *is* eternal life! God *always* was, and *always* will be. We cannot rationalize or understand this with our finite human minds. We can only praise God that He has given us His enlightening word to affirm to us that the Father and the Son ARE eternal life! It is through God's word, regardless of our total incapacity to understand it (just like dead and stinking Lazarus), that we are assured of eternal life *because God is that life, and He now lives in us!*

LIVING WATER FOR TODAY:

*Even God, who **gives life to the dead** and calls into being that which does not exist.*—ROMANS 4:17B

For today, experience the true freedom and joy in knowing that you are no better or more capable than dead and stinking Lazarus in deserving or choosing God's life. But like Lazarus, Jesus has come to *your* tomb and called *you* forth into eternal life! **His**— *forever full of joy and pleasure*—**abundant life** *(Psalm 16:11)*. **PTL!**

APRIL 11

*"And **He gave Him authority to execute judgment**, because He is the Son of Man."*
—JOHN 5:27

This is a fearful verse to some Christians, yet understanding the true meaning of the word *"judgment"* discards all that fear. In God's wisdom and mercy, we can often look to scripture to explain scripture. I frequently turn to Strong's Concordance to look up the Greek word used in a particular verse, and then locate every other place in scripture where that same Greek word is used. This process produces both the spectrum of meaning attributed to the word I am looking up, and also the context in which each meaning is rendered into English. It is amazing the clarity that scripture brings to scripture when applying this method to verses we initially may not fully understand.

Such is the case in today's verse. The same word for *judgment* in *John 5:27* is also used in *John 9:39*, where Jesus explains the kind of *judgment* He came into the world to bring: *"And Jesus said, 'For judgment I came into this world, so that those who do not see may see, and those who see may become blind.'"* The Living Bible translates this same verse with greater clarity: *"Then Jesus told him, 'I have come into the world to give sight to those who are spiritually blind* [meaning us] *and to show those who think they see* [those who think they know everything and are the purveyors of truth] *that they are blind.'"*

Day by day and verse by verse Jesus continues to bring us along this journey of *judgment* or *enlightenment* or *understanding* as a modern day English equivalent for this process. By God's mercy and grace He continues to show us more and more of our blindness, while His radiance renews our minds *(Ephesians 4:23)* and transforms us from glory to glory *(2 Corinthians 3:18)*. Like the blind man, all believers now say: *once I was blind, but now I see! PTL!*

LIVING WATER FOR TODAY:

*"One thing I do know, that though **I was blind, now I see**."*
—JOHN 9:25B

For today, be comforted that God has you on His journey where He continues to shed light (understanding) on verses that take you deeper and deeper into knowing Him. He continues to brighten the path that He has ordained for you to travel in this world. And as that path brightens, *you grow in more peace and trusting God with (and for) everything!*

ILLUSTRATING JOHN 9:25

This verse is illustrative of something very practical for us to understand as Christians. It comes near the end of a long pericope of scripture describing how Jesus healed a man who was blind from birth. As we see repeatedly in scripture, Jesus performed this miracle on the Sabbath, and this troubled the religious leaders intensely. They first questioned the healed man. Then they questioned whether he was truly blind. Then they questioned the man's parents. Then they started over, questioning once more the formerly blind man. Then they accused Jesus of being a sinner for healing on the Sabbath. Finally, the man had enough. We read in *John 9:25: "He then answered, 'Whether He is a sinner, I do not know; one thing I do know, that though **I was blind, now I see**."'*

This is a good insight for us as Christians. We can come across people who are skeptical or do not believe. Our temptation is to try to convince them or tell them what they need to do. Taking a lesson from this formerly blind man, the most powerful (and effective) thing we can do when presented with the opportunity to share our experiences of Christ, is simply to talk to the person about what Jesus means to us personally, and then, trust Jesus to give them sight. No amount of persuasive argument in our human effort will do anything. *Only God can bring sight to the blind.*

Another good example of this is found in *Luke 8:39*, where we read about a demon-possessed man who Jesus healed. The man was so grateful that he pleaded with Jesus to allow him to remain. But Jesus refused and gave him this command: *"'Return to your house and **describe what great things God has done for you.**' So he went away, proclaiming throughout the whole city what great things Jesus had done for him."*

We don't need to have a doctorate degree in biblical and theological studies. We don't need to memorize a lot of verses. We don't need a multi-step plan of salvation. We don't need to argue with anyone at all. All we need do is share what great things Jesus has done for us—then trust Jesus to make the blind see, and expose those who think they know so much as being truly blind.

APRIL 12

*"Do not marvel at this; for an hour is coming, in which all who are in the tombs will hear His voice, ²⁹and will come forth; **those who did the good deeds to a resurrection of life**, those who committed the evil deeds to a resurrection of judgment."*
—JOHN 5:28-29

The little phrase, *"those who did the good deeds"* used to scare me to death. For half of my life I thought the *good deeds* referenced in this verse referred to things like: (i) attending church services, (ii) teaching Sunday school, (iii) reading my Bible daily, (iv) praying unceasingly, (v) tithing on the gross (not net) of my income; (vi) giving generously *over* my tithe, (vii) and witnessing every day. I could go on and on with this list I thought were the *good deeds* referred to in *John 5:29*. The truly frightening part was I could readily recognize a plethora of sinful *evil deeds* in my life daily, but the *good deeds* always seemed inadequate and in short supply. I hated reading these words in scripture.

Praise the Lord! The gospel's good news, however, is that these activities are *not* the *good deeds* referred to in these verses. Jesus is referring to a resurrection of both believers and unbelievers, which tells us that both will be resurrected with new bodies that will express the character of the one resurrected. The *good deeds* are belief in God, turning to God, praying to Him, loving Him, praising Him, hating sin (even though we still sin). These are the *good deeds* that Jesus is referring to. And the freedom producing question is this: Who causes us to believe? Who draws us to think of Him, read scripture, and pray to Him? The answer to all these questions is *God alone does this work in us! The good deeds Jesus is referring to are not ours but HIS!* We have *nothing* to boast in but God!

LIVING WATER FOR TODAY:

*For by grace you have been saved through faith; and that not of yourselves, it is the gift of God; ⁹**not as a result of works, so that no one may boast.** ¹⁰**For we are His workmanship,** created in Christ Jesus for good works, which God prepared beforehand so that we would walk in them.*—EPHESIANS 2:8-10

For today, rejoice in the Lord that you are HIS workmanship. He placed His fountain of life ("Living Water") *in you*, to fill you with belief in Him, worship of Him, praying to Him, and love for Him and others. These are the works God calls you to walk in, which He Himself is producing in you. *PTL! And again, PTL!*

APRIL 13

*"I can do nothing on My own initiative. As I hear, I judge; and My judgment is just, because I do not seek My own will, but the will of Him who sent Me. ³¹If I alone testify about Myself, My testimony is not true. ³²There is another who testifies of Me, and I know that the testimony which He gives about Me is true. ³³You have sent to John, and he has testified to the truth. ³⁴But the testimony which I receive is not from man, but I say these things **so that you may be saved**."*

—JOHN 5:30-34

These verses contain a wonderful message of comfort and love. Jesus tells us He is the manifestation of God's will and that He never acts on His own initiative independent of His Father. Why is this important? It is important because Jesus is revealing the sole purpose for why He came to accomplish everything He is doing in the gospels (and Old and New Testaments) through His life, death, and resurrection. Think about this for a moment. *Every* miracle He performs, *every* word He speaks, *every* action He takes, *EVERYTHING* is for *one* purpose: "*so that you may be saved*" through belief in Him.

For the first 40 years of my life, I added so much complicated human performance and doctrinal baggage to God's simple gospel. I thought it was my responsibility to live up to all the high standards set forth in scripture. That turned God's word into an endless source of fear, bondage, and guilt for me. These last 40 years, however, have been a progressive realization of increasing freedom and joy as I journey through scripture, recognizing that Jesus has fulfilled *every* word, commandment, and requirement for me. God has done it *all!* He is *all* I need! Scripture is *always* good news to me now.

LIVING WATER FOR TODAY:

Be anxious for nothing, but in everything by prayer and supplication with thanksgiving let your requests be made known to God. ⁷And the peace of God, which surpasses all comprehension, will guard your hearts and your minds in Christ Jesus.—PHILIPPIANS 4:6-7

For today, take comfort in the journey the Lord has you on. It is His journey: He is in control. He is bringing you through all the trials, difficulties, and challenges in your life to a place where you can totally rest in Him—where you are not *trying* to be *anxious for nothing*, but you ARE *anxious for nothing* because an all-sovereign, all-loving *God* has etched His word deeper and deeper into your heart and mind.

APRIL 14

*"He was the lamp that was burning and was shining and you were willing to rejoice for a while in his light. ^{36}**But the testimony which I have is greater than the testimony of John;** for the works which the Father has given Me to accomplish—the very works that I do—testify about Me, that the Father has sent Me. ^{37}And the Father who sent Me, He has testified of Me. You have neither heard His voice at any time nor seen His form."*
—JOHN 5:35-37

In these verses, Jesus is speaking directly to the religious leaders who were so offended when He healed the crippled man by the pool of Bethesda (both because He did so on the Sabbath, and because He referenced God as His Father making Him equal to God). Jesus gives the Jewish leaders four "witnesses" that each testify concerning Him. Three of these witnesses are contained in today's verses. *First*, Jesus reminds them that John the Baptist, who the Jews initially rejoiced to receive his testimony, was testifying as a witness about Jesus *(John 1:14-18)*. *Second*, Jesus points to the very works (miracles) He was performing as giving witness that God had sent Him. *Third*, Jesus declares that the Father Himself is a witness to His Son and has testified of Him *(John 5:37)*.

How blind were the hearts of these religious leaders! They rejoiced in John the Baptist's message so long as he spoke in generalities, but they abandoned him when he got specific about Jesus. Then, they rejected Jesus' miracles on the grounds that they were performed on the Sabbath. In truth, His miracles were something they could not control so they began planning to put Jesus to death *(John 5:18)*. *Finally*, Jesus spoke a truth that utterly destroyed the foundation of their human authority. Doesn't every religious leader claim their authority is based on their closeness to God? Yet Jesus told all those listening that these religious leaders had never heard the witness of God's voice at all. What a scathing indictment of the true condition of these leader's hearts and minds.

LIVING WATER FOR TODAY:

Great are the works of the LORD; *They are studied by all who delight in them.*—PSALM 111:2

For today, with a heart full of thanksgiving, consider again the journey of your own life. Consider how God has chosen, enlightened, nourished, blessed, comforted, protected, sustained, counseled, guided, and drawn you to Him. There is no greater comfort for the present and for the future! God's faithfulness *to you!*

April 15

"You do not have His word abiding in you, for you do not believe Him whom He sent.
³⁹You search the Scriptures because you think that in them you have eternal life;
*it is these that testify about Me; ⁴⁰and **you are unwilling to come to Me so that***
you may have life."

—John 5:38-40

The fourth "witness" Jesus referenced is in today's verses. God's word in scripture testifies of Jesus. To understand what Jesus is saying here, we must first grasp a foundational belief held within Jewish culture at the time. Jewish scholars believed that the very study of holy scriptures (the Old Testament), would bring them eternal life. The concept was *not* that it would teach them *the source of life* (Christ Jesus), but only that the continual study of scripture (or knowledge alone) would result in life.

With that in mind, it is easier to see why these religious leaders did not understand Jesus telling them that the holy words they have been studying their entire lives, are the very words that testify about Him. Why? The answer is found in *where understanding comes from.* They did not understand because, *"You do not have His word abiding in you, for you do not believe Him whom He sent."* In *1 John 4:13*, the same author as the Gospel of John, we learn why they did not understand: *"By this we know that we abide in Him and He in us, because **He has given us of His Spirit.**"* So, God's Spirit in you and me gives us true knowledge of who Jesus is: *The God of all creation and Savior of the world!* Did these religious leaders study scripture and know it forwards and backwards? Yes. Did they observe with their own eyes the physical miracles that Jesus performed? Yes. Yet their eyes remained blind. They could not recognize or understand who stood before them. God had not given them His abiding Spirit, and without the Spirit of God, spiritual understanding is impossible.

Living Water for Today:

By this we know that we abide in Him and He in us,
*because **He has given us of His Spirit.**—1 John 4:13*

For today, praise God, that out of His great love for you He chose to put His Spirit in you and give you understanding *(Galatians 1:15-16a)*. That is your total salvation! It can't be lost, tarnished, or diminished because it is all God's mercy toward you.

APRIL 16

*"I do not receive glory from men; *42*but I know you, that **you do not have the love of** **God in yourselves.** *43*I have come in My Father's name, and you do not receive Me; if another comes in his own name, you will receive him."*

—JOHN 5:41-43

As we continue day by day through what Jesus is telling these religious leaders, it is becoming increasingly clear how ridiculous it was for them not to accept Him. He now further emphasizes this fact by pointing out that they would readily receive any ordinary person who came into their midst making claims in their own name, while at the same time rejecting Him (Jesus) who had performed many physical miracles in front of them and who obviously came from God. How completely absurd is this?

This is not just a dramatic encounter for us to read as though we are a bystander. Remember, *every* word of God is intended for each of us personally. What are we to conclude from these words spoken by Jesus? I will tell you what God has spoken to me through these verses. If there is any remaining thread of a thought that we somehow muster up *our own* belief in Jesus as our Savior, these verses put an unequivocal end to this unscriptural fantasy. These religious leaders daily searched the scriptures with fervor and commitment. They lived their lives with ironclad discipline in accordance with the Mosaic Law. They were "good" people. By contrast, for the first half of my adult life I didn't want too much God. I was convinced He wanted to take away all the fun in my life. If eternal life had *anything* to do with our performance, these religious leaders would be far more eligible than me in terms of living a pure life humanly. But that pure human living yielded them *nothing but blindness regarding God's eternal life.*

LIVING WATER FOR TODAY:

Whoever believes that Jesus is the Christ is born of God, *and whoever loves the Father loves the child born of Him.*—1 JOHN 5:1

For today, dwell on the fact that *you believe in Christ,* and your belief didn't cause you to become born of God, but it is evidence that *God chose you* to be born of Him *(John 15:16).* Your life may be far from perfect, yet God chose to put His Spirit and love in you. As a result of this loving act of God's mercy and grace, *you believe.* And once again, your believing is proof positive that you have eternal life! *PTL! PTL!*

APRIL 17

*"How can you believe, when you receive glory from one another and **you do not seek the glory that is from the one and only God?**"*

—JOHN 5:44

Jesus keeps digging deeper with these religious leaders. Now he is exposing their hidden motives for why they search and study the scriptures so diligently. It was not because they had a hunger and thirst to know God. Their real motives were to impress each other and receive approval and praise for how brilliant and knowledgeable they were (and how upright they lived according to Mosaic Law). This is what Jesus meant by the phrase, *"when you receive glory from one another"* rather than approval from God.

This was not an isolated problem experienced only by these religious leaders. Jesus is speaking to *every* Christian here. It is part of our fallen flesh to seek approval from others. We can be a pastor, part of a music ministry, Sunday school teacher, or regular church goer, you name it, our motivation can slip into obtaining approval (glory) from others, with only a secondary thought for God. This is a reason many Christians can feel "burned out" with all their church activities.

Unlike the religious leaders of Jesus' day, God has placed His Spirit within us! The Apostle Paul writes in *2 Corinthians 3:3-5* that *"you are a letter of Christ ... written not with ink but with the **Spirit of the living God**, not on tablets of stone but on **tablets of human hearts**. ⁴Such confidence we have through Christ toward God. ⁵Not that we are adequate in ourselves to consider anything as coming from ourselves, **but our adequacy is from God.**"* Paul says we ARE—*present tense, currently and ongoing, not something we have to strive to be or some day become*—a letter of Christ written on our hearts by the Spirit of the living God! Our loving God keeps drawing us back to Him. His Spirit keeps writing on our hearts daily.

LIVING WATER FOR TODAY:

*Being manifested that **you are a letter of Christ** ... written not with ink but with the Spirit of the living God, not on tablets of stone but on tablets of human hearts.*—2 CORINTHIANS 3:3

For today, approach God's word for the sole purpose of seeking Him afresh. Then just be sensitive to what He is impressing on your heart. You can trust Him to write on your heart all He wants you to know and when He wants you to know it—*a priceless peace!*

A PERSONAL TESTIMONY

RECEIVING GLORY FROM MEN

I was a preacher's kid, and that got me started teaching a Sunday school class early on in my life. I would study the Bible primarily to develop notes to teach a class on a topic or a book of the Bible. Later in life, by the light of *John 5:44*, I recognized that in those earlier years my primary motive was to be viewed by those attending my class as a "good teacher" or a "good student of God's word." To say this using Jesus' words, I studied the Bible to *"receive glory"* from those listening. It was one of the biggest ways I considered myself to be serving God. But all my studying and teaching didn't help me feel saved. I thought it would, but it didn't. No matter what I taught, it had no impact on my personal stress.

I was also taught that I needed to witness to at least one person a day. Being in business, I would go on a business lunch with a vendor or potential customer, often for the first time, and feel a suffocating inward pressure to talk to them about God. Two emotions raged within me during these times. Part of me didn't want to embarrass myself or lose business and part of me struggled with the thought that I am trying to sell this person something that I wasn't sure of myself. How do I tell this person that God is a God of peace, while I am taking six Valium a day to deal with my own personal stress? This was my life for 40 years. This is why I can relate to Jesus' words to the religious leaders. It was Jesus saying to me, *"the very scriptures you so diligently study speak of Me, but you are blind to it."*

One day I was called to a hospital room to see my cousin, who was near death from an advanced stage of cancer. I hated hospitals but had no choice other than to go see my beloved friend, who had been a childhood buddy and now had a wife and children just like me. When I entered the room, I was overwhelmed by the profound peace my cousin had. He had more peace dying than I had living. The experience was so powerful it brought me to my knees before God beseeching Him with the prayer that *I would give up everything I had to experience the same peace of God that my cousin had.*

By God's mercy, it was not long before God led me to *Philippians 3:10, "That I may know Him and the power of His resurrection...."* Since then, I first study scripture to experience the fresh joy, love, and freedom that comes from growing deeper in knowing Him.

April 18

"Do not think that I will accuse you before the Father; the one who accuses you is Moses, in whom you have set your hope. ⁴⁶For if you believed Moses, you would believe Me, for he wrote about Me. ⁴⁷But if you do not believe his writings, how will you believe My words?"
—JOHN 5:45-47

In these last three verses, Jesus delivers His final rebuke to these nonbelieving religious leaders by referring to Moses who wrote the Law and who was highly respected by the Jewish people. Following the Mosaic Law was a deep source of pride for them. You can imagine the reaction when Jesus said that a *real* understanding of the Law would lead them to a belief in Christ, the One standing right in front of them. How is that possible?

A key component of the Law is *human performance—obey* and be blessed; *disobey* and be cursed—a simple cause-and-effect relationship with God *(Deuteronomy 11:26-28)*. Many thought this meant a person could be "good enough" to receive God's approval. The Law was given by God and contained a *perfect* standard. God's word declared that if they failed in any part of the Law, they failed in all of it *(James 2:10)*. They must keep *all* the Law, *all* the time, because that is what God's holiness and righteousness required.

What every Jewish person should have realized quickly is that *no one*, no matter how hard they tried, could keep *all* of what was required by God in the Law. The Apostle Paul in *Romans 3:20* said, *"Because by the works of the Law, no flesh will be justified in His sight; for through the Law comes the knowledge of sin."* *The Living Bible* is helpful here. *"Now do you see it? No one can ever be made right in God's sight by doing what the law commands. For the more we know of God's laws, the clearer it becomes that we aren't obeying them; his laws serve only to make us see that we are sinners."* This is the essence of Jesus' entire message to these leaders: *all of you are sinners in need of a Savior, who is standing right in front of you.*

LIVING WATER FOR TODAY:

*Of Him all the prophets bear witness that through His name **everyone who believes in Him receives forgiveness of sins**.*—ACTS 10:43

For today, recognize that every single prophet of old bore witness to the fact that *all* your sins, *all* your failures, *all* your shortcomings, *all* the things you don't like about yourself, are *completely forgiven* because you believe in Christ Jesus. *PTL!*

LIVING WATER FROM JOHN 5:25-47

April 9	When Jesus speaks His word into us, we believe.
April 10	The Father and Son are eternal life and have called us forth into this life.
April 11	Jesus came to give sight to the spiritually blind.
April 12	We are God's workmanship created in Christ Jesus for good works, which God prepared beforehand so that we would walk in them.
April 13	Jesus is the manifestation of God's will.
April 14	The testimony of Jesus is greater than man's; the Father who sent Him also testified about Him.
April 15	"By this we know that we abide in Him and He in us, because He has given us of His Spirit" *(1 John 4:13)*.
April 16	The result of God's loving act of mercy and grace is belief in Jesus.
April 17	The Spirit of the Living God writes on our hearts that our adequacy is from God.
April 18	We are all sinners in need of a Savior; everyone who believes in Jesus receives forgiveness of sins.

PRAYER

Father, I worship and praise You for Your mercy in choosing me and granting me Your Spirit, who daily writes on my heart a progressive understanding of You.
In my flesh, I am blind. I am just like these religious leaders trying to live my life separate from You in my own human efforts. This always leads to failure. I would be without any hope without Your Son Jesus, whom You sent to put belief in me for forgiveness of my sins, and to rescue me from eternal death. To You, I am filled with thanksgiving, worship, and praise. In Your
Son's precious name,
Amen.

JESUS SATISFIES!

———

JOHN 6:1-21

APRIL 19

Therefore Jesus, lifting up His eyes and seeing that a large crowd was coming to Him, said to Philip, "Where are we to buy bread, so that these may eat?" ⁶This He was saying to test him, for He Himself knew what He was intending to do. ⁷Philip answered Him, "Two hundred denarii worth of bread is not sufficient for them, for everyone to receive a little."

—JOHN 6:5-7

We have all been in situations just like Philip. From Philip's perspective, the situation looked insufficient and unsolvable. There was no way they could feed all these people. But did it look dire to the Lord? Of course not! He had already started to orchestrate the solution when He caused the little boy (or his mother) to think about packing a lunch that morning. So why do our circumstances often look scary and impossible to us? There is only one reason: because we can't see as God sees. Does anything look bleak or scary to God? Does anything look hopeless to Him? It certainly does to us because we can't see as God sees. We can't see that God already has it all handled. Or we can't see the end result of what we see today. All we see is the storm raging all around us and it looks hopeless. But God sees His purpose and the end result of all of it.

Here is something even more exciting. If you are a person who marks your book, put two large asterisks by this paragraph! We also can't see the good God is accomplishing in and through what looks like a crisis to us, today. This is what *Romans 8:28* is telling us. God is working ALL things together *for our good.* Are you worried about the path that your child is taking in their life? You may be worried sick about this or that, but right while you are worrying about the mess you see, God is working it all out for His glory, for your good, and for the good of your child's life. *PTL!* You just can't see it yet.

LIVING WATER FOR TODAY:

*And we know that **God causes all things to work together for good** to those who love God, to those who are called according to His purpose.*—ROMANS 8:28

For today, acknowledge that you believe and love God because you have been called by Him according to His purpose. Because of this reality, be assured that God is working *ALL* things together for your good today, even when you can't recognize it…yet. *PTL!*

April 20

*This He was saying to test him, for **He Himself knew what He was intending to do.***
—JOHN 6:6

This verse is one that I have never forgotten since the first time I read it because it makes clear that Jesus is the One in complete control of the situation. Jesus' question was not a "test" that Philip could "pass" or "fail." It was a means to draw His disciples' attention to something important that was about to happen. Jesus was not pondering the problem like Philip was. He already knew what He was going to do to feed this large crowd. That very morning He had placed on the heart of a young boy (or his mother) to pack a small lunch for the day. This was God's doing. Perhaps the small boy's mother and father were in the crowd with him, and as far as they knew, it was a lunch for the three of them and nothing more. *But God had other plans!*

Another verse I have never forgotten is *Genesis 50:20.* This Old Testament verse teaches us the same principle of God being in absolute control. It is one of the most compelling verses in all of scripture for its clarity and power. Joseph is speaking to his brothers, the same brothers who years before, through spite and jealousy, threw Joseph into a pit and then sold him into slavery to be carried off into Egypt to live a life of untold misery. It had been a profound injustice done him by the very brothers he was now addressing. When the brothers realized who it was that spoke to them, they were fearful because of what they had done to him many years before.

But this horrific injustice did not turn Joseph from God. He remained steadfast in his confidence that the mighty hand of God would control all things for his good. So much so, that he could say to his brothers, *"you meant evil against me, but God meant it for good."*

LIVING WATER FOR TODAY:

*As for you, you meant evil against me, **but God meant it for good in order to bring about this present result**, to preserve many people alive.*—GENESIS 50:20

For today, be comforted in this liberating truth: whatever problems you are facing, whatever injustice you are enduring, recognize that none of it is a waste. *God is using all of it to bring about His good work in you and through you, according to His purpose.*

APRIL 21

*One of His disciples, Andrew, Simon Peter's brother, said to Him, ⁹"**There is a lad here who has five barley loaves and two fish, but what are these for so many people?"** ¹⁰Jesus said, "Have the people sit down." Now there was much grass in the place. So the men sat down, in number about five thousand. ¹¹Jesus then took the loaves, and having given thanks, He distributed to those who were seated; likewise also of the fish as much as they wanted.*

—JOHN 6:8-11

In John, Jesus usually performs miracles on His own. Healing the crippled man of 38 years by the pool of Bethesda *(April 1-2)* is a good example. But at other times, while God's work is still His, He uses the actions of human agents to accomplish His purpose. So it is in today's verses. We don't ever have to stress over our life's ministry because God will always draw us to see and act according to what He would have us do.

For example, why did Andrew observe that one little boy had a tiny lunch of five barley loaves and two fish immediately after Philip had emphatically stated that it would take a year's wages in bread to give each a small bit *(John 6:7)*? Why would a small boy think to anticipate needing to bring a lunch that day? Did he think of it or was it his mother? Why would this little boy be willing to offer up all that he had (as little as it was) so that Jesus could use it to feed a multitude? All these human actions are good examples of how God works in our lives. He put this miracle in motion long before He had the crowd sit down. My guess is this little boy was not fretting about how little he had to share, but only excited to see what Jesus would do with what he had.

So it is with us today. God may show us some need, cause us to say something, or touch our hearts to act in some way to care for others. Do we focus on how little we have, or do we trust God to use whatever we have and whoever we are, to work His love and care into the lives of those He brings us in contact with? Again, *it is His work, not ours!*

LIVING WATER FOR TODAY:

*But to each one is given **the manifestation of the Spirit** for the common good.*—1 CORINTHIANS 12:7

For today, be confident that God has given you the precise *"manifestation of the Spirit"* (in terms of time, vision, interest, finances, gifts, and talents) that He purposes to use to minister through you to others. *PTL!* This is a wonderful freedom.

APRIL 22

*Jesus then took the loaves, and having given thanks, He distributed to those who were seated; likewise also of the fish as much as they wanted. ¹²**When they were filled**, He said to His disciples, "Gather up the leftover fragments so that nothing will be lost."*

—JOHN 6:11-12

Perhaps ten thousand people (five thousand men and another five thousand women and children) were following Jesus by this time because they saw the miracles He was performing. Jesus went up on a mountain (the Golan Heights today) and sat down with his disciples. No one needed to tell Him that the crowd grew hungry. He was highly attuned to the needs of those following Him (as He is with each of us today).

On *April 21* we looked at the little boy's five-loaves-and-two-fish lunch, but today's verses contain something even more comforting. These verses give us a wonderful insight into God's character. Our God is not aloof and remote, but present and attentive. He is a God who anticipates our needs and initiates circumstances that increasingly draw us to Him day by day, who is the only source of true satisfaction to us. This miracle, feeding the large crowd until they were *filled*, illustrates how Jesus alone anticipates, initiates, and satisfies all our needs. Nothing else but God can do this.

Early on in my life I thought getting married and having kids would do that. It didn't. Then I thought building a career and making money must be the missing element to happiness. No matter how much money I made, it was never enough. None of these earthly things fully satisfy. Why? Because the only thing that truly satisfies is God's life. Only God can fill us with His life: full of His peace, love, joy, contentment, and fulfillment. Jesus, in performing this miracle, gives us an insight into a God who loves to fully satisfy us from His infinite abundance. Do you hunger for more love, happiness, companionship, or fulfillment in life? Jesus will *fully satisfy your hunger* in His timing.

LIVING WATER FOR TODAY:

*The eyes of all look to You, and You give them their food in due time. ¹⁶**You open Your hand and satisfy the desire of every living thing.**—*PSALM 145:15-16

For today, turn to Jesus with your hunger and desires, knowing that from His open hand He will satisfy those desires in His time, according to His purpose. *Be comforted!*

APRIL 23

And they came to John and said to him, "Rabbi, He who was with you beyond the Jordan, to whom you have testified, behold, He is baptizing and all are coming to Him." ²⁷John answered and said, "A man can receive nothing unless it has been given him from heaven."

—JOHN 3:26-27

Many Christians have told me that they feel guilty about not doing enough for God. Like the little boy with only five loaves and two fish, they feel that caring for one grandchild or spouse at home is too small an offering to God. "I'm not feeding the multitudes, just my elderly parents," they might say. Consider for a moment a truth that will bring life-changing freedom to you in this matter of "serving God." Do you think that little boy was fretting over how little he had to offer Jesus? Or was he excited to see what Jesus would do with what little he had? Here is this freedom-truth: *The little boy just entrusted what he had to Jesus, and Jesus did the rest.* So it is with us today.

We have seen this wonderful freedom-truth before in *John 3:26-27*. Here it is in *The Living Bible*: "*So they came to John and said, 'Master, the man you met on the other side of the Jordan River—the one you said was the Messiah—he is baptizing too, and everybody is going over there instead of coming here to us.' ²⁷John replied, 'God in heaven appoints each man's work.'"* John's answer reveals this truth: *God appoints every person's work.* Has He appointed you to care for a child or spouse? Has He appointed you to pray for others? Don't minimize the ministry of your prayers. I have a friend who was an Apache helicopter pilot in Afghanistan. He told me that he could always tell when it was morning in America because he felt people's prayers supporting and protecting him. That was work appointed by God to be done.

LIVING WATER FOR TODAY:

Declaring the end from the beginning, and from ancient times things which have not been done, saying, "My purpose will be established, and I will accomplish all My good pleasure."

—ISAIAH 46:10

For today, carry this verse with you. Meditate on it and watch the Lord melt away all your worries and fears about all manner of things in your life. God has promised you *personally* that *HE* will accomplish *ALL* His purpose and good pleasure in your life. *PTL!*

April 24

My fruit is better than gold, even pure gold, and my yield better than choicest silver. ²⁰I walk in the way of righteousness, in the midst of the paths of justice, ²¹to endow those who love me with wealth, that I may fill their treasuries.

—PROVERBS 8:19-21

When I first read these verses, my personal life was a stressful mess. I looked pretty good on the outside at church, but my private life subsisted on popping Valium every day to keep the stress from overwhelming me. I plodded along in a fog, with a marriage that was gradually deteriorating, with more kids than I wanted to have, and with a business that never produced the level of income I thought I needed. When I first read words like "gold," "silver," and "fill their treasuries" I stopped reading. I wanted to discover what this was all about.

I will never forget what I found. It utterly blew my mind. To my surprise, the phrase *"My fruit"* is not referring to the psalmist, but to God. It refers to what God accomplishes *in us* over our lifetimes. Not just a ticket to heaven, but day by day. What He accomplishes in us is better than gold, even pure gold (no matter how wealthy we are). The verses go on, referring to God in the first person: *"my yield is better than choicest silver,"* and *"I walk in the way of righteousness ... that I may fill their treasuries."* What is it that God is filling our treasuries with? He is filling us with His wisdom, love, peace, joy, contentment, and fulfillment, until we have no unfulfilled desires. *Praise God!*

These verses are not about us doing something for God, but God doing everything for us until we are *filled* to the point where we have no unfulfilled desires. Imagine that! We no longer desire to feel more secure, which causes us to stress and strive for more worldly things, because God has become our security. We no longer desire for more of man's approval because we know that we are fully and eternally approved of by God.

LIVING WATER FOR TODAY:

*For **He has satisfied** the thirsty soul, and the hungry soul
He has filled with what is good.—*PSALM 107:9

For today, be comforted that God is at work in you *(Philippians 2:13)*, filling your thirsty/hungry soul with all the goodness of His own life! *Praise the Lord!*

A PERSONAL TESTIMONY

KNOWING GOD IN A DEEPER WAY

Every three years our company holds a National Leadership Conference (NLC). Usually, my wife and I, along with other executives making up a selection committee, pre-visit the locations we are considering for the next NLC. I remember visiting a five-star resort in the Bahamas for this reason.

When we got there, a lady representing the resort met us and spent the entire day with us, showing us a plethora of attractions, the pristine gardens, the immaculate rooms, and an impressive panoply of foods from a variety of cuisines. At some point during the day, she made a reference to God. As we walked along, I responded, "You know, I've got a great God-story to share with you some time." I just left it at that and would not have mentioned it again.

When evening arrived, she offered to take us to dinner, and we gladly accepted. During that dinner she reminded me of my earlier comment about a "God-story." So, I shared with her about the visit I made to my cousin who was near death from an advanced stage of cancer (*see* page 191). I told her how stressful my life was prior to this visit and how overwhelmed I was by the profound peace my cousin had. He had more peace dying than I had living. The experience was so powerful it brought me to my knees before God beseeching Him with the prayer that *I would give up everything I had to experience the same peace of God that my cousin had.*

At this point, she reached for her napkin and began to sob. As my wife comforted her, she told us of her quadriplegic son who was close to 20 years old. She shared how stressed she's been, worried sick that she would not be able to work long enough to save the money it would take to care for him when she is gone. Through her tears, she shared, "I just realized that I don't need any more money, I just need to know God in a deeper way." How wonderful is the faith that God brought to her? *I just need to know God in a deeper way.*

David says in *Psalm 94:19*, *"When my anxious thoughts* [like worry and stress] *multiply within me, Your consolations* [or knowing God in a deeper way through His word] *delight my soul."* It is my personal and constant testimony through decades of life's trials, that Jesus anticipates my every need and deeply satisfies *me* through His word. *Praise the Lord!*

April 25

*Now when evening came, His disciples went down to the sea, ¹⁷and after getting into a boat, they started to cross the sea to Capernaum. It had already become dark, and Jesus had not yet come to them. ¹⁸**The sea began to be stirred up** because a strong wind was blowing.*
—John 6:16-18

I n *Mark 6:45* we learn that Jesus took His disciples down to the boat and sent them ahead while He dispersed the multitude and returned to the mountain to pray. In His absence, as nightfall deepened and the disciples were still in transit to Capernaum, a strong wind arose and violently stirred up the waters. This certainly was perceived by the disciples as a life-threatening situation with the pounding waves threatening to overwhelm them. Yet, where was Jesus? Did the onset of this strong storm catch Him by surprise? Of course not! Scripture tells us that He is the One who created all things *(John 1:3)*, so he had complete control over this very storm. He could have calmed it with a single word while still on the mountain, yet He allowed it to gain strength. Nevertheless, to the disciples' perception, Jesus was not there when they needed Him.

Isn't that how we often perceive our own troubles? We feel tossed about in the middle of a maelstrom, and Jesus is nowhere to be found. But is that true? He is the One who is allowing the storm to exist in the first place. If He could solve all our troubles with a single word, yet He allows them to continue, then these "troubles" are accomplishing something important in our lives. God's intention is not to scare us or make us miserable, but to strengthen our faith and bring us into an abiding joy, even in the midst of our troubles (*see* DAY 1 *"Consider it all joy … when you encounter various trials" James 1:2* in *Joy for Today*: DEVOTIONAL STUDIES FROM JAMES FOR EVERYDAY LIFE).

LIVING WATER FOR TODAY:

*Consider it all joy, my brethren, **when you encounter various trials**, ³knowing that the testing* [exercise] *of your faith produces endurance. ⁴And let endurance have its perfect result, so that **you may be perfect and complete,** lacking in nothing.*—James 1:2-4

For today, recognize that God allows trials into your life to exercise your faith in a unique way that completes His *Romans 8:28* transforming work in you until you are a person who is full of joy and peace in every situation—*a perfect reflection of Christ in you!*

APRIL 26

Then, when they had rowed about three or four miles, they saw Jesus walking on the sea and drawing near to the boat; and they were frightened. ²⁰But He said to them, "It is I; do not be afraid."

—JOHN 6:19-20

When we find ourselves in the midst of troubles, particularly when they are the result of our own doing, we are tempted to believe that Jesus has abandoned us. On *April 25* we discovered that this is *never* the case. Rather, God is allowing troubles to touch our lives so He can perform His *Romans 8:28* good work in us. Here is another insight that is also true: when we are amid our troubles, while we are brooding in our thoughts that God has abandoned us or is punishing us in some way for our sins, we can easily fail to recognize the form Jesus uses to come to us *"walking on the sea* [of our troubles] *and drawing near to* [our] *boat."* We misidentify Him as something fearful and frightening.

Ask yourself, could Jesus have simply appeared directly into the boat? Yes, He could have done that easily. Then why did He choose to approach the boat by walking on the water? My sense is that Jesus was demonstrating to His disciples (and to us) that He is in control of *ALL* our circumstances and that we (His children) are as perfectly safe in the midst of our "troubled boat" as we are when standing on solid ground. He wants us to know that when He wants the "storms" in our lives to end, they will end. Meanwhile He is using them for our good. He is in complete control. When He approached the boat, Jesus wasn't being tossed by the wind or waves, He was walking on calm water. He was not being affected by the storm, but rather, was controlling the precise intensity and duration of the storm. So it is with our troubles today.

LIVING WATER FOR TODAY:

The LORD has established His throne in the heavens, and ***His sovereignty rules over all.*** —PSALM 103:19

For today, whatever difficulties you are facing in your life, recognize that your personal Lord and Savior Jesus is sovereign over *every single one of them*. He has allowed them to happen and is actively working through all of them for your good according to His purpose. *PTL!* What a comfort!

April 27

*So they were willing to receive Him into the boat, **and immediately the boat was at the land** to which they were going.*

—John 6:21

This verse is sometimes used to argue that we each must be "willing to receive" Jesus into "our boat." This attempt to personalize the interpretation of this verse robs it of true meaning. The *English Standard Version* reads, *"Then they were glad to take him into the boat"*; and the *New Living Translation* says, *"Then they were eager to let him in the boat."* This verse is referring to the disciples' collective response to Jesus' arrival. Their fear was blinding them, but once He spoke, their anxiety changed to gladness, and they were eager to have Him in the boat with them.

When considering today's verse, I have two questions for you. *First*, were the disciples at any greater risk in the storm than they were on land? Many of us feel that we are in a storm today as we read this devotional. Perhaps we are being buffeted by worries about a child, a job, someone's health, family finances, or relatives—you fill in the blank. We hunger for more calm in our lives, yet the storm feels unrelenting. But are we at any greater risk, no matter how much storm we feel around us, *when God is sovereign and in total control of everything?* In truth, the disciples (and us) are equally secure in stormy and calm times *because we are under the all-knowing, divine care of our Almighty God.*

Second, did God purpose to use the storm to reveal that He would perform miracles to care for His disciples (and you and me)? The answer should be obvious. He purposely sent His disciples ahead of Him while He remained behind to pray. He could have calmed the storm from the mountain, yet He chose to miraculously walk on water to reach them amid its violence. And God is performing miracles to protect us every day!

Living Water for Today:

Casting all your anxiety on Him, *because He cares for you.*—1 Peter 5:7

For today, do exactly what this scripture encourages you to do: Cast ALL your anxiety upon Jesus. Not some, or only the deep anxiety that you cannot handle yourself, but ALL your anxiety! He not only cares for you but will guard your heart and mind with the peace of God which surpasses all comprehension *(Philippians 4:7)*. PTL!

LIVING WATER FROM JOHN 6:1-21

April 19	God is working all things together for our good today, even when we can't recognize them—yet!
April 20	God is in complete control and using our problems to bring about His excellent work in and through us.
April 21	God has given each one of us a manifestation of the Spirit to minister to others in need.
April 22	Only God can fill us with His infinite abundance of peace, love, joy, and contentment.
April 23	God appoints every person's work, regardless of its apparent insignificance to us, according to His good pleasure.
April 24	God is filling our treasuries with all the goodness of His life until we have no unfulfilled desires.
April 25	God allows the trials in our lives to strengthen our faith in us, that we may be lacking in nothing.
April 26	Jesus is sovereign over every difficulty we face, working through all of them for our good.
April 27	Under the all-knowing, divine care of Almighty God, we are equally secure during stormy and calm times.

PRAYER

Father, You have demonstrated repeatedly in scripture that You are always willing to care for Your children and satisfy them deeply with Your love and peace, including times when, to our eyes, You perform miracles to care for us, to feed us, and hold us safe from our human storms. Our hearts swell in worship and praise to You, knowing that we are always safe and secure in Your Son Jesus, no matter what is happening in our lives each day. You are our rock and salvation, both eternally and each and every day. Thank You, dear Father, for Your faithfulness in caring for our every need, even when we don't understand what we truly need ourselves. In Your Son's precious name, Amen.

My Living Water Thoughts

BELIEVING IN CHRIST PLEASES GOD

———

JOHN 6:22-71

APRIL 28

*Jesus answered them and said, "Truly, truly, I say to you, you seek Me, not because you saw signs, but because you ate of the loaves and were filled. ²⁷Do not work for the food which perishes, but for the food which endures to eternal life, **which the Son of Man will give to you**, for on Him the Father, even God, has set His seal." ²⁸Therefore they said to Him, "What shall we do, so that we may work the works of God?"*

—JOHN 6:26-28

The crowd that Jesus had fed the day before finds Him again in Capernaum. They ask how He got there, but Jesus was not interested in small talk. He cut right through to what was really on their hearts. He tells them that they were not following Him because they saw miracles that only God could perform, but because of something far more basic: Jesus had fed them *for free*. Stop and put this in context. The Jewish people lived under the Mosaic Law which focused on *human performance—obey* and be blessed; *disobey* and be cursed *(Deuteronomy 11:26-28)*. There are no free lunches in this belief system. You must perform to receive a blessing from God. It is never just given to you *for free*, but that is exactly what Jesus had done. *He fed them all until they were full for free!*

Down through the ages, this general attitude has persisted. We are told that nothing is truly free. We must work for our paycheck. We must do certain things to get certain things or accomplish certain things. This is entirely contrary to God's way! His way focuses on *"the food which endures to eternal life, which the Son of Man **will freely give to you."*** The crowd, while still in a works-based mindset, asked Jesus *"What shall we do, so that we may work the works of God?"* Jesus' glorious answer is revealed tomorrow.

LIVING WATER FOR TODAY:

*The God who made the world and all things in it, since He is Lord of heaven and earth, does not dwell in temples made with hands; ²⁵**nor is He served by human hands**, as though He needed anything, since **He Himself gives to all people life and breath and all things**.*

—ACTS 17:24-25

For today, consider how much your upbringing has imprinted you with the notion that you must work to please God, rather than recognizing that eternal life (God's life, the Christian life) is all a *free* gift to you *from* God. *Your belief in Christ is evidence (not the cause) of God freely working in you. PTL! It is all free!*

April 29

*Jesus answered and said to them, "This is the work **of** God, **that you believe in Him whom He has sent.**"*

—John 6:29

In this short verse, Jesus makes two powerful statements by answering the crowd's question from two perspectives. First, from the crowd's works-based perspective, He is saying that God considers *our believing in His Son Jesus* as our complete work for God (which fully pleases Him). Second, from God's perspective, He reveals that the *work of God* is God's own divine work *in us* that produces our belief in Christ.

This verse is a great example of why it is so important to pay close attention to the little words in scripture. Look at the word "of" in this verse. It is easy to read over it, but it actually embodies the grandest of spiritual truths in the entire verse. Jesus tells us that it is the work OF God, not the work of man, that yields eternal life. The word "of" means "out of" or "from" God. Jesus is speaking of a work that flows *out of* or *from* God—that our believing in Christ is the resulting work of God in us and comes entirely from God.

Here is one more marvelous point. It is amazing how scripture expands and enlightens other scripture. We see this same principle from *John 6:29* in the book of *Acts*. A man named Apollos was encouraged to travel to Achaia to aid the church there. In *Acts 18:27b* we read, *"and when he had arrived, he greatly helped those who had **believed through grace.**"* The phrase *believed through grace* means they believed through God's enabling work of grace in them, or they believed through God's gift of belief to them.

Living Water for Today:

*For by grace you have been **saved through faith; and that not of yourselves, it is the gift of God;** [9]not as a result of works, so that no one may boast.*—Ephesians 2:8-9

For today, give thanks to God for this verse and how it dovetails with *John 6:29* to make it clear that you are eternally saved through faith (belief) in Jesus alone; and further, that your faith is not something you can boast about as though you worked to produce it yourself. There is great freedom in knowing that your faith is entirely a gift from God, which means that it is forever strong and stable in the face of every trial. You can never lose it. *PTL!*

This verse reveals one of the most thought-provoking truths in all of scripture. Jesus answers the crowd by telling them: *"This is the work of God, **that you believe in Him** [referring to Christ] **whom He** [God] **has sent."*** There is a belief today among some Christians (I know because I grew up under it), that by inviting Jesus into our life we are saved, which is like a "Get into Heaven Free ticket" for when we die. In the meantime, during our life, we need to work for that same God to please Him and show Him our appreciation for that gift of salvation. We need to be good disciples: witnessing to someone every day, helping out in our church, tithing, praying, reading our Bible more, and quitting all our bad habits. This concept was perfectly encapsulated in a sign I once saw outside a church. It read, *"Have you made God smile today?"* In earlier years, I would have driven away thinking, *did I make Him smile today?* Now, I praise God for what scripture declares: *Our belief in Christ, which God has given us, is what pleases God.* Far from making me lazy or giving me a "license to sin," just knowing that it is Christ alone that pleases God frees me to be sensitive to His leading day by day.

Whether we believe God chose us, or we choose God; whether we believe in free will, or the lack thereof; whether we must pray a specific prayer to invite Christ Jesus into our life or that it is God's unilateral decision to save us, Christians are divided by all these matters. If I go to lunch with someone who wishes to argue over any of these topics, I try to avoid it completely. But one thing unifies. There is real freedom in *John 6:29* for all of us, and it is the source of our true unity in Christ. The New Testament repeatedly declares, scores of times, that **we are saved simply by believing in Jesus Christ as our Savior.** He accomplished everything God demanded of us. That's why Jesus said on the cross: *it is finished*.

I don't care what church a person attends, or how many different doctrines we disagree on; if God has brought faith into that person's life to believe that Jesus Christ is God's Son sent to be the sacrifice for our sins, I am gloriously united with that person! Praise the Lord, we are all equal children of God!

APRIL 30

*So they said to Him, "What then do You do for a sign, so that we may see, and believe You?
What work do You perform? ³¹Our fathers ate the manna in the wilderness; as it is written,
'HE GAVE THEM BREAD OUT OF HEAVEN TO EAT.'" ³²Jesus then said to them, "Truly, truly,
I say to you, it is not Moses who has given you the bread out of heaven, but it is My Father
who gives you the true bread out of heaven. ³³For the bread of God is that which comes down
out of heaven, and gives life to the world." ³⁴Then they said to Him, "Lord, always give
us this bread." ³⁵Jesus said to them, "I am the bread of life; he who comes to Me will not
hunger, and he who believes in Me will never thirst. ³⁶But I said to you that you have seen
Me, and yet do not believe."*

—JOHN 6:30-36

S cripture has a wonderful way of communicating the real heart-condition of those
in the crowd who were following Jesus. They ask Jesus, *"What then do You do for
a sign, so that we may see, and believe You?"* You might be thinking: *are these people
serious?* It was only the day before when Jesus fed all of them from two small fish and
five barley loaves. These same people are now asking Jesus for a sign so they can see
and believe as if the previous day's miracle never happened. This pure sophistry
exposes their blindness!

But for those who believe, these verses are full of power and insight. Where does
our salvation come from? From our heavenly Father. Where does our faith and believing
come from? Again, from our heavenly Father. *"For the bread of God is that which comes
down **out of heaven**, and gives life to the world."* When the crowd asks for Jesus to keep
feeding them, He gives them the first of seven "I AM" descriptions we will see in John:
I AM the bread of Life. This is reminiscent of God's self-description in *Exodus 3:14.*

LIVING WATER FOR TODAY:

*These things I have **written to you who believe** in the
name of the Son of God, so that **you may know that you
have eternal life.**—*1 JOHN 5:13

For today, no matter how much you are struggling with hardship, worry, or sin from
your flesh, know that all of it will pass because there is one unchanging God who
has given you belief in His Son and through that belief, He is relentlessly working all
things together for your good *(Romans 8:28)*. What a priceless freedom!

May 1

*"All that the Father gives Me will come to Me; and the one who comes to Me **I will certainly not cast out**. ⁴⁴No one can come to Me unless the Father who sent Me **draws him;** and I will raise him up on the last day." ⁶⁵And He was saying, "For this reason I have said to you, that no one can come to Me **unless it has been granted him from the Father."***
—JOHN 6:37, 44, 65

Thus far, Jesus has made clear to the crowd that they cannot receive eternal life because they do not *believe*. The crowd gave Him the flimsy excuse that they needed to see a sign from Him before they could believe, even though they had all participated in exactly such a miraculous sign the day before when Jesus fed the 10,000.

When I read these verses, I often reach for a Kleenex. Jesus didn't leave us reading only about those who *fail* to believe (and thereby fail to receive eternal life). He also revealed insights into God's most magnificent miracle of all: our salvation resulting in eternal life! God *chose us* before the foundation of the world to be holy and blameless before Him *(Ephesians 1:4)*. To accomplish this, He *gave us* to Jesus *(John 6:37)*, and actively *draws us (John 6:44)* and *grants us* to come to Him *(John 6:65)*. To "draw" means to "induce to come" or "induce to believe"; and to "grant" means to grant or gift us with the faith to believe in Christ. So again, we see our belief in Christ comes from God.

Here is the exciting part. Jesus uses the little word *ALL* to convey a powerful absolute—*everyone* that the Father has given to Jesus *WILL* come to Jesus! There are no exceptions. There is no requirement that we accept because *we are the gift* being given from Father to Son. Jesus doesn't say that "a lot," or "many," or "a majority" will come. No, Jesus said *ALL* that the Father has given Him *will* come. Does Jesus then decide to accept some and reject others? No! He says that *"the one who comes to Me I will certainly not cast out."*

LIVING WATER FOR TODAY:

*Just as **He chose us in Him before the foundation of the world**, that we would be holy and blameless before Him. In love* ...—EPHESIANS 1:4

For today, abide in this wonderful truth: God has chosen *you* before the foundation of the world (before He created anything) to be holy and blameless before Him in Christ Jesus. Not by the way you act, but by the righteousness of Christ abiding in you. *PTL!*

MAY 2

*Jesus said to them, "**I am the bread of life**; he who comes to Me **will not hunger**, and he who believes in Me **will never thirst**. ³⁶But I said to you that you have seen Me, and yet do not believe. ³⁷All that the Father gives Me will come to Me, and the one who comes to Me I will certainly not cast out. ³⁸For I have come down from heaven, not to do My own will, but the will of Him who sent Me. ³⁹This is the will of Him who sent Me, that of all that He has given Me I lose nothing, but raise it up on the last day."*
—John 6:35-39

I know a dear Christian who once told me how he had lived most of his life in fear because he was taught that if he died with any unconfessed sin in his life he would not go to heaven. For decades I was also tormented by worry that I could lose my salvation. Yes, "you are saved by God's grace" I was told, but then came the catch—I still needed to be a good disciple of Christ. In other words, it still came back to my performance. But what if I didn't witness *enough*, pray *enough*, tithe *enough*, attend church *enough*, or (God forbid) I had a lustful thought, what then? The answer was, "Well, maybe you weren't saved in the first place." Thank God for today's freedom-verses from John.

Verse 35 tells us the glorious truth about how secure our salvation really is. It says, *"he who believes in Me **will never thirst**."* To *never thirst* means believers will *never* be without their eternal life. Also *verse 37* says: *"All that the Father gives Me will come to Me, and the one who comes to Me I will certainly not cast out."* "But Daryl," some have said to me, "maybe Jesus doesn't cast us out, but we can cast *ourselves* out from our salvation, if we at some point choose not to believe in Christ." In response, I never argue. I merely refer them to *verse 39*, *"This is the will of Him who sent Me, that of all that He has given Me **I lose nothing**."* Scripture is clear: All who God has chosen—come to Jesus. All that come to Jesus—believe. All that believe, He loses *none* of them. *PTL!*

LIVING WATER FOR TODAY:

*But when the kindness of God our Savior and His love for mankind appeared, ⁵**He saved us**, not on the basis of deeds which we have done in righteousness, but **according to His mercy**, by the washing of regeneration and renewing by the Holy Spirit.*—Titus 3:4-5

For today, consider all that God has done for you without expecting you to do anything in return—how permanent your salvation really is in Christ—*you are as secure as Christ!*

MAY 3

*"It is written in the prophets, 'AND THEY SHALL ALL BE TAUGHT OF GOD.' **Everyone who has heard and learned from the Father, comes to Me.**"*

—JOHN 6:45

What a wonderful verse, full of assurance! Jesus is referencing from the Old Testament *Isaiah 54:13* and *Jeremiah 31:34* that prophesied about Him. *Isaiah 54:13* tells us that *"All your sons will be taught of the LORD; and the well-being of your sons will be great."* Today's verse echoes that prophesy. To be *taught of God* means God grants a person to *hear* and *learn* from Him. This is a reference to God's work in us *(John 6:29)* which actively draws us to His Son Jesus *(John 6:44)*. What is the result of this teaching? All who are taught (or drawn) by God come to Jesus *(John 6:45)* and believe in Him *(John 6:29)*. None of us would ever think about God or believe in Him on our own *(Romans 3:11-12)*. Only God drawing us, and granting us belief in Jesus, *is what saves us.*

Here is how *The Living Bible* translates *John 6:45*: *"As it is written in the Scriptures, 'They shall all be taught of God.' Those the Father speaks to, who learn the truth from him, **will be attracted to me.**"* Many think that our belief *initiates* our attraction to Jesus. But these verses tell us the opposite: our belief is the *result* of God attracting us to His Son.

Why is this important? If our attraction to God is a *result* of God's work rather than sourced in us, then our attraction to God is *evidence* that we are eternally saved. The test is not whether we act perfect or have smooth circumstances. The absolute test of our eternal salvation is the existence in our heart of an attraction to God-things. *PTL!*

LIVING WATER FOR TODAY:

*"They will not teach again, each man his neighbor and each man his brother, saying, 'Know the LORD,' for **they will all know Me**, from the least of them to the greatest of them,"declares the LORD, "for **I will forgive their iniquity, and their sin I will remember no more.**"*—JEREMIAH 31:34

For today, rejoice that you have been chosen by God to know the Lord. He has granted you the glorious blessing of both hearing and learning from Him as He teaches you. Your sins and iniquity no longer keep you separated from Him because He has forgiven them all and remembers them no more. *PTL!*

MAY 4

*"Truly, truly, I say to you, **he who believes has eternal life.**"*
—JOHN 6:47

This verse from Jesus' own mouth teaches the simplest, yet most powerful, of gospels. It is yet another verse from scores of verses in John that declares the same *life-giving* truth:

He who believes.

HE WHO BELIEVES.

HE WHO BELIEVES HAS ETERNAL LIFE!

Forgive me for repeating this glorious freedom-truth from God's word again and again. Has this phrase seized your heart in its life-changing embrace? I know from my own experience that the more God infuses this scriptural truth into my heart, the more He strips away religious baggage and preconceived notions of what salvation, eternal life, and being a Christian is all about. *It drives me to my knees in worship and praise to Him!*

My salvation is not something I strive for or work at. It is not based on my Christian heritage or being the son of a preacher. It is not the result of my willingness to pray a certain prayer or testify before an assembly of believers. In fact, it isn't anything I can boast of at all. It is *ALL* God's work! We are eternally saved solely because God decided to choose us, grant us belief in His Son, and give us into the caring hands of Jesus. And one more glorious point: The present tense verb *has* in the phrase *"he who believes **has** eternal life"* is active and indicative, meaning a *permanent and irrevocable possession. PTL!*

LIVING WATER FOR TODAY:

*For God so loved the world, that He gave His only begotten
Son, that **whoever believes in Him** shall not perish,
but have eternal life.*—JOHN 3:16

For today, appreciate how simple, yet powerful, God's message is for you. It is not *whoever* works, labors, strives, or achieves, but *whoever believes* in God's Son has eternal life. True freedom in Christ comes when all preconceived assumptions and all ifs, ands, or buts concerning God's word are set aside, freeing you to listen and be taught directly from God concerning what His word says. *PTL! **Whoever believes!***

MAY 5

As a result of this many of His disciples withdrew and were not walking with Him any-more. ⁶⁷So Jesus said to the twelve, "You do not want to go away also, do you?" ⁶⁸Simon Peter answered Him, "Lord, to whom shall we go? You have words of eternal life. ⁶⁹We have believed and have come to know that You are the Holy One of God."
—JOHN 6:66-69

Through this entire conversation with the crowd, Jesus spoke piercing words to them—words that they could not understand yet could not avoid. He spoke to their deepest need for eternal life. Yet, what motivated the crowd was nothing deeper than following Him in hopes of participating in another free lunch or dinner. What do you think the crowd had in mind when they told him they needed to see a sign and then immediately told Him about their fathers being given manna in the wilderness out of heaven? *They wanted another free meal!* Jesus told them His Father was the One who gave their fathers that manna, and now gave them His Son as the Bread of Life. Jesus invited them to eat and drink of Him and receive eternal life. This was too much for the crowd to hear.

Verse 66 picks up the narrative where many of His disciples (meaning many in the crowd who had been following Him) withdrew from following any longer. Seeing this, Jesus turned to his group of 12 disciples and asked if any of them were going to leave as well. Peter gave the reply, *"Lord, to whom shall we go? You have words of eternal life. We have believed and have come to know that You are the Holy One of God."*

Out of the vast thousands in the crowd that day, how did Peter know to say that? The crowd was mostly hanging out waiting for another free meal, but Peter recognized Jesus as the Holy One of God, whose very words are eternal life. How did Peter know this? The answer to that question is revealed in tomorrow's devotional verses.

LIVING WATER FOR TODAY:

But know that the LORD has set apart the godly man for Himself; the LORD hears when I call to Him.—PSALM 4:3

For today, rejoice that you have been set apart by the Lord to have His eternal life. This is not only a one-time event for heaven one day. God's hears you every time you call (pray) to Him. *He always hears you so just continue to pray! PTL!*

MAY 6

*He said to them, "But who do you say that I am?" ¹⁶Simon Peter answered, "You are the Christ, the Son of the living God." ¹⁷And Jesus said to him, "Blessed are you, Simon Barjona, because **flesh and blood did not reveal this to you, but My Father who is in heaven.**"*

—MATTHEW 16:15-17

To the extent we know anything about the 12 disciples, scripture reveals the most about Peter. Yes, we know of Judas betraying Jesus, but God's word tells us the most about Peter's day-to-day reactions, ego, and self-delusions. We know how aggressive he was, carrying a sword even though he was walking in the presence of Almighty God who could certainly protect him from harm. We know how impetuous he was, using that sword to cut off the ear of one sent to arrest Jesus as though Jesus couldn't take care of Himself. And we know that this same Peter denied Jesus three times in a matter of hours. In other words, he was pretty much like us with all our human frailties.

It was this Peter who answered Jesus' question, "But who do you say that I am?" Peter did not hesitate. *"You are the Christ, the Son of the living God,"* he said. Jesus answered, *"flesh and blood did not reveal this to you, but My Father who is in heaven."* What a glorious revelation Jesus has given us in His answer. Today, we believe *exactly* what Peter believed: *Jesus is the Christ, the Son of the living God!* Peter did not arrive at this answer based on anything he acquired during his flesh and blood life. This understanding could only come directly from God. For us, no amount of hard work in our church, no amount of study in seminary, no amount of reading scriptures, none of it has brought us to this understanding. Only our Heavenly Father—Almighty God Himself—revealed this to us. We, along with Peter, believe in a truth that only God could reveal. This is again *irrefutable evidence* that we have received eternal life. *PTL!*

LIVING WATER FOR TODAY:

*Now I say this, brethren, that **flesh and blood cannot inherit the kingdom of God;** nor does the perishable inherit the imperishable.*—1 CORINTHIANS 15:50

For today, grab a tissue and rejoice that you believe today exactly what Peter believed: *that Jesus is the Christ, the Son of the living God!* And God says to you: *"Blessed* [eternally joyful and happy] *are you." PTL!*

A QUESTION TO CONSIDER

WHY IS THIS SO IMPORTANT FOR US TO UNDERSTAND?

Over the last several days we have been prayerfully considering Jesus' own spoken words in *John 6* concerning belief, and the source of the belief that results in eternal life. As we have learned from these John 6 verses, if the kind of belief that produces eternal life is all from God and not from us, then four truths become apparent:

First, this truth *removes our pride (and judgmental attitudes)*. There is no room for prideful thinking; that we somehow independently believed in Christ and others did not. There is no pride when we understand that our salvation is all God's grace and mercy toward us. And there are no grounds for judgment, when we are no more capable of believing on our own than those who do not believe.

Second, this truth *eliminates an argumentative spirit*. We no longer have our fleshly appetite to argue with people, as well-intentioned as we may be, trying to convince them to believe in Christ. It takes us out of the picture other than joyfully sharing about what Jesus has done in our own lives. We can now leave it to God to draw them and grant them belief in His Son Jesus. It is no longer about our debating skills, but Christ.

Third, this truth *frees us from feeling responsible for another person's salvation*. God is well able to bring those He has chosen to His Son precisely when it pleases Him to do so *(Galatians 1:15-16)*. No amount of our manipulation or self-effort can accomplish it.

Fourth, this truth *removes any boasting*. In those times when someone is attracted to the Lord through our caring for them, it is God who is drawing them, not us or our exceptional skill. We have nothing to boast in but God's mercy and grace toward us!

EPHESIANS 2:8-9

*"For by grace you have been saved through faith; and that not of yourselves,
it is the gift of God; 'not as a result of works, so that no one may boast."*

LIVING WATER FROM JOHN 6:22-71

April 28	The food which endures to eternal life, which the Son of Man shall give to you, is FREE!
April 29	Belief in Christ is the resulting work of God in us and comes entirely from Him.
April 30	The bread of God is that which comes down from heaven and gives life to the world.
May 1	All (everyone) that the Father has given to Jesus will come to Him.
May 2	He who believes in Jesus shall never thirst; our eternal life is secure in Christ forever.
May 3	Everyone who has heard and learned from the Father, comes to Jesus.
May 4	"He who believes has eternal life" means our eternal life is a permanent and irrevocable possession.
May 5	Jesus, the Holy One of God, speaks the words of eternal life.
May 6	Jesus is the Christ, the Son of the living God.

PRAYER

Father, You are the living God! Like Peter, I believe Your Son Jesus is the Christ. I believe He is my Savior and Redeemer. I believe that but for Your working in me, choosing me before the foundation of the world, granting me life-saving belief, drawing me to Your Son, and giving me eternally into His care and protection, I would still be dead in my trespasses and sins, and hopelessly blind in darkness. Your word is clear—only a belief sourced from You can eternally save me. I can do nothing to save myself. I am no better than anyone else. I have nothing to boast in. You alone deserve all my praise and worship. What a glorious freedom—from stress, worry, anxiety, and guilt—from the exhaustion of striving for salvation through my own effort. I cannot worship and praise You enough! In Your Son's glorious and victorious name, Amen.

JESUS CONTROLS
OUR
CIRCUMSTANCES

———

JOHN 7:1-53

A SPECIAL WORD TO THE READER...

I have previously shared that the greatest fear I harbored for nearly half of my adult life was the fear of whether I would truly wake up in heaven when I died *(see page 159)*. The second most debilitating fear I struggled with is addressed in the upcoming devotionals that explore *John 7:1-53 (May 7-12)*. This secondary fear was a close runner-up to my primary fear. It was, in fact, the more tenacious, pernicious, and relentless of my fears. The resulting doubt that infused my mind was subtle—yet all-encompassing—raising its ugly head in any number of situations and circumstances. The fearful worry: **"Am I in God's will?"** would infect my thinking and rarely stopped there. More questions followed: *What really **IS** God's will? How do I find God's will for my life, and will I know it when I see it? If I see it, how do I do it? What happens when I fall out of God's will (if I can ever get into it in the first place)?* Or, to put it another way, *how do I stay in God's will if that's possible?* And perhaps the most pervasive iteration of this worry: *Are the problems I am facing right now in my life the result of me being out of God's will?* It is fair to say during this stretch of my life that knowing God's will was profoundly more elusive, confusing, and stressful than it was comforting, peaceful, and reassuring.

Over the next few days of devotionals, we will explore two glorious truths: (i) that Jesus is controlling all our daily circumstances; and (ii) that God has put us in His will forever! And He (not us) will never allow us to fall out of His will! Reading this, you may be filled with genuine "what if" questions, like: *"Aren't all my bad choices or sinful thoughts and actions evidence that I am **out** of God's will?" "What if I made a bad choice and now, I am suffering the consequences?"* Or *"what if I can't break free from a destructive sin or habit? Surely, I must be out of God will!"* I can only tell you that I have entertained all these questions myself and completely understand where you are coming from. But what we will consider in the following days, as the Holy Spirit enlightens us within, will bring us immense peace and freedom daily, until we have nothing left to say but **praise the Lord, praise the Lord!**

MAY 7

*"Go up to the feast yourselves; I do not go up to this feast because My time has not yet fully come." ⁹Having said these things to them, He stayed in Galilee. ¹⁰But when His brothers had gone up to the feast, then **He Himself also went up, not publicly, but as if, in secret.***

—JOHN 7:8-10

I n *John 6:4* we read about the Passover feast, and now in *John 7:2* we come to the eight-day celebration Feast of Tabernacles. This means the Apostle John has jumped about six months ahead in his narrative of Jesus' sojourn on earth. Things are now heating up with growing opposition from the Jewish leaders, including repeated references to threats on His life *(John 7:1, 13, 19, 25, 30, 32, 44; 8:37, 40, 59).* But scripture repeatedly tells us that it was not Jesus' time *(John 2:4; 7:6, 8, 30; 8:20).* The phrase *My time* in *verse eight* refers to Jesus acting in accordance with the will of His Father. God protected His Son in every circumstance until the time was exactly right *(John 12:23, 27; 13:1; 16:32; 17:1).* Jesus does the same in the lives of each and every believer.

Some question whether Jesus lied to His brothers when He told them that He would not go to the feast. This is not the case. His brothers tried to convince Jesus to *publicly participate in the feast as a pilgrim* in the same way they planned to participate. To do this, Jewish families would travel as pilgrims to Jerusalem and construct primitive shelters out of leaves and branches. They would then live in these shelters for the duration of the eight-day feast to commemorate God's faithful blessings upon the Israeli people as they wandered in the desert wilderness. Jesus would not go to the feast as a pilgrim, but He would go to deliver a prophetic message from God for which he awaited His time.

LIVING WATER FOR TODAY:

*"For whoever does the will of My Father who is in heaven, **he** is My brother and sister and mother."*—MATTHEW 12:50

For today, meditate on this verse, praying that God will grant you insight into the cause-and-effect order in the verse. You do not acquire membership in God's family by successfully doing the Father's will. Living out God's will in your life is the evidence and result of God choosing you to be in His family in the first place. *PTL!*

CONNECTING THE THEOLOGICAL DOTS:

God reveals in *John 7:1-53* how He was controlling Jesus' circumstances for His protection until His perfect hour had arrived. To see God's working in this way is very comforting. Let's take a closer look at God's care in protecting Jesus:

In *John 7:25-30* Jesus arrives at the feast and is speaking publicly, declaring that He is from the Father. Some of the people do recognize Him as the Christ but are puzzled why the leaders (who want to kill Jesus), don't seem to recognize Him and have said nothing to Him. God was blinding the Jewish leaders' understanding to protect Jesus. *Verse 30* tells us that *"no man laid his hand on Him, because His hour had not yet come."*

By this time, *John 7:31-33* tells us that many of the crowd believed in Jesus. It was causing such a ruckus that the Jewish leaders heard the crowd and sent officers to seize Him. Yet again, these officers could not lay hands on Him because, as Jesus said in *verse 33*, He was with them for a little while longer.

In *John 7:40-44*, at just the right time, God raised up a dispute among the people concerning the identity of Jesus. One group declaring that Jesus was the Prophet that Moses had prophesied; while others doubted that such a Prophet could come out of Galilee. This indecision blunted the resolve to seize Jesus; again, God protected Him.

Then in *John 7:45-46* the temple officers came back to the Jewish leaders, having failed to seize Jesus as commanded. Their answer: *"Never has a man spoken the way this man speaks."* Jesus' own words were so powerful that they protected Him from capture. Finally, in *John 8:20* Jesus is in the temple's treasury teaching openly, yet no one seized Him, *"because His hour had not yet come."*

This entire narrative is a demonstration of how God guides our circumstances and protects us each day according to His will. We sometimes wish some things in our life were different. We may wish we had a different job, stronger finances, better health, or less trouble with family members. How much easier life would be, if only [fill in the blank]. But God is all-knowing! He knows our every circumstance and He allows all things into our life, just at the right moment, for His glory and our eternal good. *PTL!*

MAY 8

*And **we know** that God causes **all things** to work together for good to those who love God, to those who are called according to His purpose.*
—ROMANS 8:28

God knows our every circumstance. He allows every detail in our life to be there in His perfect timing. The phrase *"we know"* in this verse refers to a fact, something we have confidence in as true, that God causes ***ALL THINGS*** to work for our good. Ask yourself this question: What does the phrase *"all things"* in this verse exclude? Does it exclude a rebellious child? Does it exclude all the wrong choices we have made in life? What exactly does it exclude? The answer is self-evident. ALL THINGS is an absolute! Nothing is excluded. That rebellious child is not excluded, nor are any of our mistakes in life, including the very worst of them. *God works **all things** for His glory and our good.*

For the first 30-years of my life I worshipped the unholy trinity of money, success, and glory (hunger for respect from others). How God could be controlling, allowing, and working all my fleshly cesspool of selfishness during those years for His glory and my good was beyond my comprehension. Yet today, I wouldn't change any of it. Only by living half my life enslaved to my self has brought me to my knees in humble worship to God for His unfathomable mercy and love for me. I lived not wanting too much of God for fear He would take the fun out my life. I lived only wanting enough God to get me into heaven when I died. But God loved me more than that and had other plans. He knew how empty, tired, and stressed I was. He worked every circumstance in my early years to the point where I became burned out; then He brought me to my cousin's death bed to show me a man who had more peace dying than I had living. Even my beloved cousin's tragic death worked for my good.

LIVING WATER FOR TODAY:

*As for you, you meant evil against me, **but God meant it for good** in order to bring about this present result, to preserve many people alive.*—GENESIS 50:20

For today, with thanksgiving and great worship in your heart, recall as many circumstances in your life as God brings to your mind where things looked dire, only to see them later as life-changing blessings for your good. Rejoice with a full heart of praise, for God has worked all these things for His glory, and for your good. *PTL!*

MAY 9

*But when it was now the midst of the feast Jesus went up into the temple, and began to teach. ¹⁵The Jews then were astonished, saying, "**How has this man become learned, having never been educated?**" ¹⁶So Jesus answered them, and said, "My teaching is not Mine, but His who sent Me. ¹⁷If anyone is willing to do His will, he will know of the teaching, whether it is of God or whether I speak from Myself."*
—JOHN 7:14-17

In the middle of the feast, when the greatest number of people would be there to listen, Jesus went up to the temple and began to teach. *"The Jews"* referred to in *verse 15* were a different group than the Jewish crowd in attendance. These were the learned Jews who marveled at Jesus' teaching. According to them, He had no schooling or rabbi to teach Him! We would say today that he had no seminary training. Jesus answered their grumblings directly, declaring that His teaching came from His heavenly Father.

The Lord's reply here is so comforting! God was speaking through Him; and by extension, He was speaking to us. We need no seminary training to recognize that Jesus' words are God's words spoken to us. Anyone who *"is willing to do His will, he will know of the teaching, whether it is of God."* Some misinterpret this verse, thinking it requires a person to be willing to do God's will *BEFORE* they can understand His words. This is opposite to the context of the entire book of John. It is God who draws us and puts His will in us which is willing to do His will *(Philippians 2:13)*. We cannot muster saving belief on our own! Anyone who desires God's will (referring to every Christian), will be blessed by God with the knowledge that Jesus' words are God's words. *We will know when we read scripture that God is speaking to us!*

LIVING WATER FOR TODAY:

*For since in the wisdom of God the world through
its wisdom **did not come to know God**, God was well-
pleased through the foolishness of the message preached
to save those **who believe.** —1 CORINTHIANS 1:21*

For today, appreciate that you *know* God in a different way from how the world knows Him. Rejoice in the gospel's message: ***Christ died for you on the cross.*** This is foolishness to the world's wisdom, *but precious truth to you who believes in Christ as your Savior.* God has given you that *knowing* of Him in an experiential and life-saving way!

MAY 10

*"If anyone is willing to do His will, **he will know** of the teaching, whether it is of God or whether I speak from Myself. ¹⁸He who speaks from himself seeks his own glory; but He who is seeking the glory of the One who sent Him, He is true, and there is no unrighteousness in Him."*

—JOHN 7:17-18

The phrase *"he will know"* comes from the Greek word γινώσκω ("ginōskō") which in the book of John refers to an active fellowship with God. It doesn't mean something grasped as an intellectual understanding; but rather, something known experientially. For example, the foundation of every Christian's experience of God's love is on an individual and personal level—we feel it, not just understand that "God is love" in our head. We also feel His love as it spreads to others through us. A *"ginōskō knowing"* means to experience God's eternal life (God's quality of life) personally every day; it goes much deeper than knowing a lot of scripture and doctrine. One of the earliest church fathers, Augustine, put it this way: *"Understanding is the reward* [result] *of faith ... What is 'If any man be willing to do his will'? It is the same thing as to believe"* (quoted in John 7:17 note section, NASB, 1531) We have already seen many times in John: *belief is given to us from God!*

Here is some more freedom from *verse 17*. It says if a person is *"willing to do His will,"* not if a person *"DOES God's will."* To be willing means to desire God's will. Does that mean we must be perfect in doing God's will to understand His teaching? Not at all. In fact, that is impossible. Every Christian still deals with the daily warring of our flesh against the Spirit. But all believers have one thing in common: *we all desire God and are attracted to His will.* Some say this teaches "too much grace" and leads to a "license to sin." This same old argument was used against the Apostle Paul. Tomorrow, we look at Paul's answer to this criticism in *Romans 6:17-18.*

LIVING WATER FOR TODAY:

*Friendship with God is reserved for those who reverence him. **With them alone he shares the secrets of his promises.*** —PSALM 25:14 (TLB)

For today, draw close to God as His dear friend. Know Him a little more today as He shares His secrets and promises of renewing your mind and transforming you with His own quality of life in you. *PTL!*

MAY 11

But thanks be to God that though you were slaves of sin, you became obedient from the heart to that form of teaching to which you were committed, [18]*and **having been freed from sin, you became slaves of righteousness.***

—ROMANS 6:17-18

From time to time I am approached by someone with concerns that if too much grace is taught it will lead Christians to adopt a lifestyle of sin, full of every conceivable debauchery the world has to offer. *"Why not?"* they say to me, *"if a person is already saved unconditionally?"* Well, today's verses in *Romans* reveal a REALLY BIG "why not."

Romans 6:17-18 assures us that it is *IMPOSSIBLE* for any true believer to freely engage in a *constant* lifestyle of fleshly sin. I didn't say that we don't sin or make wrong choices. We all do that. What is impossible for any believer is to be *re*-enslaved back to sin as the controlling master in our life once God has eternally saved us. God has chosen us and granted us life-saving belief in Jesus. The Apostle Paul explains it this way: we all were once slaves to sin, but now, having been freed from our slavery to sin (through Christ Jesus' work on the cross), we have become slaves to righteousness. Sin is no longer our master. Jesus, who is our righteousness *(1 Corinthians 1:30)* is now our master. *PTL!*

The word "slave" in today's verses brings frequent tears to my eyes. It is from the Greek word δοῦλος ("duolos"), which means "one whose will (referring to our human will) is swallowed up by the will of another" (referring to God's will). Paul is saying that every true believer has God's will (righteousness) as their heart's primary desire. This does not mean that we live it every day, but only that it is God's will we desire. This is what Paul illustrates from his own life in *Romans 7:21-22*. He finds that he has both evil in his flesh and God in his "inner man." He concludes: *"Therefore there is now no condemnation for those who are in Christ Jesus." (Romans 8:1)*. PTL!

LIVING WATER FOR TODAY:

*And now you are free from your old master, sin; and **you have become slaves to your new master, righteousness.**—*ROMANS 6:18 (TLB)

For today, don't be discouraged that you still do sinful things or have sinful thoughts; *rejoice rather that you desire God in your heart!* That is *evidence* God has saved you!

The fact that "we are always in God's will" flies in the face of what most of us (me included) have been taught our whole lives; but God's word teaches what it teaches:

Philippians 2:13: *"For it is God who is* [present tense and continuous] *at work in you* [believers], *both to will* [grow our desire for Him] *and to work for His good pleasure."*

Romans 8:14: *"For all who are* [present tense and continuous] *being led by the Spirit of God* [every Christian], *these are sons of God."*

2 Corinthians 9:8: *"And God is able to make all grace* [every blessing] *abound to you, so that always having all sufficiency in everything, you may have an abundance for every good deed."* In *Isaiah 46:10* God also declares, *"My purpose will be established, and I will accomplish all My good pleasure."* Does that include God accomplishing all His good pleasure with, and in, and through us? Yes!

Ephesians 2:10: *For we are* [present tense and continuous] *His work-manship* [not IF we let Him. We ARE His workmanship], *created in Christ Jesus* [He is the Creator God, and we are the created] *for good works* [referring to what God desires to accomplish in our life], *which God prepared beforehand* [long before we were born, God determined what would come into our lives, and what specific things He would accomplish in and through us] *so that we would* (as a matter of fact) *walk in them.*

Ezekiel 36:26-27: *"Moreover, I will give you a new heart and put a new spirit within you; and I will remove the heart of stone from your flesh and give you a heart of flesh. ²⁷ I will put My Spirit within you **and cause you** to walk in My statutes, and you will be careful to observe My ordinances."*

Proverbs 20:24 (TLB): *"Since the Lord is directing our steps, why try to understand everything that happens along the way?"*

It doesn't matter if we understand what God is doing daily in our life. To be in God's will is not that we walk without sin every day (that's for glory). God's will relates to His progressive transformation of our lives over the course of our lives for His glory and our good!

May 12

Now on the last day, the great day of the feast, Jesus stood and cried out, saying, "If any-one is thirsty, let him come to Me and drink. ³⁸He who believes in Me, as the Scripture said, 'From his innermost being will flow rivers of living water.'" ³⁹But this He spoke of the Spirit, whom those who believed in Him were to receive; for the Spirit was not yet given, because Jesus was not yet glorified.

—John 7:37-39

I thought scripture was complicated for so many years, but it really is simple when we don't try to force our human qualifiers on it. Today's verse says: *"He who believes in Me ... From his innermost being* [spirit] *will flow rivers of living water."* Does it say he who believes AND lives an upright and sinless life? No. Does it say he who believes AND has gotten victory over all their bad habits? No. John repeats scores of times in his gospel that *belief is the only criteria* for experiencing this living water flowing from within us. What does this flowing, living water refer to? It means we will experience a growing desire for and understanding of God's word; a growing understanding of how sinful our lives are apart from Christ; a growing comfort in prayer; and a growing love for others.

This verse is informing us of a glorious freedom-fact! This is not a conditional goal that we attempt to attain, it is a *fact* that exists for every person (Christian) who believes. It is an event that became fact when Jesus was glorified, and the Spirit was given. It is the Spirit who accomplishes this flow of living water from within us. The *flow* is the writing of the Spirit on our hearts: *"Being manifested that **you are a letter of Christ** ... written not with ink but with the Spirit of the living God" (2 Corinthians 3:3).* It is God, not us. The simple truth is: If you believe in Christ Jesus as your Lord, that *belief is evidence that God has chosen you, redeemed you, saved you, dwells in you, and is **writing on your heart forever!***

Living Water for Today:

*But we all, with unveiled face, beholding as in a mirror the glory of the Lord, **are being transformed into the same image from glory to glory,** just as from the Lord, the Spirit.*—2 Corinthians 3:18

***For today**, though you may have troubles like all the Corinthians did, you are a letter of Christ that manifests more and more of Christ as God's Spirit writes on your heart, progressively transforming you from glory to glory into a true mirror image of Him!*

A PERSONAL TESTIMONY

GOD'S WILL OR COINCIDENCE?

My wife and I travel to Phoenix to visit my brother each winter. I purchase tickets weeks in advance when we make this trip, but a recent trip had to be delayed by one day because a dear friend of mine had died and his memorial service was scheduled for the day of our departure. So one day later we were on the plane, and who should come on board just before the door closed but a long-time friend and attendee of one of my Bible studies from years past! Turns out, she and her girlfriend (who was already somewhere on the plane) were also traveling to Phoenix. We gladly took the opportunity to catch up. She asked how we were doing and whether I had written any more books. I told her that I had, referring to a daily devotional in the book of *James* called *Joy for Today*. She asked if she could get a copy. It just so happened that my brother had asked me to bring him four copies and we ended up bringing six, so we gave one to her and the other to her friend.

Eight days later we were flying home and these same two ladies were on the plane. Coincidence, right? Our friend then told us the following: "We were not scheduled to come back today, but last night while we were in our hotel room, I was reading your devotional when my friend received a phone call that her son had just attempted suicide. She was shaking in fear that she could not get home in time to see him alive. When she got off the phone, I said to her, 'I know you are extremely troubled, but let me just read these first few devotionals to you.' I can't put into words the power of God's word to lift us up out of that urgent crisis and comfort us."

We all hugged and I told her, "You know what is even more comforting? Think about this: the God who created us knew in His timing what you would be dealing with in exactly that hour. He even worked (years before) through an email from a friend that encouraged me to write the *Joy for Today* book in the first place. Then consider the change of our flight for one day and you having the thought to ask if I had written any more books, or the thought that we should bring two extra books for no apparent reason so we had those books to share with you. All so God could minister to you with His word in your time of need." *You be the judge: God's will or coincidence?*

LIVING WATER FROM JOHN 7:1-53

May 7	God protected Jesus in every circumstance, according to His will, until Jesus' time had fully come.
May 8	God works all things for His glory and our good.
May 9	Jesus declared that His teaching was not His own but came from God who sent Him.
May 10	Believers desire to know God and are attracted to do His will.
May 11	We have been freed from our slavery to sin and have become slaves of righteousness.
May 12	Rivers of living water (the Holy Spirit) flow from the inmost being of anyone who believes (trusts) in Christ.

PRAYER

*Father, what comfort there is in knowing that You
hold me securely in Your will moment by moment and
day by day. While I get distracted by each sin I commit,
Your will is something much more encompassing
and grand. Your Son died on the cross to remove from
my ledger every sin I have ever committed or ever will
commit. As Your word declares in Proverbs 4:18,
You have me on Your ever-brightening path
of the righteous, which gets brighter and
brighter until the full dawn. Thank You and
I praise You for placing **me** in Your will.
In Your Son's precious name,
Amen.*

MY LIVING WATER THOUGHTS

WE ARE ALL LOSERS

———

JOHN 8:1-32

TIME FOR A QUIZ!

Let's begin this section with a little quiz. There is a lot of freedom in the answers:

Can any of us make ourselves more "godly" than God makes us?
No! Every Christian is a child of God. We have Christ in us! Right now we are all exactly who God would have us to be in this moment in life (and tomorrow, and the next day)!

Did God say *"I will accomplish all my good pleasure"*?
Yes! In Isaiah 46:10, which makes us all, 24/7, day after day, vessels of God's mercy! He doesn't delegate this work to us or anyone else. He does ALL the work Himself!

Does scripture indicate that *"no purpose of [God] can be thwarted"*?
Yes! Scripture says that in Job 42:2, which means that none of us can thwart (slow down, frustrate, modify, or prevent) any aspect of God's will for us! Praise God! Praise God! Praise God!

What freedom there is in the answers to these questions! God is the Creator! We are but dust *(Psalms 103:14)*. He is the Potter, we are just clay He molds *(Romans 9:20-24)*. What can the clay do for itself? Can it help the Potter? Can it prevent the Potter from doing what He intends to do to shape the clay? No! The clay can neither facilitate nor inhibit what God is doing, or the timing in which He desires to do it. In truth, the lump of clay can't even get itself on the Potter's wheel in the first place, let alone take part in the shaping of what God has in store for it. *What a freedom this is!*

YOU are a child of God. *YOU* have Christ in you! In spite of all the things Paul addressed in his letter to the Christians in Philippi, he began it with a vitally important truth: *"I am confident of this very thing"* ... that the God who began His good work in your life will continue that work until it is completed *(Philippians 1:6)*.

This truth from Philippians is the same for us today.

God has done it all ... He is all we need!

We are just clay in the hands of our all-loving Father God!

MAY 13

*They said to Him, "Teacher, this woman has been caught in adultery, in the very act.
⁵Now in the Law Moses commanded us to stone such women; what then do You say?"
⁶They were saying this, testing Him, so that they might have grounds for accusing Him.
But Jesus stooped down and with His finger wrote on the ground. ⁷But when they
persisted in asking Him, He straightened up, and said to them, "**He who is without sin
among you, let him be the first to throw a stone at her.**"*

—JOHN 8:4-7

The Christian environment I grew up in held an upspoken assumption that there was a hierarchy of sins. No one said so outright by listing them in order, but it was there. To my perception, divorce was the biggest sin, followed closely by adultery, then abortion, then possibly a drinking or substance addiction. As you can imagine, people in that environment, who fell into any of these enumerated sins, felt permanently tarnished and unaccepted by others (while those who had not, often felt proud and judgmental).

Verse seven tells us that with God, there is no hierarchy of sins. We are all equal losers when it comes to being sinful before God. These religious leaders thought they had cornered Jesus into a no-win situation, but Jesus cut through to their own real condition, stripping away all their pride and judgment: *"He who is without sin among you, let him be the first to throw a stone at her."*

My granddaughter has a little plaque near her dinner table. It reads "Don't judge someone just because they sin differently than you." I love that! Before God, we have all sinned (equally) and fall (equally) short of the glory of God *(Romans 3:23)*.

LIVING WATER FOR TODAY:

*For **all have sinned and fall short** of the glory of God,
²⁴being justified as a gift by His grace through the
redemption which is in Christ Jesus.—ROMANS 3:23-24*

For today, acknowledge two vital truths: (i) that God does not grade sin on a curve—you and everyone you know have sinned and fallen equally short of God's glory; and (ii), that God has redeemed you from those very same sins (whatever they are) through the gift He has given you in Christ Jesus. There is no room for personal pride or a judgmental attitude, only praise and worship to Him. *PTL!*

May 14

Again He stooped down and wrote on the ground. ⁹When they heard it, they began to go out one by one, beginning with the older ones, and He was left alone, and the woman, where she was, in the center of the court. ¹⁰Straightening up, Jesus said to her, "Woman, where are they? Did no one condemn you?" ¹¹She said, "No one, Lord." And Jesus said, "I do not condemn you, either. Go. From now on sin no more."

—John 8:8-11

Here is the second time within a couple of verses that the Apostle John tells us Jesus stooped down and wrote on the ground. By God's leading, John made note of these back-to-back events, yet was apparently not inspired to tell us *why* Jesus did this or *what* was written. Isn't that interesting? God calls us to accept by faith many things in scripture that cannot be grasped by the finite human mind during our time on earth. How did God create all things out of nothing? How is He a God with no beginning or ending? Why does He choose one person for glory and not another? All these truths we must take by faith. One thing we do know for certain, though. Whether God's word is written in dirt or in our modern-day Bible, it is powerful! It affected each accuser in a personal way, beginning with the older (with more life experiences of sin in their lives).

In *verse 11*, when everyone had faded from the scene—no doubt driven away by images of their own sinful lives—Jesus asks the woman if anyone condemned her. She said: *"No one, Lord."* This is where He tells her something miraculous. He says, *"I do not condemn you, either. Go. From now on sin no more."* Now, Jesus is not telling her to try harder not to sin anymore. Rather, He is pronouncing her a *new creation in Christ!* Because the resurrected Christ now lives in her she cannot continue in a lifestyle of sin. Prior to this encounter with Jesus, she was in total bondage to sin. All she could do was live as a slave in bondage to evil. Now that Christ has come into her life, *SHE IS FREE!*

Living Water for Today:

*And now you are free from your old master, sin; and **you have become slaves to your new master, righteousness.**—*Romans 6:18 (TLB)

For today, like the woman caught in adultery, in the midst of your sin, God does not condemn you because He has already forgiven you. He has given you a new desire in your heart for Him. He has made you a "slave of righteousness." *PTL!*

MAY 15

*Then Jesus again spoke to them, saying, "**I am the Light of the world**; he who follows Me will not walk in the darkness, but will have the Light of life."*
—JOHN 8:12

When considering the meaning of the previous phrase in *verse 11, "From now on sin no more,"* the first and most important consideration is the context. The very next verse gives us some life-changing information. Jesus is speaking to the crowd again, saying, *"**I am the Light of the world**; he who follows Me will not walk in the darkness, but will have the Light of life."* This is the second "I AM" statement in John from the mouth of Jesus. It is Jesus explaining what He meant in the previous verse.

Jesus is telling us that those who follow Him—which refers to all believers who have faith in Christ—are those who no longer walk in darkness but have within them the Light of life. The Spirit of God abides in us, enlightening and influencing our daily lives. This does not mean that we never again fail or sin. But it means we have God's sinless life living in us. Praise God! We saw this same concept when discussing the Greek word δοῦλος ("doulos") from *Romans 6:17-18 (May 11)*, which means "one whose will (referring to our human will) is swallowed up by the will of another" (referring to God's will). We no longer continually desire sin, but rather, our heart increasingly hungers for righteousness! PTL!

So, Jesus is not telling the woman caught in adultery to try harder not to sin. Rather, He is pronouncing her a *new creation in Christ*. Prior to meeting Jesus, she was in total bondage to sin, a slave to her evil flesh. But now that Christ has come into her life, *she is free!* With the power of the resurrected Christ living in her she cannot continue in a lifestyle that only desires sin. Christ has set her free—*to desire God-things!*

LIVING WATER FOR TODAY:

*Therefore there is now **no condemnation for those who are in Christ Jesus**.*—ROMANS 8:1

For today, as you meditate on these words, feel all the guilt and self-condemnation that plagues you melt away as you recognize the truth contained in this verse: There is NO condemnation from God toward you, either in this life or ever in eternity, because you are *in* Christ Jesus! *PTL!*

May 16

*So the Pharisees said to Him, "You are testifying about Yourself; Your testimony is not true." [14]Jesus answered and said to them, "**Even if I testify about Myself, My testimony is true**, for I know where I came from and where I am going; but you do not know where I come from or where I am going."*

—John 8:13-14

As educated as the Pharisees were, they were certainly wrong-minded when it came to spiritual matters and faith. Jesus was performing all manner of miracles openly in their midst, and in the process, spoke of His Father and He being the Son. The Pharisees were not at all confused that Jesus was referring to Almighty God (as His Father), nor to Himself as the Son of God. It is a short path of logic to conclude that such testimony made Jesus equal to God. The Pharisees could not tolerate such a notion! They latched on to a rule found in the Mosaic Law *(Deuteronomy 17:6, 19:15)* that applied to resolving arguments between disputants, what we would call today as a trial.

During this formal dispute resolution process, the Mosaic Law required at least two witnesses testify to establish a truth about something. Of course, just because there is only one person testifying doesn't make the matter false (it could be entirely true, having only one witness), but the Mosaic Law required a second witness in such a formal trial to corroborate the truth. What the Pharisees attempted to do in these verses was twist this original rule to fit their hidden agenda. They took the baseless position that since Jesus was testifying about Himself (He was only *one* witness), which to them made His testimony false. This is not what the Mosaic Law established. The truth Jesus spoke was not determined by the number of witnesses but by the *source* of the information spoken.

Living Water for Today:

The testimony of the LORD is sure, *making wise the simple.*—Psalm 19:7b

For today, take a deep breath and let it out slowly. When you seek "wisdom" in the testimony of many sources (people, books, TV, magazines) regarding a choice you must make, it often leads to a cacophony of noise and complexity. But God's wisdom comes from just His testimony alone (His word). He alone will make you know His way. God doesn't need anyone or anything else to help Him. He Is All We Need! *PTL!*

MAY 17

"You judge according to the flesh; I am not judging anyone. [16]But even if I do judge, My judgment is true; for I am not alone in it, but I and the Father who sent Me. [17]Even in your law it has been written that the testimony of two men is true. [18]I am He who testifies about Myself, and the Father who sent Me testifies about Me."

—JOHN 8:15-18

I love these verses for how gracious, yet uncompromising, Jesus is concerning the truth of His and His Father's relationship. Jesus begins His response by telling the Pharisees their judgment of Him based on their human thinking *"according to the flesh"* is wrong. They have no clue about God's greater plan of salvation for humanity and how Jesus is God's divine agent, specifically sent by God to bring about this plan. Jesus tells them that He is not judging anyone for failing to understand using only their own fleshly human thinking. They need God to grant them understanding *(see May 1).*

Here is where it gets interesting. While Jesus does not judge them for having only a finite, fleshly human mind to grasp spiritual things, He does not let them off the hook from the truth itself. Consider for a moment what the Pharisees were most troubled by: *that Jesus was referring to God as His Father and Himself as the Son.* In these verses He goes right back to this very principle. He cites the same Mosaic Law that the Pharisees were attempting to use regarding the testimony of at least two witnesses to establish the truth *(Deuteronomy 17:6, 19:15).* Jesus then doubles down on the glorious spiritual truth that He and the Father are ONE! He tells the Pharisees, who must be absolutely appalled at this point, that even if He was judging, His judgment would be true because He testifies *AND His Father adds a second testimony,* to the truth of what Jesus is declaring.

LIVING WATER FOR TODAY:

*The one who believes in the Son of God has the testimony in himself; the one who does not believe God has made Him a liar, because he has not believed in the testimony that God has given concerning His Son. [11]And **the testimony is this, that God has given us eternal life, and this life is in His Son.**—*1 JOHN 5:10-11

For today, consider with celebration God's testimony concerning His Son Jesus: that God has given YOU eternal life and this life is in His Son, and His Son is IN YOU! *Praise the Lord!*

May 18

*He said therefore again to them, "I go away, and you will seek Me, and will die in your sin; where I am going, you cannot come." ²²So the Jews were saying, "Surely He will not kill Himself, will He, since He says, 'Where I am going, you cannot come'?" ²³And He was saying to them, "You are from below, I am from above; you are of this world, I am not of this world. ²⁴I said therefore to you, that you shall die in your sins; for **unless you believe that I am He, you will die in your sins.**"*

—JOHN 8:21-24

What freedom there is in these verses! As befuddled as the Pharisees appear to be, Jesus is simply referring to His upcoming crucifixion and return to heaven. That's what He means when He says, *"Where I am going, you cannot come."* Then He once again declares the gloriously liberating truth repeated throughout the book of John: BELIEF is the sole basis for our eternal salvation! Remember, I have mentioned from the beginning of these devotionals that there are scores of references in the Gospel of John to the fact that *belief* (that Jesus is our Savior) is the sole requirement for eternal life with God. Here is yet another one of those references.

There is enormous freedom in these words from Jesus. It is not belief AND something else, like going to church, teaching Sunday School, tithing, reading your Bible, praying without ceasing, failing less, or quitting your bad habits, etc. In scripture it is always and only *belief* that makes the difference between *"you shall die in your sins"* versus *"whoever believes in Him shall not perish, but have everlasting life" (John 3:16).*

What do these verses mean to us? Jesus is making a distinction between *belief* in Him and *working* for Him. Remember He is speaking directly to the Pharisees. These are not barroom brawlers. These men have given their entire lives to following the Mosaic Law to please God, yet Jesus puts them and all humanity into two groups: You are either in the group of those who *believe* OR those who are *in sin*. There is *nothing* in between.

LIVING WATER FOR TODAY:

*Who is the one who overcomes the world, **but he who believes that Jesus is the Son of God**?*—1 JOHN 5:5

For today, rest from all the concerns you have in this world; for God's word promises that you will overcome all of them because you believe in Jesus as the Son of God. *Praise the Lord!*

MAY 19

So they were saying to Him, "Who are You?" Jesus said to them, "What have I been saying to you from the beginning? ²⁶I have many things to speak and to judge concerning you, but He who sent Me is true; and the things which I heard from Him, these I speak to the world." ²⁷They did not realize that He had been speaking to them about the Father. ²⁸So Jesus said, "When you lift up the Son of Man, then you will know that I am He, and I do nothing on My own initiative, but I speak these things as the Father taught Me. ²⁹And He who sent Me is with Me; He has not left Me alone, for I always do the things that are pleasing to Him." ³⁰As He spoke these things, many came to believe in Him.

—JOHN 8:25-30

These verses reflect the mental confusion the Pharisees were going through. One moment they are accusing Jesus of calling God His own Father *(John 5:18, April 6)*, and the next moment they are asking Him *"Who are You?"* Jesus patiently reminds them of what He has been saying about Himself from the beginning. He is a messenger sent by God to speak divine truth to humanity. Then He gives them an impactful prophecy: *"When you lift up the Son of Man, then you will know that I am He, and I do nothing on My own initiative, but I speak these things as the Father taught Me."*

From our modern perspective, it is obvious that Jesus was referring to the immediate future when these same religious leaders would have Him lifted up on a Roman cross and crucified. They would bury Him in a tomb, roll a huge stone in front of its entrance, but in three days the stone would be rolled aside, and Jesus would be gone. Jesus is telling them that then they will know who He really is. They will know He is the Son of God because *no one can rise from the dead but God Himself or someone God has raised.*

What a statement! What encouragement for us! Jesus rose from the dead because He IS eternal life, and *His life resides in us daily.*

LIVING WATER FOR TODAY:

Jesus said to him, "I am the way, and the truth, and the life; no one comes to the Father but through Me."—JOHN 14:6

For today, consider that Jesus IS eternal LIFE—and His life resides *IN YOU!* Your human flesh may die, but the *true you* never will. *PTL!*

MAY 20

As He spoke these things, many believed in Him. ³¹Then Jesus said to those Jews who believed Him, "If you abide in My word, you are My disciples indeed. ³²And you shall know the truth, and the truth shall make you free."

—JOHN 8:30-32 NKJV

What a contrast between how Jesus speaks to the Pharisees and religious leaders and how He speaks to those in the crowd that His Father has chosen to grant belief *(February 26)*. To the Pharisees and religious leaders He speaks as though they are still under the Law *(compare today's verses to those immediately following in John 8:33-59)*, but to those in the crowd who truly believe He gives a respite of grace. On *May 14* we learned about the woman caught in adultery. Jesus wrote His words in dirt and all her accusers slinked away quietly. When He asked her who had judged her, she responded *"No one, Lord."* Even before the cross, she was a true believer in her Lord and Savior Jesus. His response was one of grace to a believer, *"I do not condemn you either. Go. From now on sin no more."* We saw that Jesus was not commanding her to try her best not to sin but was, in truth, transferring her into the kingdom of Light as a *new creation in Christ*.

So it is with all true believers in today's verses. As a result of Jesus' spoken words of the coming cross, many believed in Him. I doubt this occurred overtly, but rather, the Spirit of God was blowing on them inwardly *(March 9)*, giving life-saving belief to those the Father had chosen to grant it. To those, Jesus spoke grace: *"Abide in My word ... And you shall know the truth, and the truth shall make you free."* Just like the woman caught in adultery Jesus spoke grace to them even before the cross. At that moment, God made them *new creations in Christ*. Jesus didn't tell them to obey the Law but to abide in His words concerning the coming cross. Just as He commanded of His disciples in *Acts 1:4*, *"to wait for what the Father had promised,"* Jesus was gathering true believers to Himself.

LIVING WATER FOR TODAY:

*"But the Helper, **the Holy Spirit**, whom the Father will send in My name, He **will teach you all things**, and bring to your remembrance all that I said to you."*—JOHN 14:26

For today, give thanks to God that His Spirit draws you, teaches you, and brings remembrance of His life-giving words to you, *that cause you to abide in Him for everything, every day, and forever*. What a glorious, loving, merciful, gracious God! Praise Him!

UNDERSTANDING JOHN 8:30-32

John 8:30-32 is often confusing to many Christians. They read *"If you continue in My word, then you are truly disciples of Mine"* and get focused on the word "IF." In modern English, it suggests something conditional. Something we must do to keep ourselves "believing in Christ" to remain "saved." While this is one way to interpret these verses, it is inconsistent with the rest of the book of John. Throughout John, BELIEF granted to us from God is the only basis for salvation.

The Apostle John revisits this concept of "abiding" in *1 John 4:16*, and further clarifies its meaning: *"We have come to know and have believed the love which God has for us. God is love, and the one who abides in love abides in God, and God abides in him."* What precedes everything is given at the end of the verse. The reason we live our life abiding in God's love is ***because God abides in us!*** When John talks about abiding he is referring to *our condition* as believers in God, living out our lives in God's love and safe in the care of God Himself.

Abiding is not a *conditional requirement* that we do to please God. He is already pleased with us *in Christ*. Our "condition" is that of being "at rest," in the love of God because God abides in us! *What a glorious condition this is!* John wrote this letter as an encouragement to believers living among the early churches who were suffering great persecution. It remains a source of joy and enormous encouragement for us today amid our trials and tribulations!

There is nothing about abiding that depends on us to act in a certain way or do a certain thing. It is entirely the result of God's great love for us, placing us in Himself where we can abide in total peace in His love *forever!*

ROMANS 5:8

"But God demonstrates His own love toward us, in that while we were yet sinners, Christ died for us."

LIVING WATER FROM JOHN 8:1-32

May 13	All have sinned and fall short of God's glory; but we are justified freely by His grace through redemption in Christ Jesus.
May 14	We are free from our old master (sin) and have become slaves to our new master (righteousness).
May 15	Jesus is the Light of the world; those who follow Him will have the Light of life enlightening and influencing them every day.
May 16	God's wisdom comes from His testimony alone— the testimony of His word.
May 17	And the testimony is this: that God has given us eternal life and this life is in His Son Jesus AND in us!
May 18	There are only two classifications of people: either God grants a person belief (and life) in Jesus His Son, or they die in their sins.
May 19	Jesus is the way, the truth, and the life; and the way to the Father is through His Son Jesus.
May 20	*"... abide in My word ... And you shall know the truth, and the truth shall make you free" (John 8:31-32 NKJV).*

PRAYER

Father, I am no better than the woman caught in adultery.
Before You revealed Yourself in me, I was a miserable slave
to my fleshly desires and hungers, yet never satisfied with
any of it. How I praise You for the faith You have granted
me, to believe in Your Son Jesus as my Savior. What free-
dom there is in knowing that You do not condemn me for
my sins but have taken them all away and replaced them
with a continual desire to praise and worship You. What
mercy and grace this is! Thank you also for the faith You
have granted me to trust that You are still working at Your
pace and in Your timing to perfect in me that which You
have started. Regardless of episodes of sin from my flesh,
You are faithfully working to transform me from glory to
glory into the image of Your Son. I praise You dear God!
In Your Son's precious name,
Amen.

My Living Water Thoughts

PRAISE GOD
HIS WORD
IS AT HOME
IN US

———

JOHN 8:33-59

MAY 21

*They answered Him, "We are Abraham's descendants and have never yet been enslaved to anyone; how is it that You say, 'You will become free'?" ³⁴Jesus answered them, "Truly, truly, I say to you, everyone who commits sin is the slave of sin. ³⁵The slave does not remain in the house forever; the son does remain forever. ³⁶So **if the Son makes you free, you will be free indeed.**"*

—JOHN 8:33-36

On *May 20* we read the Lord's message of grace to those in the crowd who believed in Jesus as He spoke of His coming crucifixion. He told those believers to: "... *abide in My word ... And you shall know the truth* [referring to Himself], *and the truth shall make you free."* Others in the crowd, however, thought Jesus was referring to political suppression. I guess this is understandable since Jerusalem was being occupied by the Romans at the time. Given that fact, their response was somewhat delusional. They said, *"We are Abraham's descendants and have never been enslaved to anyone."* As usual, they were missing the point. Jesus wasn't speaking of political enslavement; *He was referring to being a slave of sin and the freedom He offers from such a painful and hopeless life*.

Nevertheless, Jesus uses their earthly understanding of slavery as a teaching opportunity. He reminds them of what they already knew: that a slave is only temporary in a house and can be bought and sold many times between houses during his or her life. By comparison, only the son of the household is permanent. Notice Jesus' reference to the **Son** in *verse 36*. The word is capitalized, meaning Jesus was referring to Himself: *"if the Son* [Jesus] *makes you free,* **you will be free indeed.**" No more wandering about in the darkness under the enslavement of sin but transferred PERMANENTLY by Jesus into the house of our Father God *as His children*. Nothing can ever change that!

LIVING WATER FOR TODAY:

It was for freedom that Christ set us free; therefore
keep standing firm and do not be subject again to
a yoke of slavery.—GALATIANS 5:1

For today, rest in the freedom that Jesus has given you. Freedom to give up all your religious self-effort to please God, trusting that He is working His good pleasure in you in His perfect timing; freedom to abandon your worries for your troubled children, or stressful finances, or insecure employment, *freedom to trust Him for everything. PTL!*

MAY 22

*"I know that you are Abraham's descendants; yet **you seek to kill Me, because My word has no place in you.** ³⁸I speak the things which I have seen with My Father; therefore you also do the things which you heard from your father." ³⁹They answered and said to Him, "Abraham is our father." Jesus said to them, "If you are Abraham's children, do the deeds of Abraham."*

—JOHN 8:37-39

Doesn't this entire conversation between the Jewish leaders and Jesus seem upside down and crazy? Jesus has come to this earth, not of His own initiative but because His Father has Him. He is not trying to "sell" them anything. His task from His Father is to be a Messenger, to share with them the words of life, to forgive them of every sin, and infuse them with eternal life *for free.* Do they celebrate this glorious development? No! On the contrary, all they have in their hearts and minds is an obsessive desire to kill Him rather than accept Him.

Jesus tells them why this is so in *verse 37, "because My word has no place in you."* The Living Bible translates the same portion of scripture as *"because my message does not find a home within your hearts."* This is a startling statement if you think about it and explains a great deal about what is going on in the world today. It sheds light on why we are seeing such a dramatic rise in evil and lawlessness everywhere. There has been a growing trend in America over the last 20-30 years to purge from the public discourse every reference to God. Those who are advocating for this separation from God have the same "heart condition" as those Jewish leaders wanting to kill Jesus 2,000 years ago. There is no place in the hearts of many for the word of God. But praise our Lord Jesus! His word has found a home *in our hearts!* He has placed a love for His word within us!

Tomorrow, we will ask the question: *Do you want to kill Jesus?* The answer to that question is absolute evidence of your eternal salvation.

LIVING WATER FOR TODAY:

*We love, **because He first loved us.*** —1 JOHN 4:19

For today, realize afresh that without God *FIRST* loving you and being at home within you, there would be no love in your heart for Him or others. He alone *(in us)* is the source of *all* our love and kindness. He abides in you—forever! *Praise Him!*

MAY 23

"But as it is, you are seeking to kill Me, a man who has told you the truth, which I heard from God; this Abraham did not do. ⁴¹You are doing the deeds of your father." They said to Him, "We were not born of fornication; we have one Father: God." ⁴²Jesus said to them, "If God were your Father, you would love Me, for I proceeded forth and have come from God, for I have not even come on My own initiative, but He sent Me. ⁴³Why do you not understand what I am saying? It is because you cannot hear My word."

—JOHN 8:40-43

Many Christians worry about their eternal salvation. I know, I fretted endlessly with persistent doubt over my own salvation for decades. But the word of God is full of absolute evidence affirming every Christian's salvation on almost every page of scripture if we only have eyes to see it. There is nothing ambiguous or nebulous about God's word. It sets forth again and again a variety of clear tests (measured from our own life experiences) for whether a person is saved or unsaved, whether they have been chosen by God for glory, or not. These verses contain one of these tests. Jesus says, *"If God were your Father, you would love Me."* Jesus is speaking of a "heart condition" here.

Ask yourself, *do I seek to kill Jesus, or am I drawn to love Him?* Do I desire to separate myself from God and eliminate Him from everything I do in life, or do I hunger for more of Him and His word?

If you are drawn to Him, THEN GOD IS YOUR FATHER! He abides in you. The test Jesus presents here is simple: *If you love Me, then God is your Father.* What about your feelings of sinfulness? If God was not in your heart, you would never have these thoughts *(Romans 3:11)*. Such thoughts are evidence that God is at work in your life *(Philippians 2:13; 1:6)*, not that you are failing Him or losing your salvation. *PTL!*

LIVING WATER FOR TODAY:

*The one who keeps His commandments abides in Him, and He in him. **We know by this that He abides in us, by the Spirit whom He has given us.**—*1 JOHN 3:24

For today, this verse is more evidence that God abides in you and you in God. Do you ever think about God, or experience the Spirit of God guiding and directing your decisions throughout your day? *You do because God's Spirit eternally abides in you!*

*"Which one of you convicts Me of sin? If I speak truth, why do you not believe Me? [47]**He who is of God hears the words of God**; for this reason you do not hear them, because you are not of God."*

—JOHN 8:46-47

These verses are filled with rich meaning that brings me to my knees every time I read them. The phrase *"of God"* in the Greek means "out of God," or he that "comes from God," or he who is "born of God." The next word *"hears"* means "to understand and believe." Jesus is saying that every true child of God understands and believes that Jesus is their Lord and Savior. We understand who He is and why He came—He is God's gift of eternal life to us. Every true believer understands this truth. Why? Not based on anything we have studied or earned in our own effort. It is because they are *out of God!* God has put Himself in us (think of it like He has placed His own *"DNA"* in us) and this divine *DNA* enables us to understand (and believe) this truth.

It is interesting to note the order of Jesus' explanation to these Jewish leaders. He doesn't say: "you don't hear because you aren't trying hard enough to understand the words of God," or "you don't hear because you don't want to hear bad enough." No. According to Jesus, hearing the words of God is not something we try to do. It is the *result* of something else that has *already* happened. Hearing is not the path into God, but rather, hearing the words of God is the *result* that Christians experience by *already* being placed into God's household—*by God.* It is the action *initiated first by God* that *results* in a person being able to hear and understand God's speaking to them. It was not possible for these Jewish religious leaders to hear the words of God that Jesus spoke, not that they weren't trying, but that they were not *"of God."*

LIVING WATER FOR TODAY:

*God is faithful, **through whom you were called into fellowship with His Son,** Jesus Christ our Lord.* —1 CORINTHIANS 1:9

For today, rejoice in God's faithfulness to you. He did not leave it up to you to earn your place in His household. He alone called you into fellowship with His Son. It is His calling that enables you to hear the words He speaks to you. What a glorious freedom. What immense mercy and grace. *What a great confirmation (again) of your salvation! PTL!*

MAY 25

*For **the word of the cross** is foolishness to those who are perishing, **but to us who are being saved it is the power of God.***

—1 CORINTHIANS 1:18

If there was ever a verse that boils down, simplifies, and brings clarity to all the chaos and insanity we see manifested in this world today, it would be this verse. I don't think this is an accident. In God's infinite wisdom, He chose a means to eternal life that completely and totally negates any boasting that humanity might devise for itself. God's path to salvation and eternal life leaves each Christian with one and only one boast: ***GOD HAS DONE IT ALL ... HE IS ALL I NEED!*** *(1 Corinthians 1:31).*

This verse explains why we can talk with someone about simple things related to God: like what the cross represents, or Jesus' crucifixion, death, burial, and resurrection, or the joy that our salvation and eternal life brings us—and they will shake their head and conclude that we are foolish to believe such superstitions. Why? Because God—at that moment in their life—has not yet revealed His Son in them. They only have man's "wisdom" to rely on and such wisdom is completely incapable of perceiving God. Nevertheless, God through us, has planted a seed of truth in them, which God may (or may not) grow into full blossom of life-giving faith. I have seen this progressive transformation occur—from unbelief to belief—countless times during my life. We see this reflected in the Apostle Paul's life, a man who was capturing and putting Christians to death. Scripture says, *"But when God...was pleased,"* He revealed His Son in Paul *(Galatians 1:15-16).* It is not for us to decide who is saved or not saved. But a person's attitude toward the things of God is a good snapshot of their present condition before God.

LIVING WATER FOR TODAY:

*For **God has not destined us** for wrath, but **for obtaining salvation through our Lord Jesus Christ.*** —1 THESSALONIANS 5:9

For today, praise God that He revealed eternal life to you in the person of His Son Jesus, who *IS* eternal life. Rejoice that He chose you as one of His children and granted you life-saving belief—which is the divine *"listening organ"* to hear and believe the words Jesus speaks to you. You no longer need to struggle and worry about earning your salvation. *Your entire life is all in the hands of Almighty God and His Son Jesus! Praise Him!*

MAY 26

*We are from God; he who knows God listens to us; he who is not from God does not listen to us. **By this we know the spirit of truth** and the spirit of error.*

—1 JOHN 4:6

The word *"we"* that begins this verse refers to believers. The word *"from"* in the first phrase *"We are from God,"* means again "out of God," or "born of God," or "given a new (spiritual) birth from God." The fact that you and I are (i) attracted to God's word, and (ii) believe it, is evidence that we are part of God's family. *We have God's DNA in us!*

This is the only explanation for why we pray or think about God at all *(Romans 3:11)*. Prayer is not an empty ritual to us. The Spirit of God in us initiates our every prayer. Others may think that prayer is meaningless, but not us. We pray because God has transferred us into His household (His family) and placed Himself *(His DNA)* in us! We know—in unique, personal, and divine ways—what prayer means in terms of communing with our Father-God who created us and unconditionally loves us. We know experientially how God comforts, nourishes, and guides us through prayer. This is not an intellectual knowing. We know it because we are born of God.

We also enjoy fellowship with other Christians because the Spirit of God draws us to them and gives us much in common with them. We also no longer live with our ugly flesh constantly consuming us because we have God's *DNA* in us. Praise God! I don't say we never fail. We still have the warring of the flesh within every day, which makes us impatient, angry, selfish, and prideful. But at the same time, we feel the power of God at work, *always bringing us back to thoughts of Him, to scripture, and to prayer. PTL!*

Bottom line: we have God's *DNA*. It is the reason we love Him, worship Him, pray to Him, fellowship with each other ... and never want to kill Him *(John 8:37, May 22).*

LIVING WATER FOR TODAY:

But we all, with unveiled face, beholding as in a mirror the glory of the Lord, are being transformed into the same image from glory to glory, just as from the Lord, the Spirit.—2 CORINTHIANS 3:18

For today, recognize that God has not called you to transform yourself. It is the Spirit of God doing the transforming work in you today and every day. *PTL!*

MAY 27

The Jews answered and said to Him, "Do we not say rightly that You are a Samaritan and have a demon?" [49]*Jesus answered, "I do not have a demon; but I honor My Father, and* **you dishonor Me**. [50]*But* **I do not seek My glory**; *there is One who seeks and judges."*
—JOHN 8:48-50

At this point these Jewish religious leaders stooped to a new low and resorted to hurling personal insults at Jesus. As a reminder, on *March 12* we read how Judean Jews held deeply seated contempt and hostility toward Samaritan Jews, thinking them impure. In their minds, to call Jesus a Samaritan (which He was not) was as grave an insult as they could think of to demean Him. But could they make it even more offensive? They certainly tried by calling Him a Samaritan *with a demon*. How brutally offensive these religious leaders were. Having lost control of the conversation they now resorted to personal insults and name calling to intimidate and dehumanize Jesus. What was Jesus' response? Did He rebuke them with even more vitriol? Not at all.

Jesus simply (and calmly) stated three unequivocal facts: (i) He did not have a demon, (ii) they were dishonoring Him with such statements, and (iii) "*I do not seek My glory.*" How thought-provoking is this last statement! Jesus is saying that you can dishonor Him, rebuke Him, call Him every slanderous name your imagination can cook up, and generally treat Him like trash—and it won't affect Him one bit. Why? Because He came to *give us* peace, joy, wisdom from God, and eternal life. He wasn't looking for glory for Himself. He wasn't looking for love, respect, or acceptance for Himself. None of those motivations were on His mind. He had only one motivation: to *"always do the things that are pleasing"* to God. I explore this more as a personal testimony on the following page.

LIVING WATER FOR TODAY:

"And He who sent Me is with Me; **He has not left Me alone**, *for I always do the things that are pleasing to Him."*—JOHN 8:29

For today, what a joyous freedom this is! To not seek our own glory frees us from so much ugly effort, fleshly struggle, and sinful manipulation. When we are mistreated or disrespected, it does not bother us since our life is not about gaining glory for ourself; but rather, boasting in Jesus our Savior for all He has done for us. *PTL!*

A PERSONAL TESTIMONY

A TOP TEN SPIRITUAL TRUTH IN SCRIPTURE

Someone will occasionally say to me, "I'm going to be with my relatives this weekend [or for so-and-so's birthday or a particular holiday gathering] and I am really dreading it." I ask why and the answer is usually that someone there is always mean to them, or abusive in some way, or that they can't get over the anger they feel for a father who mistreated their mother when they were young. Whatever the reason, they always conclude with how uncomfortable they feel when spending time in such gatherings.

Such conversations always bring my mind back to *John 8:48-50* and Jesus' response to these despicable religious leaders. In my experience, the truth contained in these verses ranks among the top ten spiritual truths in all of scripture—a truth that God continues to etch into me as a *prayer*, an *awareness*, and a *desire* over the last four decades to this day. We all are human with our human preferences. We all find ourselves at times amongst others, or in situations that are less than comfortable. These verses give us divine perspective and a practical antidote.

As the CEO of a national corporation for over 60 years I have had my share of employees that I would prefer to avoid. If I absolutely could not avoid meeting with one of them, I felt so uncomfortable I would ask my wife to pray for me. Once the Lord began to etch this *John 8:48-50* truth on my heart, I began to see the same principle revealed throughout scripture. I began to thank God for His word, and these verses in John would come alive, Jesus saying to me: *"I didn't do things because I wanted to be liked or accepted. My sole purpose in walking this earth, was for people to feel God's eternal love, total forgiveness, and complete acceptance. I still desire for them to feel this love, forgiveness, and acceptance through you."*

I have also come to realize a corollary truth that is equally important, which I want to now pass on to you. The next time you are in an uncomfortable situation or family get-together, may the Lord bring to your remembrance any number of verses from His word that say the same thing, such as *Psalm 107:9* (which we explore in our *May 28* daily devotional) that it is *ONLY THE LORD*, not your in-laws, not that gnarly relative or co-worker, not your parents or spouse; it is *ONLY THE LORD* that can meet your need for feeling loved and accepted. And He is faithful to do it! *Praise the Lord!*

MAY 28

*For He has satisfied the thirsty soul, and the hungry soul **He has filled with what is good.***
—PSALM 107:9

W hen I begin to sense a "void" feeling within as I get ready to go somewhere. Perhaps a trickle of tension creeping into my heart and thoughts concerning what I am about to experience: *How are these folks going to treat me? Will I be accepted?* I take these as indications from the Lord to "come back" into fellowship with Him. Through prayer and His word, I will ask Him to direct my path. Today's verse is often a verse that the Lord leads me to. No more than a couple of minutes in His word and I feel Him start to nourish and fill me. The "void" is soon gone, and the tension is dissipated.

I've experienced this divine renewal hundreds of times over the years. I have no doubt that many of you have experienced the same. When a dread in wanting to go somewhere begins to creep in, I begin to pray (and even ask my wife to pray for me). Within the next hour or next day, instead of not wanting to go (or do what I was dreading), I feel just the opposite. How amazing is that? I'm looking forward to going or doing whatever it was that I was previously anxious about. Why? Because God is at home in us and He makes His presence within us fresh and new as we turn to Him in prayer and in His word. *He is greater than all our anxieties (1 John 4:4)!*

My experience is that God often replaces my dread with the same heart He gave Paul in *2 Corinthians 12:15-16.* Paul told the Corinthians that he would gladly, not reluctantly, but gladly (meaning happily, joyfully, and freely) *"spend and be expended for your souls."* Paul is saying that it doesn't matter how you treat him: *"If I love you more, am I to be loved less? **But be that as it may**...."* For Paul, *"whatever treatment you give me is okay."*

LIVING WATER FOR TODAY:

*You are from God, little children, and have overcome them; **because greater is He who is in you than he who is in the world.***—1 JOHN 4:4

***For today**, pause to enjoy both Psalm 107:9 and 1 John 4:4 throughout your day.* You are *never* left alone with anxiety and a sense of void (thirst and hunger) within. The God in you is always greater and will fill those feelings of hunger and thirst with Himself. *PTL!*

MAY 29

*"Truly, truly, I say to you, if **anyone keeps My word he will never see death.**" ⁵²The Jews said to Him, "Now we know that You have a demon. Abraham died, and the prophets also; and You say, 'If anyone keeps My word, he will never taste of death.' ⁵³Surely You are not greater than our father Abraham, who died? The prophets died too; whom do You make Yourself out to be?"*

—JOHN 8:51-53

We are reaching the end of this oddly disconnected conversation between Jesus and the Jewish leaders that John was inspired by God to record in his gospel. This entire chapter is a good example of what is often referred to as a "collective monologue." The religious leaders are speaking at one level, not hearing or understanding anything of what Jesus is teaching them. By contrast, each time the Jewish leaders respond, Jesus reveals yet a deeper truth that is even more mind-blowing and powerfully profound than His prior revelation! The result is two threads of conversation, which appear superficially to be woven together, taking place without any real exchange of information. One conversation is completely human and earthly without insight, while the other is divine wisdom from God.

Having read the *May 23, 24,* and *26* devotionals, you recognize the style John uses to prove that every Christian has eternal life. It is not working hard to "keep the Lord's word" that produces the result of "never seeing death." The *cause* and *effect* is actually the opposite. For those whom God has chosen to never see death, those are the ones who keep His word. If you apply John's test to your own experience, ask yourself, "Do I think about God?" "Am I drawn to the things of God, to prayer, and His word?" If you think along those lines at all, even if you are angry at God for something, then you *know* you have been called by God to never see death. *PTL!*

LIVING WATER FOR TODAY:

He who did not spare His own Son, but delivered Him over for us all, how will He not also with Him freely give us all things?—ROMANS 8:32

For today, rejoice that your life is cared for daily by your Heavenly Father, who spares nothing to provide you eternal life *and every good thing you need throughout this life. PTL!*

MAY 30

*"Your father Abraham rejoiced to see My day, and **he saw it and was glad.**"*
—JOHN 8:56

Talk about a mind-blowing declaration to these Jewish religious leaders! Jesus refers to Abraham, the person these Jews most admired, and tells them, *"Your father Abraham rejoiced to see My day, and **he saw it and was glad.**"* I can't imagine the tsunami of utter shock that must have swept over them at that revelation. Jesus is now telling them that He has firsthand knowledge of Abraham's response of rejoicing and gladness (from over 1,500 years ago) when first learning the details of God's good news gospel and the coming day of Christ to bless His people—and that all of it was contained in scripture.

Jesus was telling these leaders that Abraham knew that this very day would come when Jesus (the Christ) would come to earth, walk amidst His people, teach them, heal them, and offer them salvation—FREE. Yes, Abraham knew about Christ way back then and saw this day as vividly as these leaders were experiencing it firsthand; but Abraham, unlike them, saw all of it and was THRILLED! *He rejoiced and was glad!*

Why is it important for us to recognize that the gospel existed centuries before Christ came to earth? Because it explains how Jesus could pronounce the Samaritan woman at the well *(John 4)*, the ill man by the pool of Bethesda *(John 5)*, and the woman caught in adultery *(John 8)*, as forgiven in the present tense. God is not limited or bound by time or dispensations. The gospel of mercy and grace was as real, vibrant, and available to Abraham prior to the cross as it is to us after the cross. The Kingdom of God is eternal and exulted—in Abraham's day, in Jesus' day, and in our own day—yes, even *TODAY!*

LIVING WATER FOR TODAY:

The Scripture, foreseeing that God would justify the Gentiles by faith, preached the gospel beforehand to Abraham, saying, "ALL THE NATIONS WILL BE BLESSED IN YOU." —GALATIANS 3:8

For today, meditate on the scope of God's infinite greatness, how He saw every sin, and trial, and difficulty that would besiege you, eons before you were born. He saw all of it hung on the cross and dealt with by His Son. Likewise, He chose to bless you and grant you eternal life *long before you were born!* What abundant love, mercy, and grace! *PTL!*

MAY 31

Jesus said to them, "Truly, truly, I say to you, before Abraham was born, I am." ⁵⁹Therefore they picked up stones to throw at Him, but Jesus hid Himself and went out of the temple.
—JOHN 8:58-59

In these final two verses, Jesus brings the Jewish leaders to the breaking point of their human understanding. There is absolutely no confusion as to what the term "I am" is referring. To the Jews, the term "I am" refers exclusively to deity. It is a direct reference to *Exodus 3:14* where God answered a question from Moses, referring to Himself as the "I AM." Jesus using this specific term did not do so by accident. It was not a slip of the tongue or coincidental (and the meaning was not lost on these Jewish leaders). To them, this was equal to declaring, "I, Jesus, am the Jehovah God of the Old Testament."

To us who believe, this phrase *"I AM"* is wonderful and buckles our knees. Through the enlightening power of the Holy Spirit, it brings us great joy. It reminds us, once again, how God chose to reveal who Christ truly is to us—the How-Great-Thou-Art Almighty God, our Savior, Redeemer, Sanctification and Righteousness, Comforter, and our daily Guide. *He is everything to us!* By contrast, God did not reveal this to these Jewish leaders. His word had no place in them *(John 8:37)*. Without God's enlightenment, what Jesus said was an abomination they simply could not tolerate! Jesus had finally gone too far! They could take no more! They began to scramble around, looking for stones to hurl at Him. They wanted to stone Him to death *on the spot (see May 22)!* As they scurried about looking for stones (probably not finding many inside the Temple grounds), Jesus quietly slipped away from them. His hour was not yet come *(John 7:30)*.

LIVING WATER FOR TODAY:

God said to Moses, "I AM WHO I AM"; and He said, "Thus you shall say to the sons of Israel, 'I AM has sent me to you.'"—EXODUS 3:14

For today, take great comfort in the fact that your God is the great I AM! He is not remote or allusive. He is not only in the past or the future. He is always *in the present with you*; and He is always active, working all things together for your good *(Romans 8:28)* even when you are not aware of it. You need comfort today? **Jesus—the How-Great-Thou-Art God, the Creator of everything—is your "I AM!"**

LIVING WATER FROM JOHN 8:33-59

May 21	We are no longer slaves of sin; Christ has freed us!
May 22	Praise God! He first loved us and continues to grow His love in us by placing His word in our hearts.
May 23	The Spirit of God, opens our hearts to His word.
May 24	God's calling enables us to hear Him speak to us.
May 25	The word of the cross is the power of God.
May 26	The Spirit is why we can discern truth from error.
May 27	Jesus did not come to seek His own glory; His motivation was to always do the things that were pleasing to God.
May 28	When we have anxious thoughts, God makes His presence fresh as we turn to Him and His word.
May 29	Our life is cared for daily by our Heavenly Father who gives us a desire to turn to His word.
May 30	God's infinite greatness: He chose to bless us and grant us eternal life long before we were born.
May 31	God said to Moses and Jesus said to the Jewish leaders: "I AM"; what comfort that He is our great I AM.

PRAYER

*Father, I praise You that Your word is at home in me. Your gospel of mercy and grace is eternal! Your gospel is readily revealed throughout scripture, in Old and New Testaments alike. By Your mercy, grant me the eyes to see Your good news on every page of scripture. All my efforts to constrain You into the limits of time with my myopic theology and religious ideas are nothing more than vanity. The glorious good news begins with the fact that YOU CHOSE ME! Long before I was even born, and could do anything to earn it, You chose me to be a vessel of mercy to hold Your glory. It drops me to my knees in continual worship to You. You—Father, Son, and Holy Spirit—are **my** Great I AM! You are always present and active in my life. I need nothing else but You. I have nothing to boast of but You. In Your Son's precious name, I pray.*

Amen.

My Living Water Thoughts

_____

_____

_____

_____

_____

_____

_____

_____

_____

_____

_____

_____

_____

_____

_____

_____

_____

_____

_____

_____

_____

_____

_____

_____

_____

_____

_____

ALL OUR CIRCUMSTANCES ARE GOOD

———

JOHN 9:1-41

JUNE 1

*As He passed by, He saw a man blind from birth. ²And His disciples asked Him, "Rabbi, who sinned, this man or his parents, that he would be born blind?" ³Jesus answered, "It was neither that this man sinned, nor his parents; **but it was so that the works of God might be displayed in him.**"*

—JOHN 9:1-3

When considering all the circumstances in our lives, two perspectives are most common. The *first* is a godless perspective, that everything is a coincidence. A bunch of unrelated and unconnected happenstances. There is no meaning or benefit to any of it. The *second* is a misguided religious perspective as reflected in the attitude displayed by the disciples in these verses. They rushed to the judgment: *Who sinned, the man or his parents?* It is easy for us to fall into this same blame game. When we find ourselves in a vexing situation, we can erroneously assume that God is punishing us.

Praise God, however, there is a *third* perspective revealed in these verses. Jesus said it had nothing to do with the man (or his parents) sinning, *"but it was so that the works of God might be displayed in him."* Note that the *"works of God"* were not displayed *TO* him, but *IN* him. The word "that" in this phrase means God allowed (and used) this man's blindness as an opportunity to display His miraculous works, and to reveal Himself in a way that demonstrates what His eternal purpose is truly all about.

Let's think about this. So, God knows every difficulty we will face throughout our life before we were even born. He is sovereign over all of it and chooses to use it all to produce something glorious in us, like the forging of a diamond from a lump of coal in the furnace of life. He uses all our stress, worries, and difficulties to strengthen our faith in Him, which daily transforms us a bit more into His Son's image *(2 Corinthians 3:18)* which ultimately leads us deeper into experiencing His great love, mercy, and peace.

LIVING WATER FOR TODAY:

*And we know that **God causes all things to work together for good** to those who love God, to those who are called according to His purpose.*—ROMANS 8:28

For today, rejoice that God is using ALL THINGS, not some things or only good and spiritual things, but ALL THINGS in your life (no matter how devastating or uncomfortable) *for your good*, according to His glorious purpose *for you!*

JUNE 2

*When He had said this, He spat on the ground, and made clay of the spittle, and applied the clay to his eyes, ⁷and said to him, "Go, wash in the pool of Siloam" (which is translated, Sent). So he went away and washed, **and came back seeing**. ⁸Therefore the neighbors, and those who previously saw him as a beggar, were saying, "**Is not this the one who used to sit and beg?**"*

—JOHN 9:6-8

With the understanding that God is sovereign over everything and is working all things together for our good *(Romans 8:28)*, let's look deeper into the *"works of God"* in this blind man's life. The man himself, being blind from birth, lived entirely in darkness and was described by his neighbors as the one *"who used to sit and beg" (verse eight)*. Otherwise, scripture is silent about this man. We learn only that he lived a deeply challenging, limited, and pitiful life. Pitiful, yes, except for ONE important thing—God chose to give him a radically new life of light and sight. Jesus stopped and spoke to him! By God's mercy he heard and obeyed by faith. To what end? Instantly, the days of sitting in darkness and begging were gone. This man's entire remaining life had suddenly transformed into a brilliant beacon to the miraculous power of God shining amid darkness and unbelief.

Had you been that blind man, would you trade that miracle from Jesus for anything? Would you give it up in exchange for having your sight from birth? Undoubtedly, he wouldn't. I have asked many who have gone through great tragedy or hardship: *If you had a choice, would you change anything?* The answer I get universally from them is no, because through it all God strengthened their faith and drew them closer to Him. In the end, they realized that **God causes all things to work together for their good**. *PTL!*

LIVING WATER FOR TODAY:

*And as for you, you meant evil against me, **but God meant it for good in order to bring about this present result**, to preserve many people alive.* —GENESIS 50:20

For today, recognize that every single circumstance and event in your life is being used by God to grow and strengthen faith *in you* and to bring *you* progressively into a deeper daily experience of His love, forgiveness, patience, kindness, mercy, and grace until you are filled to overflowing with worship and praise to Him. *PTL!*

JUNE 3

So they were saying to him, "How then were your eyes opened?" *[11]He answered, "The man who is called Jesus made clay, and anointed my eyes, and said to me, 'Go to Siloam and wash'; so I went away and washed, and I received sight."*
—JOHN 9:10-11

When the *"works of God"* were displayed by God in this blind man's life the people around him noticed. Not only did they notice, but they also came to him asking for an explanation: *"How then were your eyes opened?"* The change in him made their inquiry timely, real, and relevant to their own lives. When he identified Jesus, the crowd asked *(verse 12) "where is He?"* So, the blind man was witnessing for Jesus and didn't even know it. *He just told them about his personal experience and what Jesus accomplished in his life.*

I have spoken to scores of Christians over the years who are terrified of witnessing. They love the Lord dearly but hate the possibility of getting into an argument, or being ridiculed, or just saying something wrong. The whole experience feels forced and artificial. I was one of these folks for the first 20 years of my Christian life. I was taught that I needed to witness to at least two people every day before I laid down to sleep. The stress of that burden made me miserable. It caused me to force the "gospel" conversation at inappropriate times at work and eventually led me to question my own salvation. But, praise God, scripture reveals a method far more normal and compelling.

Take another look at the cover of this book. Observe the scattering of boulders and rocks that represent all the hard circumstances in our lives. Then focus on the living stream of water flowing through all those hard places. *THAT WATER TAKES THE HARD OUT OF LIFE!* And as it does, God is changing us in ways that others notice. Like the formerly blind man in these verses, this is our testimony and witness.

LIVING WATER FOR TODAY:

*This is the day which the LORD has made; **let us rejoice and be glad in it.*** —PSALM 118:24

For today, whatever circumstance or worry strikes you, remember, THIS DAY is the day the LORD has made. He is sovereign over every thing in it that affects your life. There is nothing left for you to do but rejoice and be glad in it. He is accomplishing His perfect, good will in and through every hour of every day. *PTL!*

JUNE 4

*Now it was a Sabbath on the day when Jesus made the clay and opened his eyes. [15]Then the Pharisees also were asking him again how he received his sight. And he said to them, "He applied clay to my eyes, and I washed, and I see." [16]Therefore some of the Pharisees were saying, "This man is not from God, because He does not keep the Sabbath." But others were saying, **"How can a man who is a sinner perform such signs?"** And there was a division among them. [17]So they said to the blind man again, What do you say about Him, since He opened your eyes?" And he said, **"He is a prophet."***

—JOHN 9:14-17

The *"works of God"* which began with one blind man, rapidly spread to affect the lives of his neighbors and the crowd around him; and now has expanded to the attention of the Pharisees (the religious leaders). Remember, it was these same leaders who were scrambling to pick up stones to put Jesus to death at the end of the previous chapter *(John 8:59, May 31)*. This narrative demonstrates how God is sovereign over everything and everyone; and is working in all people's lives in different ways, just as He does in all our lives today and everyday.

These verses also provide another example of how God the Father protects His Son (and us). On *May 7* (and the following page 226) we saw how God raised a dispute among the religious leaders to distract them from their evil intention to put Jesus to death. Here again in today's verses we see God raising up a disagreement among the Pharisees that had the effect of thwarting any concerted effort to harm Jesus.

The former blind man is also growing spiritually as the Lord continues to enlighten him. Look at his expanded perception of who Jesus is: He was a "man" *(verse 11)*, a "prophet" *(verse 17)*, someone who should be followed by disciples *(verse 27)*, to one who is "from God" *(verse 33)*, and finally, to the One who is Lord and worthy of worship *(verse 38). PTL!*

LIVING WATER FOR TODAY:

Surely goodness and lovingkindness will follow me all the days of my life, and I will dwell in the house of the LORD *forever.* —PSALM 23:6

For today, just as surely as God was growing truth, faith, and understanding in the blind man, He is growing the same in you, for His glory and your good. *PTL!*

JUNE 5

*The Jews then did not believe it of him, that he had been blind and had received sight, until they called the parents of the very one who had received his sight, [19]and questioned them, saying, "Is this your son, who you say was born blind? Then how does he now see?" [20]His parents answered them and said, "**We know that this is our son, and that he was born blind;** [21]**but how he now sees, we do not know**; or who opened his eyes, we do not know. Ask him; he is of age, he will speak for himself." [22]His parents said this because they were afraid of the Jews; for the Jews had already agreed that if anyone confessed Him to be Christ, he was to be put out of the synagogue. [23]For this reason his parents said, "He is of age; ask him."*

—JOHN 9:18-23

The situation with the blind man is now getting out of control for the religious leaders. They made the mistake of asking him *in public* who he thought Jesus was. His answer was unequivocal: *"He is a prophet."* You can imagine that answer being repeated in whispered tones as it rippled through the crowd.

In response, the Pharisees quickly moved on to the man's parents in a cynical attempt to prove that this apparent miracle had some other explanation. No luck there! While the parents readily acknowledged that this was their son—and he was born blind—they would contribute nothing further. They obviously held an opinion—probably believing their son's explanation about being healed by Jesus—but were afraid to say anything because they knew the religious leaders were secretly biased against Jesus.

Before we think too harshly of the parents, ask yourself what you would have done. To be *"put out of the synagogue"* meant total alienation from Jewish society and all temple ceremonies (meaning, cut off from God), which often also meant the loss of any ability to make a living. For these parents, this was not a price they were willing to pay since they knew the religious leaders questioning them were *already closed-minded to the truth.*

LIVING WATER FOR TODAY:

*Now may the **God of hope fill you with all joy and peace in believing**, so that you will abound in hope by the power of the Holy Spirit.* —ROMANS 15:13

For today, when you are amid cynicism or criticism, the Holy Spirit brings you enduring hope *as He fills you with joy and peace through your believing in Him!*

JUNE 6

*So a second time they called the man who had been blind, and said to him, "Give glory to God; we know that this man is a sinner." ²⁵He then answered, "Whether He is a sinner, I do not know; **one thing I do know, that though I was blind, now I see.**"*
—JOHN 9:24-25

When the Pharisees reached a dead end with the man's parents, they returned to the formerly blind man; this time with a twist of theology to confuse and leaven his testimony. But the man was having nothing to do with their attempted manipulation. All the man knew and would testify to was: *"though I was blind, now I see."* What do you suppose he was referring to when he declared: *"now I see?"*

Let's put this phrase in context. In *verse five* Jesus said, *"I am the Light of the world."* It is apparent from the context that Jesus not only gave this man *physical sight*, but also granted him *spiritual insight. First*, his eyes were opened to see who Christ is. He is Lord and worthy of worship *(verse 38). Second*, when Jesus says He brings light to the world, He is bringing divine understanding. This is reflected in the man's wise answer to the Pharisee's hyper-technical interpretation of the interplay between sin and the Sabbath.

For us today, the Lord has opened our eyes to see that God's word, both written in the Bible and on the tablets of our hearts, is the only blueprint for lasting peace in our lives. Without God's light in our hearts, all paths lead to despair and misery. There is no peace in a good job and good income alone, or in the addition of a marriage, family, and nice house. Only God's word brings light and insight, giving us the understanding that He is working all things together for our good, keeping us safe on His ever-brightening path of the righteous *(Proverbs 4:18)*; where we find His peace, joy, and deep satisfaction in *whatever He has us doing today.*

LIVING WATER FOR TODAY:

***Rejoice in the Lord always;** again I will say, rejoice!*
—PHILIPPIANS 4:4

For today, *rejoice!* Every trial and tribulation you face is an opportunity to rejoice some more. God has chosen you and given you His light. Once you were blind but now you see! You see with renewed faith that He is daily working all things together *for your good*. Again, I say, *rejoice!*

JUNE 7

*The man answered and said to them, "Well, **here is an amazing thing, that you do not know where He is from, and yet He opened my eyes.** [31]We know that God does not hear sinners; but if anyone is God-fearing and does His will, He hears him. [32]Since the beginning of time it has never been heard that anyone opened the eyes of a person born blind. [33]If this man were not from God, He could do nothing." [34]They answered him, "You were born entirely in sins, and are you teaching us?" So they put him out.*
—JOHN 9:30-34

What a difference there is between the Pharisees ("knowing" God through their dead, religious perspective), and the formerly blind man (knowing Him as the living and present God experientially). In *verse 24*, the Pharisees tell this man to *"give glory to God"* because somehow God caused the man to see, even though they "know" with certainty that Jesus is a sinner. What is their evidence? He healed on the Sabbath! Yet in *verse 29* they claim to not know where Jesus comes from, even though their earlier conclusion that He is a sinner pretty much precludes the possibility that He is from God.

Imagine if you were this man who had just received sight. Your life is exploding all around you with color and light. You are seeing everything for the first time in your life. How exhilarating this moment must have been for him. That is the picture of our Christian life in Christ, full of exciting insight as Christ guides and continually reveals Himself to us. At that moment, nothing could have been more *irrelevant* to this man than the delusional conversation these Pharisees were having before him. Finally, he says, *"here is an amazing thing"* that you Pharisees do not know where He is from. For his willingness to speak truth to power, he also fell under their judgment of being a sinner and was put out of the synagogue. *Do you think this rejection troubled him?*

LIVING WATER FOR TODAY:

You will make known to me the path of life; in Your presence is fullness of joy; in Your right hand there are pleasures forever. —PSALM 16:11

For today, what a blessing it is to have a living relationship with God, who is leading you each day! He gives you sight to see in every circumstance and makes known to you the *"path of life"*: the decisions He would have you make today. *PTL!*

JUNE 8

*Jesus heard that they had put him out, and finding him, He said, "**Do you believe in the Son of Man?**" 36He answered, "Who is He, Lord, that I may believe in Him?" 37Jesus said to him, "You have both seen Him, and He is the one who is talking with you." 38And he said, "**Lord, I believe.**" And he worshipped Him.*

—JOHN 9:35-38

These verses contain the climax to what we have been observing in the man's growing awareness of who Jesus is. Jesus is the one who seeks out and engages this man (not the other way around). He asks him if he believes in the *"Son of Man."* This is Jesus' most common reference to Himself. It is used 84 times in the gospels and never used by anyone other than Jesus. It is a reference to *Daniel 7:13-14* where the Son of Man is pictured as a heavenly figure who in the end times is entrusted by God with authority, glory, and sovereign power. Jesus uses the phrase *"Son of Man"* again here as a messianic title that the previously blind man fully understood.

Up until now, this man knew only one thing: *once I was blind, now I see*. He had no interest in entering a theological debate over whether it was a sin to heal on the Sabbath. After all, HE was the one who had been healed! But finding himself in the Lord's presence again there was no need to convince him of anything. By this time, God had granted him life-saving belief.

This pattern is always the same in scripture. God who initiates contact with us and has one question: *"Do you **believe** in the Son of Man?"* From Abraham to us, **belief alone is reckoned as righteousness by God**. Like Abraham, God grants us belief to recognize who Jesus is, and what His saving sacrifice on the cross means to us.

LIVING WATER FOR TODAY:

*Even so **Abraham BELIEVED GOD, AND IT WAS RECKONED TO HIM AS RIGHTEOUSNESS.** 9So then those who are of faith are blessed with Abraham, the believer.*—GALATIANS 3:6, 9

For today, enjoy the blessings that flow from your simple belief in God and His Son Jesus. Abraham was far from perfect, but he was blessed by God solely because of his belief. You are equally blessed today, amid this dark world with all its troubles, God is working all things into a blessing for you—THE BELIEVER! *PTL!*

JUNE 9

*Brethren, my heart's desire and **my prayer to God for them is for their salvation.***

—ROMANS 10:1

I recently had someone come up to me and say (I'm paraphrasing here), "It's hard, Daryl, to get excited about God opening my eyes to see and believe in Christ when I have so many relatives who still can't see (and I fear they won't be saved)." The Apostle Paul had these same feelings for his own countrymen—the Jewish people. He prayed earnestly for their salvation. We learned from Paul earlier in *Romans* that, apart from God drawing a person to believe, no one even thinks about God, let alone prays for others to know God *(Romans 3:11)*. What are we to conclude from this?

No part of our flesh would pray for others. Like Paul, who was burdened and praying fervently for his countrymen, such prayers are solely by inspiration from God. Would God place that burden on your heart for a particular relative, or anyone for that matter, only to not grant the very prayer that He prompted you to pray?

This explains a lot about God's plan to save people. We are so human, and like Paul says, we see in a mirror dimly *(1 Corinthians 13:12)*, we can see only in part. We can't fully understand everything that God is doing in another person's life. We can't connect all the dots in a way that seems fair to us. But we can have confidence that God has placed the thought in us to pray for a particular person for a reason. God will take that prayer and work it in a way that leads to the fulfillment of His purpose. ***Those prayers are never inspired, only to be unanswered and forgotten.*** You can trust in Almighty God for this.

LIVING WATER FOR TODAY:

*The effective prayer of a righteous man can
accomplish much.* —JAMES 5:16B

For today, rest in the comfort of knowing that it is God who has inspired you to pray for those you are concerned about, and that He will answer your prayers for them in His timing and for His purpose and glory. With that assurance in mind, enjoy again *Philippians 4:6, "**Be anxious for nothing**, but in everything by prayer and supplication with thanksgiving let your requests be made known to God."*

A PERSONAL TESTIMONY:

YOU WILL BELIEVE WHEN GOD GIVES YOU BELIEF

I know we are all miserably human in our frailties. We are waiting for glory, when we will finally be freed from our fleshly worries and struggles. Because we are human, we often worry ourselves sick over loved ones who do not yet appear to have a life-saving belief in Jesus as their Savior and Lord. Caught up in this worry, we lose sight of the freedom-truths contained in *Romans 8:28*, that *"God causes all things to work together for good"* and Paul's own personal testimony in *Galatians 1:15-16* where he shared that he came to believe in the Lord *"when God was pleased to reveal His Son in me."* May the Lord allow us to see (and have faith in) His glorious works in our lives and those around us!

My wife Sherryl's sister from Fresno used to visit us often in Anaheim, California. Our family was her family ... our kids, her kids. That is how close we were. I will never forget her telling me one time in our kitchen, "Daryl, I wish I could believe as you and Sherryl do, but I just can't. I can't make myself believe." I said, "I know you can't. Don't worry about it. When God wants you to believe, you will."

This went on for probably 25 years of visits to our home. One day, we got a little card from her in the mail. She wrote that she had been reading the *Living Bible* we left for her. She then made this stunning declaration: *"I believe in Jesus now."*

When we worry and stress over this or that loved one not receiving eternal life or being with us in heaven, we pray and pray because we love them so much, then one day the Lord opens their eyes to see and believe. What is left for us to do for the remainder of our lives? I'll tell you what I do. I have nothing more to do but praise God because He is the One, *in His timing*, that causes all of us to see and believe. *Praise the Lord!*

JUNE 10

Jesus said to him, "You have both seen Him, and He is the one who is talking with you." *³⁸And he said, "**Lord, I believe.**" And he worshiped Him.*

—JOHN 9:37-38

What a beautiful example of Jesus' compassion. This man didn't have to look for Jesus. The Lord knew exactly what happened to him and where to find him, just as He always knows about us. Jesus came to him in the exact moment the man was experiencing alienation and rejection. What was Jesus' response? Jesus revealed Himself fully as the *Son of Man* in a way that comforted him and made him feel loved and cared for.

How do we know this? In *verse 38*, the phrase *"and he worshiped Him"* literally means the man threw a kiss toward Jesus. This is an indication of how deeply affectionate and appreciative the man now felt toward the Lord. Yes, he is kicked out, alienated, rejected, but the Lord comes along and conveys *His immense love for him and how he now belongs to Him.*

These verses impact me deeply because I talk to so many who have felt "put out" by a family member, Christian friend, a marriage, or even a church against their will. Jesus knows our situation every time we are feeling put out and rejected. He is right there conveying how much He loves us, how much He will never put us out, and how much He is always caring for us. PTL!

At times like these, I can never forget *Isaiah 49:15-16: "Can a woman forget her nursing child and have no compassion on the son of her womb? Even these may forget, but I will not forget you. ¹⁶Behold, I have inscribed you* [each of our names] *on the palms of My hands."*

LIVING WATER FOR TODAY:

*Make sure that your character is free from the love of money, being content with what you have; for He Himself has said, "**I WILL NEVER DESERT YOU, NOR WILL I EVER FORSAKE YOU,**" ⁶so that we confidently say, "**THE LORD IS MY HELPER, I WILL NOT BE AFRAID. WHAT WILL MAN DO TO ME?**"* —HEBREWS 13:5-6

***For today**,* how can you not praise the Lord, and then praise Him again…and again? The God who makes blind men see is the same God who assures you that He is always, 24/7, caring for you. Praise God! How blessed are you! How blessed are we all!

LIVING WATER FROM JOHN 9:1-41

June 1	God works all our difficulties together for our good.
June 2	The blind man is an example of God's mercy and miraculous power giving him a new life of light and sight.
June 3	By sharing his personal experience, the blind man was unknowingly witnessing to the neighbors.
June 4	The works of God and the blind man's testimony rapidly spread to affect the lives of many people in different ways.
June 5	The blind man's parents feared the religious leaders.
June 6	As believers one thing we do know, that though we were blind, now we see (God's word brings light and insight).
June 7	Unlike the Pharisees, the blind man believed "If this man were not from God, He could do nothing."
June 8	From Abraham to the blind man to us, God grants us life-saving faith to see and understand who the Son of Man is.
June 9	God uses our prayers (that He has placed in us) to work all the ways that lead to the fulfillment of His purpose.
June 10	Jesus reveals Himself in a manner that comforts us and makes us feel loved.

PRAYER

*Father, I praise You that You are constantly working all
things—good and bad—together for my good and Your
glory. No matter what I am feeling at the moment, You are
with me. You will never forsake me. I am in Your arms and
You are caring for me. You are not a God of judgment to us
who believe in Your Son Jesus. You are only and always
a God of blessing, mercy, and love. We are but vessels of
clay and deserve nothing, but You have chosen to grant
us saving belief out of Your infinite love for us.
Again and again I lift my praises to You.
In the precious name of Jesus, Your Son, I pray
Amen.*

THE LORD IS MY SHEPHERD

JOHN 10:1-18

A SPECIAL WORD TO THE READER...

God gave us three primary examples in scripture to illustrate our relationship to Him: (i) the potter and the clay *(Jeremiah 18:6; Romans 9:21)*, (ii) the vine and the branches *(John 15:1-5)*, and (iii) the shepherd and the sheep *(John 10:1-18)*. The distinctive characteristic common to all three illustrations is how utterly powerless and incapable of self-help are the objects representing us. What can the clay do for itself? Can it help the potter shape it? Can it even help get itself on the potter's wheel? How about the branches, can they grow even an inch apart from the nurturing supply that flows to it through the vine? And last, what can the sheep do to guide themselves. They are completely helpless without their shepherd's protection, guidance, feeding, and care. Over the next few days, we have reached John 10, where Jesus refers to Himself as the good shepherd and we, His sheep. Many consider this one of the most glorious sections in all of scripture. Its greatness is found in Jesus' words describing what it means for Him to be our good shepherd and for us to be His sheep.

Nothing regarding God's care for us, frankly, is more comforting to me than to contemplate a good shepherd caring for His sheep. I find great comfort in asking myself specifically: *Is there any way the sheep can help the Shepherd?* The answer is none. Okay, but how about this: *Is there any way the sheep can help themselves?* Again, the answer is no. Sheep are *totally* dependent on the shepherd. Since I have kids and grandkids, and we all live in a very broken world, this is wonderfully comforting.

PRAYER:

Lord, I am trusting you completely, as a dumb sheep, to make me know what I need to know and when I need to know it. Your word promises that You will instruct me in the ways I should choose; and You will make me know Your will (Psalm 25:12, 14). I am but clay—I can do nothing for myself to deal with the circumstances I am living through. I am only a branch that needs the life-giving supply from You, from Your word in scripture, and the words You speak to me on the tablet of my heart. You know me far better than I know myself. You are the How-Great-Thou-Art Shepherd who I am trusting completely.

JUNE 11

"Truly, truly, I say to you, he who does not enter by the door into the fold of the sheep, but climbs up some other way, he is a thief and a robber. ²But he who enters by the door is a shepherd of the sheep. ³To him the doorkeeper opens, and the sheep hear his voice, and he calls his own sheep by name and leads them out."

—John 10:1-3

To understand Jesus here, we need a description of what an Eastern sheepfold (or shelter) looked like and how it operated. The sheepfold itself was a corral-like enclosure, with approximately four-feet high walls made of a conglomerate of stones, wood, rails, and tightly packed thorn bushes. Its purpose was to keep the sheep safe at night from predators and thieves. Operationally, several shepherds would keep their sheep in the same sheepfold. When morning came, each shepherd would come to the shelter and call his own sheep. Immediately, his sheep would separate out from the herd and follow the voice of their own shepherd. The sheep may not be that smart, but they could recognize their own shepherd, probably because each shepherd raised his sheep from birth and cared for them continually. They were intimately attuned to the voice they trusted.

Knowing God's voice simply means that we recognize and are attracted to Him. We are attracted to reading the Bible rather than the Quran. We are attracted to Christianity, rather than Hinduism, Buddhism, or Islam. We know God's voice alone. We gain comfort in reading His word and listening to Him speak to our hearts. God inhabits His word. When we hear it, we feel it operating within us. "We hear His voice." *PTL!*

LIVING WATER FOR TODAY:

*For the **word of God is living and active and sharper than any two-edged sword**, and **piercing** as far as the division of soul and spirit, of both joints and marrow, and **able to judge the thoughts and intentions of the heart**. ¹³And there is **no creature hidden from His sight**, but all things are open and laid bare to the eyes of Him with whom we have to do.*—Hebrews 4:12-13

For today, take comfort that you are drawn to God, by God. Because He inhabits His word, it is living and active within you. No problem, challenge, concern you have today is hidden from Him. Through it all, *He is caring for all that concerns you. PTL!*

June 12

*"When he puts forth all his own, **he goes ahead of them**, and the sheep follow him because they know his voice. ⁵A stranger they simply will not follow, but will flee from him, because they do not know the voice of strangers."*

—John 10:4-5

These verses contain two crucial statements. *First*, Jesus tells us that the shepherd goes ahead of his sheep. What a comforting thought this is for us today! Our good shepherd Jesus is always leading us, even when it does not feel like He is (or look like He is). HE IS! We dumb sheep don't need to figure it all out or know even where we are going. That is Jesus' job. He is *our* good shepherd. He has it all figured out and is working all things together to care for us. We just relax, trusting Him in all things, and listening to His voice. The Christian life—full of joy and worship to Him—is that simple.

Second, verse five says: *"**A stranger they** [the sheep] **simply will not follow**, but will flee from him."* This is a powerful statement of fact. *They simply will not follow!* That specific shepherd's sheep will *never* follow a stranger—but will flee from him. They do not know the voice of strangers. Don't be lulled to sleep by thinking this is merely *a nice thought*. IT IS MUCH MORE THAN THAT! It is written directly *about* US and *to* US! Jesus is speaking specifically about Christians right now—*today*. It means that we can **never**, ever, lose our salvation! The words *"simply will not follow, but will flee"* are the words Jesus used. They are not mine. I am quoting Him.

God's sheep will never follow a stranger's voice. That means they will never disbelieve in Christ. Not because we are humanly strong enough to "hang on" to our belief, but because God not only gives us our faith, but continues to strengthen it. *PTL!*

Living Water for Today:

Since the Lord is directing our steps, *why try to understand everything that happens along the way?* —Proverbs 20:24 TLB

For today, consider anew that Jesus is *your* good shepherd, directing everything concerning your daily care and protection. Feel your peace and contentment grow. You can completely relax, trusting Him in all things, because He is always caring for you and making His voice known to you. *He won't let you miss it. PTL!*

A PERSONAL TESTIMONY:

NOTHING ABOUT MY LIFE IS HOW I PLANNED IT!

I have become increasingly aware of one powerful truth: ***Nothing about my life is how I planned it!*** God has been working His plan all along.

I DIDN'T PLAN TO HAVE TOO MUCH GOD IN MY LIFE. As a young person, I didn't want too much God. I was certain He would make requirements of me that would take all the fun out of life. I wanted to drive a sports car, but I was certain God would only grant me a used Rambler station wagon. My father was a pastor at a local church. I feared this meant I would one day be called to the mission field, where I'd be eaten by a big snake!

I DIDN'T PLAN TO MARRY THE WOMAN I MARRIED. I was interested in another person. I wasn't looking. That is, until God stepped in and crossed my path with Sherryl, who has become my greatest earthly gift from God.

I DIDN'T PLAN TO GO INTO THE BUSINESS I'M IN. While still a college student and newly married, a graduating student offered to sell some cleaning supplies, and $600 in accounts for $2,000. I didn't want to do it. But we prayed about it and a week later Sherryl and I both felt we should. Here we are 60 years later still in this same business, which has brought countless blessings to us.

I DIDN'T PLAN TO HAVE FOUR KIDS. I only wanted two! Sherryl likes to tease me that our third child, who is now president of our company, is the child I didn't want.

I DIDN'T PLAN TO MOVE FROM CALIFORNIA TO IDAHO. But I could not deny that the growth of our company was better served by making the move.

One genuine encouragement I can give to young people today is to tell them not to waste time worrying about what they are going to be, who they are going to marry, or what they are going to do with their life! If you belong to God, He has it all planned out. He is directing your steps and you will look back in 20, 30, 40 years and recognize that you too didn't plan any of it. God has continued to bring you to the place He wanted you to be. *The mind of man plans his way, but the LORD directs his steps (Proverbs 16:9). PTL!*

JUNE 13

The LORD is my shepherd, I shall not want. ²He makes me lie down in green pastures; He leads me beside quiet waters. ³He restores my soul; He guides me in the paths of righteousness for His name's sake.

—PSALM 23:1-3

God is active throughout our lives, through all our difficulties, challenges, stresses, and problems. He is leading us, guiding us, and restoring us daily. How comforting is that? He doesn't leave us on this earth to fend for ourselves. He is not reclusive or remote. He is present and active *in us.* He leads us to quiet waters and green pastures as He causes us to experience more of Himself. That is the meaning of *"He guides me in the paths of righteousness"* from *Psalm 23:3.*

Take a moment to appreciate all the action verbs in these three verses (and who the actor is and who is being acted upon). Each of these action verbs are attributed to God as the actor, none to us. We are the object of His actions. We receive His speaking to *"lie down in green pastures."* The *green pastures* are not the times in our lives when we are free from troubles. The *green pastures* referenced here is God Himself! Amid our troubles, stresses, and difficulties, God causes us to lie down and rest in Him. He is our *green pastures (and there is nothing more nourishing for sheep than green pastures).*

Likewise, when life is churning about us like a wind-driven sea, He leads us to a place where there are quiet waters that calm and restore our soul. Where is that place of *"quiet waters"?* It is a reference again to God Himself, not to a particular circumstance.

In every aspect of our lives, God is our good, all-we-need, How-Great-Thou-Art Shepherd. He isn't guiding us to calmer circumstances, but rather, in the midst of all our problems and concerns, He is guiding us more and more into Himself.

LIVING WATER FOR TODAY:

You enlarge my steps under me, and my feet have not slipped.—2 SAMUEL 22:37

For today, like King David's Psalm of deliverance, God is actively enlarging your steps; to guide you, protect you, and care for you. From His guidance, your feet can never slip away from His daily good purpose for your life. He *is your* wonderful—greater-than-anything-on-earth—GOOD SHEPHERD. *PTL!*

JUNE 14

*This figure of speech Jesus spoke to them, but they did not understand what those things were which He had been saying to them. ⁷So Jesus said to them again, "Truly, truly, I say to you. **I am the door of the sheep.** ⁸All who came before Me are thieves and robbers, but the sheep did not hear them. ⁹I am the door; if anyone enters through Me, he will be saved, and will go in and out and find pasture. ¹⁰The thief comes only to steal and kill and destroy; I came that they may have life, and have it abundantly."*

—JOHN 10:6-10

These verses contain two wonderful freedom-truths. The <u>*first*</u> is revealed in *verses seven* and *nine*. Jesus' self-describing declaration, *"I am the door; if anyone enters through Me, he will be saved"* is yet another unequivocal statement in John that belief alone in Jesus is the sole entry point into eternal salvation. Praise God! The little phrase ***through Me*** is worthy of being underlined, circled, and highlighted in color in your Bible! ALL that come <u>THROUGH CHRIST</u> (that is, everyone who believes in Him) will be saved.

All other pathways to God are likened to robbers and thieves. Jesus is contrasting Himself to all other false teachers and teachings that purport to bring peace, happiness, salvation, apart from God. Jesus uses an I AM statement to declare that He *alone* is the door to the household of God. For the first half of my Christian life, my "religion" seemed so complicated and stressful. Now it is so simple—just ***belief in Jesus!***

The <u>second</u> freedom-truth is revealed in *verse 10*, *"that they may have life, **and have it abundantly."*** Life abundant means that God's life supplies *far more* encouragement, strength, comfort, wisdom than we will ever need to meet whatever challenges we face. If we have a situation with our spouse, kids, or co-workers, *we have more than an abundant supply of God's patience, kindness, love, and wisdom to meet that situation! PTL!*

LIVING WATER FOR TODAY:

*And **He will be the stability of your times**, a wealth of salvation, wisdom and knowledge.* —ISAIAH 33:6A

For today, focus on Christ as your abundant life! You have more of God's wisdom and strength in you than you will ever need. He will *always* make you know what to say and do in every situation. *His abundant life in you is the stability of your day ... every day! PTL!*

A PERSONAL TESTIMONY:

UNDER A MICROSCOPE

A while back, I spent time with a friend who was agonizing over his constant depression and sexual addiction. He shared with me how he had been going to one counselor after another for years trying to get relief. From our discussion, it was clear that his entire focus was on putting the failures of his flesh continually "under the microscope," instead of putting Jesus under the microscope. Here is what I mean.

My friend's counselors had the singular focus of continually probing deeper into his past, believing that if they ever discovered what sins his parents (or whomever) made him the way he was, he could then deal with the problem and find relief.

John 10:9-10 contains glorious good news for my friend and for all of us!

- *"I am the door; if anyone enters through Me, he will be saved"* **(verse 9)**
- *"and will go in and out **and find pasture"*** **(verse 9)**
- *"I came that they may have life, and have it abundantly"* **(verse 10)**

Jesus tells us that He is the door into green pastures *(Psalm 23:2)* where we can enter and find rest no matter how difficult our circumstances. The more we feed on His green pasture (and lay down to rest in Him) the more we are filled with abundance in everything needed to meet whatever challenges we have in this life. *For the word of God is living and active*, accomplishing His good pleasure in us *(Hebrews 4:12)*.

We may desire to have a little more peace in our lives right now, or perhaps not be so stressed with a particular situation. There is no peace derived from focusing on our difficulties. That was the problem my friend was experiencing. By contrast, we have God's life in us, and His life is far greater than whatever is troubling us. As we simply focus on Him through verses of scripture and prayer, His abundant life fills us with his peace and rest. It is ABUNDANT, meaning, it is FAR MORE THAN ENOUGH! Jesus is our nourishing green pasture. As we feed on Him, we experience more peace, joy, and inner-contentment than we can describe—AND more comfort in times of problems and distress than we ever thought possible *(Matthew 11:28-30). PTL!*

JUNE 15

*And the **work of righteousness will be peace**, and the **service of righteousness**, quietness and confidence forever.*

—ISAIAH 32:17

In the earlier years of my Christian walk, I was fearful of death to the point of being deeply mortified. Some of you are old enough to remember the iconic poster of "Uncle Sam" pointing his finger at you. That was my demented impression of God as a sort of Uncle Sam, pointing His finger of judgment at me daily for failing to please Him adequately. "Daryl ... you haven't witnessed to at least two people today. My patience is wearing thin with you young man!"

I remember sermons on today's verse where the "work" and the "service" was something I was supposed to do for God. As I did this work and service, God would be pleased and reward me with peace and a quiet spirit (not to mention confidence). That last term "confidence" really sent chills up my spine. I wasn't confident about anything related to God. At that point in my life, though I would never have admitted it publicly, *I wasn't certain I was even saved, though I had prayed a salvation prayer hundreds of times.*

Today, I realize that the meaning of today's verse is exactly opposite to my early understanding. The **work** and **service of righteousness** are the actions of God in us, not our struggling efforts to please Him. His **work** in us produces *peace* and a *quiet spirit* that abides in us and increasingly stabilizes our lives *(Isaiah 33:6a)*. And incredibly so, produces an utmost **confidence in Him**. We no longer fear the future. We no longer fear death! We no longer fear *anything! PTL!*

LIVING WATER FOR TODAY:

*But when this perishable will have put on the imperishable, and this mortal will have put on immortality, then will come about the saying that is written, "**DEATH IS SWALLOWED UP IN VICTORY**. [55]O DEATH, WHERE IS YOUR VICTORY? O DEATH, WHERE IS YOUR STING?"*—1 CORINTHIANS 15:54-55

For today, raise a prayer of thanksgiving in your heart to God for His work and service of righteousness in you; for He is producing a peaceful, quiet spirit, and confidence in you that surpasses all understanding *(Philippians 4:6-7). PTL!*

JUNE 16

*For **He has satisfied** the thirsty soul, and the hungry soul **He has filled with what is good.***

—PSALM 107:9

Today's verse is a small sliver of scripture that delivers a huge slice of powerful reality! In recent days we have been enjoying how the Lord is our good shepherd. How He leads us in and out of God's sheepfold. How He leads us by still waters and causes us to lay down in green pastures. As we spend time in His word, He brings His word to life in us as a living and active person, piercing and renewing our deepest thoughts. He is the Potter and we the clay, and His work is totally transformative in us.

I once thought of the Bible as nothing more than black ink on white paper. In that dead, static form, it was (for me) mostly incomprehensible—swinging erratically from something frightening to something boring. BUT NO LONGER! Now it is a candy store, full of *calorie-free chocolates* for me to eat daily and be nourished by. As we spend time in His word, *God is actively performing His works and service, creating within us a peaceful and quiet spirit, and a foundation of trust and confidence in Him.*

One way I spend more time in God's word is surprisingly simple, yet so impactful. I take verses that the Lord is touching me with and I write them on 3x5 cards or sticky notes and tape them everywhere I spend time during the day (like at my desk and in the car). I find the Lord frequently *drawing my eyes to the very verse I need* at that moment and transforming my worry and anxiety into *"still waters and green pastures."*

LIVING WATER FOR TODAY:

*Oh **give thanks to the LORD, for He is good,** for His lovingkindness is everlasting.*—PSALM 107:1

***For today**,* fill your heart with thanksgiving to the Lord, for as He lives within you He is providing everything you need to meet the challenges before you. Contemplate the many manifestations of the Lord's lovingkindness to you, even in the presence of the struggles you are currently facing. He is today, your "still water." He is caring for all that concerns you! He is all you need! He is your amazing 24/7 *good* shepherd! *Just rest in Him!*

June 17

"I am the good shepherd; the good shepherd lays down His life for the sheep. [12]He who is a hired hand, and not a shepherd, who is not the owner of the sheep, sees the wolf coming, and leaves the sheep and flees, and the wolf snatches them and scatters them. [13]He flees because he is a hired hand and is not concerned about the sheep. [14]I am the good shepherd, and I know My own and My own know Me, [15]even as the Father knows Me and I know the Father; and I lay down My life for the sheep."

—John 10:11-15

The incredible power within these verses is contained in the corollary we can easily deduce from the statements Jesus made. At the time, Jesus was speaking to Jewish religious leaders who knew only of the common practice in their culture for tending sheep. Often, a person would be hired to tend the sheep in the owner's absence. While this may include some danger associated with the job, no one expected a hired hand to give up his life for someone else's sheep. If the threat to them grew too great, it was assumed that the hired hand would ultimately put his own survival first.

Jesus contrasted Himself sharply from this typical hired hand. He is the *owner* of the sheep, He knows each of them and each of them knows Him, and He is willing to lay down His life for each of them. What we know now (that the religious leaders did not know at the time) was that Jesus' comment about laying down His life was exactly what He did for us! In the fullness of time, Jesus laid down His life on the cross to bring salvation to all His sheep—every child God the Father had given Him *(John 10:29)*.

What is the powerful corollary implied from what Jesus has stated? We must conclude that *if* Jesus loved us enough to die for us (a historical fact), *then* we can certainly trust Him to care for *everything* else about us. After all, *He now owns us and knows us by name!*

Living Water for Today:

"My Father, who has given them to Me, is greater than all; and no one is able to snatch them out of the Father's hand."—John 10:29

For today, meditate on just two truths: *First*, if Jesus was willing to pay the ultimate price by laying down His life *for you*, how much more will He do all things necessary to daily care for you? And *second*, the **confidence** you have in knowing that God is greater than all, and no one can snatch you out of His caring hands—*ever! PTL!*

June 18

*"I have other sheep, which are not of this fold; I must bring them also, and **they will hear My voice; and they will become one flock with one shepherd.**"*

—JOHN 10:16

This is a verse that many have used as a proof-text over the centuries to suggest all manner of wildly expansive interpretations regarding who God is offering salvation to. Some teach that the "other sheep" in this verse suggests that God is really the author of all religions and will eventually bring all humanity into a universal salvation. Some suggest that Jesus is referring to other dimensions in a space-time continuum, or other worlds in the universe that follow Jesus, not just our planet.

From the immediate context, however, the interpretation of *verse 16* is not so complicated or mysterious. In *verses 1-15* Jesus has been speaking to the Jewish religious leaders about God's sheepfold, referring to Israel (the Jewish people). Then in *verse 16*, He refers to *"other sheep"* in reference to the Gentiles (which includes you and me) as those who will also *"hear My voice; and **they will become one flock with one shepherd.**"* This is consistent with what Paul is referring to when he writes to the Gentile Christians in Ephesus regarding how they were once separate from Christ and excluded from the commonwealth of Israel but are now brought near by the blood of Christ, who made both groups one and has broken down the barrier between them *(Ephesians 2:12-14).*

LIVING WATER FOR TODAY:

Remember that you were at that time separate from Christ, excluded from the commonwealth of Israel, and strangers to the covenants of promise, having no hope and without God in the world. ¹³*But now in Christ Jesus you who formerly were far off have been brought near by the blood of Christ.* ¹⁴*For He Himself is our peace, **who made both groups into one** and broke down the barrier of the dividing wall.*—EPHESIANS 2:12-14

For today, rejoice from morning 'til night, that *you*—who were once far off from God, have been made near to Him solely through the shed blood of Jesus. So now, just like the chosen people of Israel, you also hear the Lord's voice and follow Him; and are completely forgiven of your sins because God has given *you* belief in Jesus as your Savior. *Praise the Lord, then praise Him again!*

JUNE 19

*He who did not spare His own Son, but delivered Him over for us all, **how will He not also with Him freely give us all things?***

—ROMANS 8:32

What an incredible verse this is! Even our finite human reasoning can grasp this logical concept. If God, to complete His salvation plan for those He has chosen, would not spare something as infinitely priceless as the life of His own Son from experiencing death on our behalf, what other possible thing could exist that He would now not freely give us? The logical answer is *nothing exists* that He would not provide us. As the scripture says, ***"how will He not also with Him** [His Son] **freely give us all things?"***

In my earlier years as a Christian, I thought this verse was referring to all the *physical things* I needed. Now I recognize the little phrase "ALL THINGS" means so much more. In fact, ask yourself this question: *What things are omitted from the "all things" referenced in this verse?* Answer: *Nothing is omitted!* God did not spare His own Son's life for us just so He could scrimp on the other needs we would have in this life. Scripture says He will also freely give us *all things*—which refers to all our physical and spiritual needs!

Here is an example: If we are sad, God knew this before we were born and is shepherding what we need. If we need more trust in Him, He is shepherding that. If we need a Christian friend, He knows, and is shepherding that for us. He is the How-Great-Thou-Art Shepherd actively working and servicing our needs, both physical and spiritual; caring about us in every respect—*every day, all the time!* What can the sheep do for itself? Nothing. *Thank you, dear God, that You provide everything we need!*

LIVING WATER FOR TODAY:

*What then shall we say to these things? **If God is for us, who is against us?***—ROMANS 8:31

For today, contemplate this simple and direct question throughout your day: If God is for YOU, who can be against you? Every thought—that God is against you, or displeased with you, or forgotten you—are utter and complete lies from the enemy of God! God did not offer up His own Son's life for you, only to put you again under bondage to anything or anyone. If God is for you—you can't ever be truly cheated, unloved, uncared-for, unappreciated ... *ever! PTL!*

JUNE 20

*Now the **God of peace**, who brought up from the dead the great Shepherd of the sheep through the blood of the eternal covenant, even Jesus our Lord, ²¹**equip you in every good thing to do His will**, working in us that which is pleasing in His sight, **through Jesus Christ**, to whom be the glory forever and ever. Amen.*

—HEBREWS 13:20-21

The ***God of peace*** is such a wonderful description for our God. The more He draws us deeper into an understanding of His work and service within us, the more we experience an ever-deepening and abiding peace in our hearts about everything.

Understanding these two verses in context is a good example of what I mean. *Verse 20* tells us that the ***God of peace*** brought up from the dead the great Shepherd of the sheep (Jesus Christ) through the blood of the eternal covenant. So far, that is easy enough to follow. But then it gets interesting because a false understanding of *verse 21* can crush a person under religious bondage, while a correct understanding of the same verse results in glorious freedom. Let's see where this *verse 21* takes us.

It says the ***God of peace*** will *"equip you in every good thing to do His will, **working in us** that which is pleasing in His sight, through Jesus Christ."* Does the verse say that the ***God of peace*** equips us with every good thing so that WE can work that which is pleasing in His sight? No! The glorious, good news from *verse 21* tells us the opposite. The ***God of peace*** has equipped us with *every good thing* (like His faith, patience, perseverance, prayer, His word, etc.). This process of "equipping" us by God is God (not us) *"**working in us** that which is pleasing in His sight, through Jesus Christ"* who is our great Shepherd! Praise God for His working in us all the things that are pleasing to Him! Do we do His will? Yes! *Not because of our effort, but because God is working His will in us! PTL!*

LIVING WATER FOR TODAY:

***For it is God who is at work in you**, both to will and to work for His good pleasure.*—PHILIPPIANS 2:13

***For today**, be confident that the God of peace is working all His perfect will in your life, in and through all your various circumstances and difficulties. Rejoice in what the Apostle Paul declared in *Philippians 1:6, "For I am confident of this very thing, that **He who began a good work in you will perfect it** until the day of Christ Jesus."*

LIVING WATER FROM JOHN 10:1-18

June 11	As we become intimately attuned to God's voice, we grow in trusting His leading in our life.
June 12	Jesus, the good shepherd, is directing everything concerning our daily care and protection.
June 13	The Lord is active throughout our lives—through all our difficulties and problems—leading us deeper into Himself.
June 14	Jesus alone is the door to eternal life.
June 15	The work and service of righteousness are the actions of God, not us.
June 16	God's word satisfies the thirsty soul, and the hungry soul He has filled with what is good.
June 17	Jesus knows each of His sheep by name and they know Him.
June 18	We who were formerly far off have been brought near and have become one flock with one great shepherd.
June 19	God who did not spare His own Son, freely gives us ALL things, which include both our physical and spiritual needs.
June 20	The God of peace has equipped us with every good thing to do His will, working in us the things that are pleasing to Him.

PRAYER

*Father, my heart is overflowing with worship and praise to
You for Your continual work and service in me. Whether
You are the potter and I am clay, or You are the vine and I
am just a branch, or You are the good shepherd and I but a
dumb sheep, the message is the same: You are the source of
everything. I can do nothing for myself without You.
In Your eternal plan of salvation for me, You did not spare
the life of Your own Son; and even now, You withhold
nothing that is good for me. You are equipping me with
every good thing that is pleasing to You. I experience faith
because you have equipped me with Your faith. I am
nurtured and guided by Your word because You have
equipped me with both Your spoken word on my heart and
the written word inspired by You for my benefit. I am safe
in Your sheepfold because You have given me Your Son
as my good shepherd, who even in the midst of turbulent
times, guides me to rest and find sustenance in Him
as my green pastures and quiet waters. Again and again
I lift my worship and praise to You.
In the precious name of Jesus, my great Shepherd.
Amen.*

GOD WILL NEVER LOSE YOU

———

JOHN 10:19-42

JUNE 21

*A division occurred again among the Jews **because of these words.***

—JOHN 10:19

God's words always affect us! Once again, the crowd was in turmoil, some saying *"He has a demon and is insane" (verse 20)*, while others were saying, *"These are not the sayings of one demon-possessed. A demon cannot open the eyes of the blind, can he?" (verse 21)*.

We have seen before how God protected His Son through timely disputes among the religious leaders concerning who Jesus was (*see May 7* and the following page 226; and *June 4* as examples). These disputes distracted them momentarily from their hearts' evil intention to harm Jesus prematurely. There was coming a perfect moment for God's grace to achieve its goal on the cross, when Jesus would lay down His life for His sheep. That perfect moment had not yet fully come.

Notice how God's word affects *every* person it touches. This was no civil discussion among a group of Jewish people who didn't personally care. It was an impassioned argument with life-or-death implications. Emotions were running hot. These Jewish leaders simply could not wrap their minds around the possibility that Almighty God, Creator of the universe, was standing there speaking to them. This is a wonderful insight for us today. We often do the same thing, by marinating in our worries and stresses, while we have the How-Great-Thou-Art Almighty God living in us, speaking His word into our hearts and affecting us in ways we simply cannot comprehend. *PTL!*

LIVING WATER FOR TODAY:

So will My word be which goes forth from My mouth;
it will not return to Me empty, without accomplishing
what I desire, and without succeeding in the matter
for which I sent it. —ISAIAH 55:11

For today, find comfort and confidence in this very thing: that God's living word, which abides in you and is given to you in scripture, never fails to accomplish what it is sent out to do. Like a potter crafting clay, God's word is sculpting every single detail of His plan for your life, your complete redemption, salvation, sanctification *(1 Corinthians 1:30)*, and total transformation from glory to glory into His image *(2 Corinthians 3:18)*, every day, amidst all your stresses, problems, and concerns. He is doing it all. *PTL!*

HOW POWERFUL AND EFFECTIVE
IS GOD'S WORD?

In my personal testimony following the *January 4* devotional, I shared my experience of visiting a missionary school in India. It took about 25 hours, in a jet flying at 600 miles per hour, to accomplish this feat. I was stunned when I realized that all this flying had only brought me halfway around this one planet earth. And our one sun is large enough to swallow up one million, four hundred thousand (1,400,000) earths! As amazing as that may seem, astronomers have been using the Hubble space telescope for years to inventory and catalog the number of suns and galaxies in the entire universe. Using the Hubble, that number has been expressed in billions. But now, in 2022, a larger and more exacting telescope (the James Webb space telescope) was launched and became operational. To their amazement, scientists have already learned that the universe is likely at least ten times *more expansive* than they had estimated before.

In *Genesis 1:3*, we read that God spoke just four words *"Let there be light"* and the sun, moon, stars, and galaxies all burst forth. Our scientists have no explanation for the existence of the entire universe other than to explain it in terms of a "big bang" theory—that the entire universe exploded out of a pinpoint of nothingness. God's record describes this same event as God speaking those four words, *"Let there be light."* Which of these two versions requires more faith for you to believe? Personally, I don't have enough faith to NOT believe in God's explanation of creation. The non-God version makes no sense at all. Billions of stars and galaxies exploding out of nothing? *Really?*

The bottom line from John is this: the God of all creation was standing there talking to these religious leaders and the crowd surrounding them. By this time, He had performed miracle after miracle right in front of them. Yet, they could not understand it. Some thought He was crazy, while others thought He had a demon.

Today, we Christians certainly don't think that Jesus was a demon. But many of us still don't comprehend any better than those religious leaders who Jesus really is—that He is the How-Great-Thou-Art Creator God, who is not only in our midst, but living in each one of us today. He is the same God who miraculously caused the blind man to see, and is now the very God who lives fully in you and me. PTL!

JUNE 22

*Declaring the end from the beginning, and from ancient times things which have not been done, saying, "**My purpose will be established, and I will accomplish all My good pleasure.**"*

—ISAIAH 46:10

The God who created everything said in today's verse, "***My purpose will be established, and I will accomplish all My good pleasure.***" This is the same God who abides in each one of us! How life-changing this is, yet many Christians do not fully understand it.

I am not saying these Christians are not believers. They *certainly* ARE believers, but many do not yet comprehend this glorious freedom-truth in an experiential way in their lives. I am not being critical or judgmental here; none of us are fully enlightened. We are all at differing points on God's ever-brightening path of the righteous *(Proverbs 4:18)*. But as we grow to understand the implications of today's verse, we find ourselves resting more and more in His care for us. We increasingly trust that He is maturing us spiritually in *HIS* timing and at *HIS* pace.

This is an understanding that only our Almighty, Creator God can reveal in us. As He does, our trust in Him deepens. We gain confidence that He has truly chosen to redeem us and live in us; and fulfill His promises to accomplish all His good pleasure in us. At some point, it finally dawns on us that *there is nothing left for us to do*, but praise and worship Him throughout our day for all that He has done (and is doing). Our old concept of "partnering with God" falls away. *We experience true joy and peace in Him!*

LIVING WATER FOR TODAY:

*Now the **God of peace**, who brought up from the dead the great Shepherd of the sheep through the blood of the eternal covenant, even Jesus our Lord, ²¹**equip you in every good thing to do His will**, working in us that which is pleasing in His sight, **through Jesus Christ**, to whom be the glory forever and ever. Amen.*—HEBREWS 13:20-21

For today, recognize our flesh wants us to believe that it can't be all God and nothing of us; but that is what scripture repeatedly tells us—God has done it all, He is all *YOU* need. Believe Jesus when He said, *"It* (all of it) *is finished!"* This will not make you lazy, *it will energize you for God's work in unfettered freedom.*

RECONCILING GOD'S GRACE
AND "COMMANDS"

For years I couldn't fit together how all of scripture talks about the grace of God and that He is accomplishing all His good pleasure *(Isaiah 46:10; Philippians 2:13, 1:6; Hebrews 4:12; Romans 1:16, 11:36; James 1:17; 1 John 3:2, 4:4; Proverbs 4:18; John 1:12-13, 3:16, 10:3-4, 14:26, 15:16; Galatians 3:1-3, 15-16; Ephesians 2:8-9; Acts 3:16, 10:47, 16:30a-31b; Psalm 27:1; 2 Corinthians 3:18, just to name a few)*; yet other sections of scripture, like *Romans 12*, seem to be chocked full of "commands" for us to try our best to accomplish on our own. How can we reconcile this?

Hebrews 13:20-21 helped me unravel this mystery: *"Now **the God of peace**, who brought up from the dead the **great Shepherd of the sheep** ... ²¹**equip you** in every good thing to do His will, **working in us that which is pleasing in His sight, through Jesus Christ, to whom be the glory forever and ever."***

First, note that Christ the great Shepherd (not us) gets all the glory. *Second*, know that God didn't fill scripture with assurances that He alone is accomplishing all His good pleasure (and His Son is the good shepherd daily directing our paths) *only to later say*, "Oh, wait a minute, scratch that—you need to do your part of the work, or you will disappoint Me (even make Me angry)." One thing we know, scripture never contradicts itself. So, how are these scriptures reconciled?

Hebrews 13:20-21 gives us the key. Jesus is our **great Shepherd** living now in us! This fact remains vibrant and true *whenever* and *wherever* we are reading in scripture. For example, we read in *1 Thessalonians 5:14*, *"be patient with everyone."* God, in this verse, is NOT telling us to reach for our bootstraps and try harder to make ourselves patient. At that moment, as we read this scripture, *God is commanding patience into us!* None of us can produce an ounce of godly patience on our own. Only the great Shepherd of the sheep is powerful enough to lead us into His patience (like the potter and the clay). Our flesh always wants to take some credit. In truth, *it is the great Shepherd who does it all.*

So, why all these exhortations and "commands" in scripture? Remember, the word of God does not go forth without accomplishing that for which it was sent *(Isaiah 55:11)*; and that His word is living and active *(Hebrews 4:12)*. In our modern day, we tend to trivialize the power of God's word as though it is merely black ink on white paper, rather than what it *truly* is: the spoken words of the How-Great-Thou-Art-Almighty-Creator God! His word never returns to Him without accomplishing that for which it was sent.

When we read, *"Be anxious for nothing" (Philippians 4:6)*, or *"Be still and know that I am God" (Psalm 46:10 NIV)*, these words are not something that simply pass in one ear and out the other. This is the *same* powerful word as those spoken by the Creator God, *"Let there be light,"* and the universe exploded into billions of galaxies. This *same* word is *still* living and active and *always* accomplishing what it was sent out to do. We may not see or feel it instantly, but it *is* working.

Think of it this way, if you had been any one of those that Jesus healed: the crippled man *(John 5:5-8)*, the blind man *(John 9:1-14)*, the woman with an 18-year affliction *(Luke 13:10-17)*, or Lazarus while he was still dead *(John 11:1-45)*, do you think any of them interpreted Jesus' words as a command, or as something they needed to apply to their life and try harder to do on their own? Jesus said, *"Get up, pick up your pallet and walk."* Do you imagine that the crippled man interpreted what Jesus said as a command for him to try harder to walk? No! He didn't even think about it—but just immediately rose up. The Lord's words were powerful and effective. They were not dependent on the crippled man's cooperation, understanding, or prior exemplary religious conduct. Each of these miracles were the same. The Lord's words did the work they were intended to do. Lazarus' experience is the most obvious. Did Lazarus, who was truly dead at the time Jesus spoke, somehow determine that Jesus' command was intended for him to rededicate himself to coming back to life on his own? Of course not! Why then, do we think that commands in scripture today are different for us?

We have all experienced feeling stressed over something, then God brings to our mind a verse like *Psalm 46:10 (NIV)* (or we read it), *"Be still and know that I am God."* These are living words spoken by God with creative power. We feel our shoulders relax. We turn to God and praise Him. Just like the crippled, the blind, the ill, and the dead, scripture is speaking the Lord's words. God's words are not a command for us to try harder, but words of creation, bringing about in us the very thing that the word declares. It is God performing His work in us *(Philippians 2:13)*. PTL!

June 23

*For this reason we also constantly thank God that when you received the word of God which you heard from us, you accepted it not as the word of men, **but for what it really is, the word of God, which also performs its work in you who believe.***

—1 Thessalonians 2:13

Here is yet another verse which declares that God's word is performing its work in us who believe *(Christians)*. Every time we read *"be patient with everyone."* *(1 Thessalonians 5:14)* God's word works a tiny bit more patience in us. This is truly a miracle! We have no capacity to be patient on our own. God is infinitely patient, and He is transforming us day by day into His own image *(2 Corinthians 3:18)*. He does this, in part, through the power of His word, working through every circumstance we find ourselves in.

This process has produced a miracle in my life no less significant than Jesus healing the cripple or giving sight to the blind man. As a young Christian, I didn't want too much God but was possessed with making more and more money. I thought money was the answer, but this compulsion left me stressed beyond my ability to cope. I was taking six Valium a day just to get by. This unhappiness bled over to my homelife—to my wife and kids. Divorce seemed to be the inevitable solution to my unhappiness.

In those years, left to my own devices, I could find no path forward other than more stress and misery. I was as helpless as the cripple, the blind man, and the dead Lazarus. But God was working in me! He drew me to His word, spoke to my heart a prayer, a thought, a verse. He brought a kind word to me from a friend. Today, I can testify with rejoicing that all these early afflictions have completely fallen away. I have nothing to boast of in myself. *ALL* the glory goes to God, and my great Shepherd, Jesus!

Living Water for Today:

*Being manifested that **you are a letter of Christ** ... written not with ink but with the Spirit of the living God.*—2 Corinthians 3:3a

For today, take comfort that your good shepherd is indwelling you, and daily leading you through His spoken and written word. He is writing His teachings, exhortations, and guidance onto the tablets of your heart; *creating (over the course of your life) an imprint that is changing you.* YOU are in God's process of making you a reflection of His word!

JUNE 24

At that time the Feast of the Dedication took place at Jerusalem; ²³it was winter, and Jesus was walking in the temple in the portico of Solomon. ²⁴The Jews then gathered around Him, and were saying to Him, "How long will You keep us in suspense? If You are the Christ, tell us plainly." ²⁵Jesus answered them, "I told you, and you do not believe; the works that I do in My Father's name, these testify of Me. ²⁶But you do not believe because you are not of My sheep. ²⁷My sheep hear My voice, and I know them, and they follow Me."
—JOHN 10:22-27

Today's verses declare an incredible affirmation of a freedom-truth for every believer—that Jesus, God's great Shepherd of the flock, *will not lose a single one of us* from His sheepfold. How glorious is that?

The context is the Feast of Dedication (which today is called Hanukkah). Hanukkah represents the reconsecration of the Temple after it was desecrated in 168 BC. It was winter, and Jesus was in Jerusalem walking in the Temple's portico of Solomon.

The Jews surrounded Him, demanding that He tell them clearly whether He was the Christ. Jesus responded that He had already done so, and all His miracles told them who He was as well. Then Jesus reveals the most amazing truth! He says, *"you do not believe because you are not of My sheep."* What? Shouldn't Jesus have said "you are not of My sheep because you do not believe?" Shouldn't our believing be the precursor to becoming one of the Lord's sheep? *Not according to Jesus.* This is only our human logic wanting to make us the center of attention. Jesus' statement is clear and unambiguous: our belief is the *result* (not the cause) of our being chosen by God to be His sheep. *PTL!*

LIVING WATER FOR TODAY:

Just as He chose us in Him before the foundation of the world, that we would be holy and blameless before Him.
—EPHESIANS 1:4

For today, be comforted by the fact that long before creation began, before God created the world you now live on, He knew you. He knew that He would create and choose YOU to be a child (a sheep) in His household. You had nothing to do with it, and therefore, you can never do anything that will "undo" it. Nothing can separate you from this immense, priceless, amazing love of God *(Romans 8:39). PTL!*

JUNE 25

*"My sheep hear My voice, and **I know them**, and they follow Me."*
—JOHN 10:27

W e talk a lot about knowing God but what is Jesus referring to when He says, *"I know them"*? On *June 11* we saw how Jesus personalized this even further. Referring to Himself as the good shepherd, He declared: *"He calls His own sheep by name."* What does it mean for God to "know" us *by name*?

First, this must be considered in the context of *Ephesians 1:4*. When He tells us that *He calls us by name* means God (the good shepherd), before He laid the foundation of the world, identified us individually, knowing everything about us: all the struggles with our flesh, all the sin in our lives, all our good and bad choices, all our desires for something other than God. Knowing all of it, our good shepherd still chose us to be part of His eternal sheepfold. God is omniscient, from beginning to end He knows it all. *He knew every unique detail making up our entire lives and He chose us anyway!* What mercy!

Second, the working shepherds in Jesus' day often named their sheep after something unique or peculiar about each individual one in their flock. By giving each sheep unique and individualized names based on these peculiar qualities, they had the ability to not only guide the entire flock but also individual sheep in the flock. Again, this leads us to worship God for His love and mercy to us. He knows each of us individually as His sheep. He knows our DNA, our personalities, our differing backgrounds, and how each of us have emerged from differing broken homes or circumstances. We each have different experiences in our individual lives right up to the present. He knows it all. He is not only a good shepherd generally, but a good shepherd *individually* to each of us!

LIVING WATER FOR TODAY:

*Just as **He chose us in Him before the foundation of the world**, that we would be holy and blameless before Him.*
—EPHESIANS 1:4

For today, take comfort in knowing that long before you became aware of your belief in God and Jesus as your personal savior, God had already chosen you before He created the universe. His love for you, and the security of your life with Him in eternity, was a higher priority than creation itself. This illustrates just how much God loves you. *PTL!*

June 26

*"And I give eternal life to them, and they will never perish; and **no one will snatch them out of My hand**. ²⁹My Father, who has given them to Me, is greater than all; and **no one is able to snatch them out of the Father's hand**. ³⁰I and the Father are one."*
—John 10:28-30

I suggest that every Christian highlight these three verses in their Bible, and maybe dog-ear this page. So whenever the enemy of our salvation tells us that we can lose it—if we have some unconfessed sin in our life, or if we are not living for the Lord as wholeheartedly as we should, or if we can lose it for whatever reason—we know where to find these verses quickly. We should put them on a 3x5 card and keep them handy.

There are those who interpret the verse, *"I and the Father are one"* as referencing the unity of the Father and the Son in the triune Godhead. This would require us to believe that Jesus suddenly jumped to a new theological topic in the midst of this conversation. The narrative's context, however, suggests a more compelling meaning—that both God the Father and Son (the good shepherd) are united in ONE PURPOSE—**the protection and preservation of our salvation!** Jesus is making an unqualified statement that the unified power of God the Father and God the Son is committed to securing our eternal life—*not just in eternity, but day by day right now.* No one is *able* [capable, crafty, or powerful enough] *to snatch us out of His hand or the Father's hand. PTL!*

Once again, remind yourself: these are the words of God! The same God who spoke but four words, *"Let there be light,"* and the entire universe containing billions of galaxies exploded into being, this same God is telling us that *nothing* can separate us from Him!

LIVING WATER FOR TODAY:

*For I am convinced that neither death, nor life, nor angels, nor principalities, nor things present, nor things to come, nor powers, ³⁹nor height, nor depth, **nor any other created thing, will be able to separate us from the love of God, which is in Christ Jesus our Lord.*** —ROMANS 8:38-39

For today, nothing can separate you from the love of God. NOTHING! *Verse 39* says **no created thing** can separate you from the love of God. *That includes you!* So ... you don't hang onto God—He hangs onto YOU! *PTL! PTL! PTL!*

JUNE 27

*"And I give eternal life to them, **and they will never perish**; and no one will snatch them out of My hand."*

—JOHN 10:28

The phrase *"**and they will never perish**"* is an emphatic term in the Greek, perhaps more accurately translated as it is in the *Amplified Bible*, *"they will never, ever* [by any means] *perish."* The Lord, here, is placing further emphasis on this glorious truth: that all of God's power is committed to His united purpose of protecting and securing our eternal life. *Praise Almighty God!* Let's consider this from two perspectives.

From the Lord's perspective, the one who spoke these encouraging words to us, He knows the enemy's relentless activity in our flesh, warring against us continually. How he buries us in guilt and doubt or thinking that our salvation depends on us. God knows the whispers from the enemy: *"Be careful not to disappoint God, He will punish you, even take back your salvation, if you make Him angry."* The enemy infuses our minds with an image of God as an aloof dictator, sitting on a cloud somewhere waiting to strike us down with lightning if we don't behave like "good" Christians. God knows the enemy's playbook, so He continues in scripture to repeat this truth, which is actively working daily to renew our minds and free us from the enemy's bondage and lies.

From John's perspective, he repeats this truth again because he wants us to be joyous, happy, and free from the burden of vain self-effort. *"But these have been written **so that you may believe** that Jesus is the Christ, the Son of God; **and that believing you may have life in His name"** (John 20:31).* Nothing in John's writings suggest our salvation is conditional or tentative. *To John, our salvation is as unchangeable as God Himself!*

LIVING WATER FOR TODAY:

*"This is the will of Him who sent Me, that of **all that He has given Me I lose nothing**, but raise it up on the last day."*—JOHN 6:39

For today, sit down in your most comfortable easy chair and let your whole being relax as you contemplate God's word. God promises you unequivocally that you (the believer) are saved eternally and *there is no possibility for you under any condition or circumstance to ever lose that salvation.* Why? Because YOU are protected by all the power of God Himself. *PTL!*

JUNE 28

For I am convinced that neither death, nor life, nor angels, nor principalities,
nor things present, nor things to come, nor powers, [39]*nor height, nor depth, nor any*
other created thing, **will be able to separate us from the love of God, which is in**
Christ Jesus our Lord.

—ROMANS 8:38-39

Yesterday's verses gave us two perspectives on the fact that we can never lose our salvation. Today's verses allow us to look at this glorious truth from yet a third perspective. The Apostle Paul takes this same absolute and unequivocal truth *(Nothing can snatch us out of the Father's or Son's hands)*, and expands it to a universal, absolute, and unequivocal fact! While you read today's verses, try your best to think of something that is **not** included in Paul's list that has the capacity to separate you from God's love. If you think of something, I want you to email me (daryl@gugf.org) and share what you have found. Over decades, I have made this request numerous times, but I have yet to receive a single reply. Why? Because *nothing* is excluded from Paul's exhaustive list, *not even us!*

Paul culminates his list with the phrase *"nor height, nor depth, nor any other created thing."* No matter how high you go or how low you feel, you are still *in* God's creation and *part of* His eternal family. Paul's list leaves only one thing out of the list: that is, GOD Himself, the Creator of everything that is on the list. And He is the One who will never allow anything to separate us from His love! *PTL!*

So, how secure is our salvation? As secure as God is! *Praise the Lord!*

LIVING WATER FOR TODAY:

Be strong and let your heart take courage, all ***you who***
***hope in the* LORD.**—PSALM 31:24

For today, rejoice in the Lord, that He has chosen you to hope and believe in Him, which daily has the effect the Lord intends for you—that your heart of faith grows stronger and is filled with confidence (courage) in His guiding and protecting you every moment of every day, all the time, and in every circumstance; even when you walk through the valley of the shadow of death, you and God are inseparable! *PTL!*

JUNE 29

*Jesus answered them, "Has it not been written in your Law, 'I SAID, **YOU ARE GODS**'?* *³⁵If he called them gods, to whom the word of God came (and the Scripture cannot be broken), ³⁶do you say of Him, whom the Father sanctified and sent into the world, 'You are blaspheming,' because I said, '**I am the Son of God**'?"*

—JOHN 10:34-36

Verse 34 has been bothersome to many Christians for centuries and has led in history to wildly distorted doctrines about God being a polytheistic God—that the earliest forms of the Jewish religion revered a pantheon of gods and only later evolved into a monotheistic faith. However, the context in which Jesus is speaking here is much simpler to understand. Jesus simply quoted *Psalm 82:6* as a verse the Jewish leaders understood well since it is part of the Hebrew scriptures they so deeply revered. If they could believe that God spoke in the heavens to a gathering of *elohim* (the Hebrew word translated in the plural as "gods"), how could they not also believe that this same God could send His Son to earth to give them life-saving deliverance? Jesus is merely using God's written word to expose their false logic and reveal their hypocrisy.

Hebrew scriptures use the word *elohim* to refer to a variety of heavenly beings (obviously to *Yahweh* Himself, the God of Israel, in thousands of places, *Genesis 2:4-5, Deuteronomy 4:35*; but also to members of *Yahweh's* counsel, *Psalm 82:1, 6*; gods and goddesses of other nations, *Judges 11:24, 1 Kings 11:33*; demons, *Deuteronomy 32:17*; the deceased human Samuel, *1 Samuel 28:13*, and angels, or the angel of *Yahweh, Genesis 35:7*). The Jewish leaders speaking with Jesus would not have confused the *elohim* referenced in *Psalm 82:6* with the *elohim* of Almighty God. All *elohim* in the Hebrew scriptures have one thing in common: they are all "residents of the spiritual world."

LIVING WATER FOR TODAY:

*I said, "You are gods, and **all of you are sons of the Most High**.* —PSALM 82:6

For today, take comfort in the fact that like those in *Psalm 82*, you are also a child of the Most High, and the Almighty *Elohim* of the Hebrew scriptures now owns you, lives in you, daily guides you, comforts and protects you, and secures your life with Him forever. *PTL!*

June 30

*Just as **He chose us in Him before the foundation of the world**, that we would be holy and blameless before Him.*

—Ephesians 1:4

Over the last ten days we have been blessed to learn how God grows in us *everything* that pleases Him *(June 21-22)*; that He is our personal great Shepherd—knowing everything about us, calling us individually by name, and caring for us daily *(June 23)*; that nothing in all of creation (including ourselves) can steal us out of His saving hands for He and the Father are one in this purpose *(June 24)*; and last, that we can NEVER lose our salvation *(June 26-28)*. With all these life-changing truths set before us, how can we not rejoice and rejoice again at today's verse. We can, without a moment's hesitancy, cast every worry, doubt, and concern that causes us anxiety onto our loving God without fear that He will reject us in any fashion. He loved us and chose us before the foundation of the world and sent His Son to cover every sin we will ever commit with His precious, sinless blood. Praise the Lord for His great mercy and grace!

God has made His salvation PERSONAL for you and me! He knows every detail about us and loves us. There is nothing in our hearts or actions that we should shy away from sharing with Him because there is nothing hidden from His sight *(Hebrews 4:12-13)*. Take today's verse without any ifs, ands, or buts and cast ALL your anxieties on Him. *Throw it all away*, knowing that your How-Great-Thou-Art good shepherd is caring for every detail of your life, every moment of every day. *PTL!*

LIVING WATER FOR TODAY:

I will be your God through all your lifetime, *yes, even when your hair is white with age. **I made you and I will care for you.** I will carry you along and be your Savior.*—Isaiah 46:4 TLB

For today, give praise in your heart to God for His unmeasurable faithfulness to you. He is the One who created you just as you are, and at every stage of your life, He is the One caring for you. You can't disappoint Him! You can't help Him! You can't separate yourself from Him! What amazing comfort and stability you have in *YOUR PERSONAL* How-Great-Thou-Art good shepherd. *PTL!*

LIVING WATER FROM JOHN 10:19-42

June 21	Almighty God living in us speaks His word into our hearts.
June 22	The God of peace equips us in every good thing to do His will and energizes us for His work in unrestrained freedom.
June 23	The word of God performs its work in us who believe.
June 24	Our belief is the result of being chosen by God, and Jesus will not lose a single one.
June 25	God knows us individually and calls us by name.
June 26	Jesus gives us eternal life, and no one can (or is able to) snatch us out of His or the Father's hand.
June 27	God's power is committed to His united purpose of protecting and securing our eternal life.
June 28	God is guiding and protecting us every moment of every day, and nothing can separate us from His love.
June 29	We are children of the Most High God and Almighty *Elohim* lives in us.
June 30	"I will be your God through all your lifetime ... I will carry you along and be your Savior" *(Isaiah 46:4 TLB)*.

PRAYER

Father, what can my heart possibly say in praise and worship to You for all these great truths from Your word. You have called me by name! Before the foundation of the world You knew me, the person I would be including all the sinfulness of my flesh, and You still loved me and chose me to be Your child as a sheep in Your sheepfold. How tenuous and frightened I can be, yet Your love for me is more stable and unchangeable than the foundations of the world itself. Nothing can remove me from Your hands.

I am Yours … I am saved … I am safe!

So, I am comforted in You. I no longer fear for my salvation. My salvation was secure before creation began. And Your creation continues in my life even up to the present day. I rejoice in Your word in Psalms 46:10, "Be still, and know that I am God." You are the One at work in me, both to will and to work Your good pleasure. You expect nothing from me! How can I adequately thank you dear God for Your love and mercy to me.

In the precious name of Jesus, my personal—
How-Great-Thou-Truly-Art—good shepherd.

Amen.

My Living Water Thoughts

My Living Water Thoughts

My Living Water Thoughts

_____

_____

_____

_____

_____

_____

_____

_____

_____

_____

_____

_____

_____

_____

_____

_____

_____

_____

_____

_____

_____

_____

_____

_____

_____

_____

My Living Water Thoughts

_____

_____

_____

_____

_____

_____

_____

_____

_____

_____

_____

_____

_____

_____

_____

_____

_____

_____

_____

_____

_____

_____

_____

_____

_____

_____

_____

MY LIVING WATER THOUGHTS

MY LIVING WATER THOUGHTS

_____
_____
_____
_____
_____
_____
_____
_____
_____
_____
_____
_____
_____
_____
_____
_____
_____
_____
_____
_____
_____
_____
_____
_____

My Living Water Thoughts

My Living Water Thoughts

_____

_____

_____

_____

_____

_____

_____

_____

_____

_____

_____

_____

_____

_____

_____

_____

_____

_____

_____

_____

_____

_____

_____

_____

_____